MW00892871

Pass the Bread Please

Francis Irmiter

Dear Father

Lord, I dedicate this book to you, may You use it to your Glory, to feed your people in word. Lord may your will, which surpasses all understanding, enrich those who read and meditate on these devotionals, may they be drawn closer to you, may that feel your presence in the words and may they hear the still whisper of your voice calling them closer. God I thank you for sending my wife into my life and the encouragement she is to me, thank you for Walter and Doug for encouraging me to write and continue to write. Father thank you for sending your Son and giving us Your words, Father draw us close to you.

For it is in the name of Jesus Christ I do pray. Amen

Cried Out

Psalm 3:4 I cried to the LORD with my voice, And He heard me from His holy hill. Selah

Does God hear you today?

In the past couple of weeks my life has seemed like a roller coaster, minute by minute up or down. Not because of anything that I had done but because of the influence of others on my life, some people just don't realize the harm that can come by their words then again maybe they do. Look here some times there is a cost to having a relationship with Christ that is different from others relationship and if they don't understand they shoot darts if it were. We have not really talked about the cost of serving God but we will.

Has your faith in Christ cost you? King David's relationship put him directly into harms way, Saul wasn't about to let this upstart take his throne so he pursued him to destroy him. Well let's face it Saul wanted David dead. Will your faith cost you your life, your friends, your family what is the price that you will pay?

So here it is thru the struggle of life that we must cry out to the Father from a cave or our home on our couch (sofa). Look at the verse again, "I cried out to the LORD with my <u>voice</u>," Is this what we do, or do we cry out in our heads and hearts not wanting others around to hear your tears. What a shame it is that we don't want to seem less then what we are, and yet we are less than what we are for closing ourselves off. David's example of crying out to the LORD, his verbalizing what was in his heart is an awesome example isn't it? How passion filled is your prayers, do they bring a tear to your eye?

"And He heard me from His holy hill," God hears you when you cry out, look by the time the trouble has built up enough for you and I to actually cry out we sometimes ask why haven't You Lord heard us but why did it take us so long to ask, why must we wait until we have been broken in heart? Is God on His holy hill today, sure He is and today He wants to hear from you, but has He, will He. I know D.A. you're a busy guy but have you taken a moment to CRY OUT TO GOD? How about your Rusty and Rod and Jesse and Brenda are your mouths silent this morning, do you only have time for just a quick silent prayer?

Oh for Pete's sake ya'll CRY OUT TO GOD and then pause and just listen, stop and be quiet this morning Julie, incline your heart toward the holy hill Bob and just stop, remember what you learned on the prayer walk and apply it today.

Selah

Warm Fuzzy

Psalm 11:4 - The LORD is in His holy temple, The LORD's throne is in heaven; His eyes behold, His eyelids test the sons of men.

I like the mornings I make no bones about it I like getting up early, even on the weekend I wake up early. Oh but to view the beauty of the new day, the quietness of it is awesome. Before the sunrise before the first fisherman or hunter crank up their 4X4 camo trucks there is a stillness that is observant, what do I mean by that well God is not only the God of the day but also the God of the night. No He is not darkness but yes He is light. So there at 4 a.m. He sits on His throne in heaven and He sees.

My question to you is what does He see in you during the day, is it righteousness or is it well not?

We go thru each day and supervise and unfortunately we get on folks when they do something wrong we don't see them doing things right we just say well that is doing the job or the task at hand. Sure I know we talk a good game about catching people doing good but it is harder for us to do because of what is ingrain in us. We are trained to look out for danger, to look for those who wish to harm us with the arrow of words or deeds.

Can I tell you about a God who is looking at you right now, yes whose eyes are even now upon you. God is not looking at you ready to pounce on your head for the ill that you may do. He is not the

God who wishes only to catch you out of line. Tell me the verse that talks about God with a thump' in stick in His hand ready to leave the throne just to smack you down? Can you show me that verse? You won't find it.

No rather God is there on His throne casting His eyes about looking at you His creation and seeing you both in good and wrong and for both there is consequence. To wrong there is conviction and correction and to good there is blessing of overwhelming abundance. Do you say where is the abundance of blessing, for starters you must be alive to read these words and to do good, isn't your very life a blessing from God, so to are you blessed when God calls you home or a loved one to His arms.

You see Gail and Beth God wishes to catch you doing good first. Is that hard to consider Bob, that God views you where you are and sees you and looks for the good, I know Kathleen that at times He views us doing wrong still He loves us not the wrong, that is why He disciplines us without using an HR manual but only His righteous judgment.

God is on His throne and He desires to give you a warm fuzzy, be ready for it, seek it and be confident that God is on His throne.

Lead me

Psalm 25 ⁴Show me Your ways, O LORD;
Teach me Your paths.
⁵Lead me in Your truth and teach me,
For You are the God of my salvation;
On You I wait all the day.
16 Turn Yourself to me, and have mercy on me,
For I am desolate and afflicted.

When was the last time you truly asked God to lead you, for Him to show you His ways? I have taken this Disc profile thing a couple of times and you are going to find this funny as to why I have taken it more than once. According to this profile I am a high D a dominating personality who wants to control everything. Some would say that I am like this others would say not, well I said not so I took it again and lo and behold it came back with the same results, then yes then I took it a third time and guess what that's right a third time it came back high D. What I haven't told you is I am also a high "I" so the D who wants to dominate things listens to the "I" who wants to creatively solve things with impute from others. The "S" and the "C" well lets just say they are on the scale somewhere toward the bottom. My point to this is only God has the right and knowledge and wisdom to be a high "D" neither you nor me.

Yet here we are always seeking the best way but often times when God has laid it out for us we think that is to simple that it shouldn't be that easy so we try to "creatively solve the problem," and in the end God has to clean up the mess. God is the best teacher there is sometimes we need to be better students and stop to not only listen but act upon what we have been taught by Him. Maybe this is a bad analogy but a map maker did not create the ground that they map out, no but rather they had to learn the ground that was created to correctly map it out, think if a map maker just wanted to draw it the way they wanted how accurate that would be.

Lead me in Your truth Oh LORD, to be taught because of who I know You to be the God of my salvation, on Him we should wait but don't often times. There is a little high "D" in all of us at times a desire to go and do and maybe a little bit of get it done so we can get it over with. God doesn't always work that way thou does He, sometimes He makes us wait could that be because we haven't learned enough yet?

Today ask God to turn Himself to you, and yes have mercy on you for are we all not desolate without His Divinity. Sometimes the hardest thing to do is sit down and to be still, but sometimes the hardest lesson is the best lesson. Wait for God and if God doesn't lead you don't go.

Example

John 13: ^{14}If I then, your Lord and Teacher, have washed your feet, you also ought to wash one another's feet. ^{15}For I have given you an example, that you should do as I have done to you. ^{16}Most assuredly, I say to you, a servant is not greater than his master; nor is he who is sent greater than he who sent him. ^{17}If you know these things, blessed are you if you do them.

"If we are the body," is an awesome song one that both encourages us and challenges us at the same time, if you haven't heard it find some one who has it on tape of cd. It asks if we are the body why aren't the body parts doing their job and teaching, reaching and healing could it be that we have some how forgotten that we are just the body and not the head and that we as the body should take direction from the head to obediently be the example of His ministry and not ours.

Christ could have demanded a lot of things, He could have commanded that things be done to please Himself and to show in a worldly fashion who the leader was, yes He could have but no He didn't. You see we can and do grow closer to God by being the servant not by taking it upon ourselves to act like the leader. The best leaders that are leaders and not dictators understand that they exist to serve those whom serve them. Christ is the best example of leadership that there ever was and ever will be and it don't matter to me how many 12 step books you read.

Leaders sometimes forget to wash the feet of those whom they lead and that is why the body has stumbled. We for some prideful humanistic fashion reason think that the church exist to be our social club, to be our place to puff us up, when really the place to be a leader is on the curb serving those whom are the least of these. Why isn't the body doing, could it be that they are not following Christ first but their own interest and if they can use the name of Christ to act socially more appealing well then so be it.

Look gird a towel about your waist and go wash some one's feet, not because you have to or because you even want to but solely because it is the example of Christ. Quit saying it is better to serve and be served and actually live it.

More than these

John 21: 15 So when they had eaten breakfast, Jesus said to Simon Peter, "Simon, son of Jonah, do you love Me more than these?"

Witnessing verses whom you love, what in the name of blue blazes are your talking about now, I love the Lord that is why I witness. Oh hang on a minute well I do only witness to those whom I am comfortable with, those who I look somewhat like those of my own skin tone, social class well Tammy's class we know that don't we. Do you David and Pat love the Lord more than these that you call friend? Alison do you love Him more than any of these so much so that you put Him first and these second.

This is a question that you have to answer, isn't it, what you think it was only written down for Peter, and yes these verses Joe have a lot of thought and can go a lot of ways but all of the ways point to one thing and that Rusty is what Jack encourages restoration of a personnel relationship with God.

Did Christ say, Simon, son of Jonah, do you love Me more than these and if you do why are you fishing? Nope, certainly not but how many of us fall back on things familiar and comfortable when we, well when we fail in our relationship with Christ either in sin or disobedience, which some would say is also sinful. Still to this day I don't know why Peter went back to fishing like I have said before he never seemed to catch anything but unless Christ told him where to cast the net, then again I go fishing and catch twigs so you can't listen to me. (Rabbit)

Have you ever asked your self this question: Do I love Christ more than _____, and then looked for evidence of that love. Love leaves a trail you can follow love, for if you truly love the Lord you and I will desire for the things of the LORD and not things of self or the world.

When then will you feed the lambs, when will you tend the sheep, when will you feed the sheep or are you set on just loving certain goats? It is your responsibility Andy and Gail and Judy and Fran to take care of the flock, a flock Helen of assorted colors and sizes. The one who has strayed the one who is hurting these sheep we should love more than these whom we associate with.

What have you answered to the question: Do I love Christ more than these, what did the evidence reveal to you and what are you going to do, go back fishing or are you going to as Christ beckoned to Peter "Follow Me."

Dinged but not pierced

Ephesians 6:16
above all, taking the shield of faith with which you will be able to quench all the fiery darts of the wicked one.

Ya ever play, when you were a kid, war? A stick would be your sword and a trashcan would be your shield and the clanging and banging of battle would ring across the neighbor hood well more like just in your back yard. Many an old broom and a couple of new ones had the handle cut off to become swords and trash can lids would be beaten till they were square or dented so they couldn't be used on trash cans anymore. You would thrust the lid out and swipe down at the other lid trying to whack it out of their hand while they were doing the same thing and who ever lost grip on the shield would pay the price for their weakness a clubbing with a wooden broom handle. Some times we don't even go into battle with a shield so how can we deflect the fiery darts? Does your shield have the tell tale sign of being assaulted, are there dings in the shield or has the shield been pierced?

"Above all, taking the shield of faith," is this how you started your day taking the shield of faith or are you fine with taking a tin look alike? It is amazing how we sometimes go to battle with the weakest battle plan, oh I'll be alright this will be fine I really am not going to get that involved so this will be all the protection I will need. WHAM! It won't be good enough. The past couple of weeks there has been one thing or the other that has just grated under my skin and even the friendly banter seemed like fiery darts to me, I went to war with a cardboard shield and was surprised when a dart got thru. Has that ever happened to you or has that just happened to me?

It is not that I don't have faith it is just that I didn't apply that faith to every situation because of being just tired of the battle and wanted something lighter. Mistake number two. No not that I wanted to get away from anything but I just kind of wanted to withdraw for a moment. A shield is worthless if you still have it slung on your back, you can only use it if you take it up and hold it in front of you, yes use two hands sometimes if need be but hold on. Call for help from those whom you seek Cry out to the Father, lay all of your cares at His feet and give Him the burden.

You see we are not lone warriors we do not stand on the hill by ourselves against the horde, no we stand as a force of one, twine together with others who share our faith in the One. We must be there to stand shoulder to shoulder with each other. When one is under assault we should not stand idly by lest their shield should be pierced.

So take up your shield and hold it in front of you and if you need help ask.

His Way

Psalm 81:13
"Oh, that My people would listen to Me, That Israel would
walk in My ways!

How well do you take direction?
When was the last time you listened to God and then did what
He said or directed you to do?

Our God is not silent, He speaks volumes each day but alas we
either are not listening or we shrug off what we hear. Can I ask you
something, has the country we live in gotten this way over night or
has the social degradation taken years to decline, what has caused it?
Could it possibly be because "My people," have stopped listening to
Him and have been relying on themselves instead?

Please tell me where it is in Gods word that we should be silent
or at the most just shake our head at disgust at what is going on in
our families, our communities, our counties, our state or our nation.
If you find it let me know, I couldn't find it.

Now for you in your shoes because that is what you can control,
just you in your size 13s or 9s you can listen to "Me," and walk
in His ways today. With each step you take today you can say I
will walk as Christ walked on the earth, no Ricardo not in sandals
necessarily but in His ways. We can reach out to the sinner without
sinning, we can help the sick with an encouraging touch, we can
obey His commands with a willing heart instead of a fleshly desire.

You see if you would place your name Judy and Gail in the place of Israel what would that mean to you, That Hugh would walk in My ways! That Connie would walk in My ways! That Nathan and Russell and Tim and Jack would walk in My ways, That Fran would walk in my ways..... What would the impact Jenna be on our communities and homes if we walked in His ways? Not tip toeing about hoping not to offend anyone or stepping so hard that we crush them but rather stepping with the purpose of being examples of Christ on this His earth.

Will you walk in the direction He sends you today or will you escape and run the opposite way.

Will He find you in rest

Matthew 25:13
"Watch therefore, for you know neither the day nor the hour in which the Son of Man is coming.

Matthew 11:28-29
Come to Me, all you who labor and are heavy laden, and I will give you rest.

Take My yoke upon you and learn from Me, for I am gentle and lowly in heart, and you will find rest for your souls.

Anger, hate, sadness, depression, hurt, worry, and stress are things that make life more abundant. Each one of these things gives you and I opportunity to turn even closer to God to be comforted, loved, healed, to have joy, peace and calmed. When He comes back will you be at rest or in rest.

Okay I am no English major, I am sure you have found that out by now, but the small words make the big words more influential don't they. I mean look at the two words before rest "at – in," what do these mean to you? The first "at" is in between a moments of not rest or you have stopped and just stayed out of the way. The second "in" is no matter what you are dealing with that you are "in rest," that stuff happens but you find that you are resting in the arms of the Lord.

I think we as humans do some of the stupidest things, that we say that we should learn from our mistakes but we don't because we repeat them from time to time. What was the last lesson you learned from a mistake you made, has it stopped the behavior that brought about the mistake.

Christ said "come to Me," and "learn from Me," the first we do the second well maybe sometimes we forget what would Jesus do and rely on what would "I" do. We often look for the times that we are at rest instead of daily being in rest. What if Christ were to come back this morning would He find you stress out because of budgets or employees or family or friends and if that were so isn't that contrary to what He has instructed you to be, yet we are human. No matter how much we try to be Christ like we are still Walter, Yvonne, Kevin, Fran, Rod, Deb, and Julie we are who we are. Learn from Christ, well He was crucified for you and I what lessons from that do you carry with you each day, salvation, forgiveness and grace, mercy.

Find rest for your soul, the rest that you can be in all of the time.

Social vs. Christ

Matthew 12: ⁶Yet I say to you that in this place there is One greater than the temple. ⁷But if you had known what this means, "I desire mercy and not sacrifice, you would not have condemned the guiltless. ⁸For the Son of Man is Lord even of the Sabbath."

Okay I am not sure of the name of this one but it seemed to fit sorta, let me ask you a question that might clarify it. Does your life at church revolve around activities and groups rather than about Christ? When the law becomes more important than Christ, well then we gotta problem don't we. I ask you this to look at your church and see what is ya'lls focus is it what we got or how can God use us.

I don't remember who said it or what movie it came from but it is true, "a little revolution is good from time to time." I know we like to think of revolution as taking over the establishment, isn't it funny thou that even after a revolution that another establishment is well established. Christ was the first peaceful revolutionist, He came not to unite but to divide, He came to establish His church, He came as a sacrifice to you and I and the guy next to you.

These verses challenge us all to keep our focus on the Lord of the Sabbath the Lord of the worship service, the Lord of our Bible study, the focus of our lives aught to be Christ and not what pennant we fly from our window. I can just see it now, these disciples walking thru the field eating this grain and some Pharisee saying that is not the way we do it, that is not what we do, the by-laws say your are supposed to vote on that. Instead of looking at the one whom the disciples came to serve, the Pharisees only saw their established law.

Is the focus of your worship on the one who said "I desire mercy and not sacrifice."

How about your daily steps, your walk of faith is it on the one who said "I desire mercy."

If all you can see is your laws then do you miss seeing the one whom the law was supposed to point to?

It makes me pull my hair out when folks say that is the way we have always done it and it is the way we will always do it and if you don't like it go to a different church. Well maybe you should go to a different church because they are not honoring God but they are honoring their social gathering.

Big "G" little "i"

Psalm 34:3
Oh, magnify the LORD with me, And let us exalt His name together.

There are many of us who think we are perfect, that the stink doesn't stick, that what we are doing is right and what you are doing is well miss guided.... Oh I think I am going to be ill. It hurts the fingers to even type that bull-oh-knee. There is one who is perfect there is one who is righteous and He is the LORD let us worship Him together instead of ourselves.

Oh, Magnify the LORD with me with some one else join together and magnify the LORD with someone. Today as you walk the talk that you have read about (not in this devo but in your private reading and study) join with another to magnify Abba Father. How encouraged do you feel when you share with some one what God means to you, what He has done for you, how He has not left you. Let the conversation be about God and not about the darts the hurdles the junk of life or you can just say don't let the conversation be about you but about GOD.

There is nothing more exciting then when we go to church on Friday and worship together, what you don't go to church on Friday, well then you must go on Saturday, no well how about on Monday, oh I know then you go on Tuesday. Then are you telling me you only go to church on Sunday really wow, you mean you only worship the Father as a group on a Sunday morning only man that's kind of ah how can I say this in a theological dramatic way. Boy are you missing out and if you don't believe me then try worshiping God on other days then just Sunday.

Look here it doesn't matter to me if you are Baptist, Church of Christ, Methodist, Spring Road Christian (that's 4 u Bob), or Catholic if your life isn't about worshiping God and lifting up Christ everyday then maybe you need to rethink your social status. All of these titles and religions don't amount to a hill of beans if they don't exalt His name when you are together.

I know people like to say that they don't need to go to church that they can be close to God out on a golf course or in a deer blind or in a mall or at a coffee table on a Sunday morning but what about coming together. It is a funny thing about worship service that is God focused you can walk away having your toes stepped on and still come away with joy and being refreshed.

Is your life about lifting up the Big "G" and becoming the small "i" the worship of your day should be about GOD not about "i" come together and exalt His name and His Glory for He has never left you and He will hear you. Cry out to Him with one voice of praise.

Gifted

Romans 12:3
For I say, through the grace given to me, to everyone who is among you, not to think of himself more highly than he ought to think, but to think soberly, as God has dealt to each one a measure of faith.

Ya ever look around and keep score of what others get as apposed to what you have been given? Never quite satisfied with the things that you have because maybe some one else was given something that has more polish or plastic on it, and well it would be just wrong if their gift cost more than yours did. Well I think a fishing story best describes what this gift envy thing is. There is a bait in my tackle box that is yes Ricardo a crank bait that I have had for over five years, the hooks are worn and some of the color has been worn off this is my it never fails bait, always do I get a strike when I use it. This bait was given to me to catch fish not to go fishing but actually to catch them. That's the kind of gift that we have been given, not to look at the others who fish and see what they have but to use whatever bait we got to cast out at the fish. You will find when you use the bait that you were given that it will work. What doesn't work is sitting head hanging down in the boat frustrated and sulking about what you don't got.

God has given you a measure of faith, are you using it or are you sitting on it?

It is a funny thing those guys in the $15K bass boats they are after the same fish that those guys who are in the $600 dollar wally-world special flat bottom boats. The fish don't care if your boat is nuclear powered quadraphonic tweaked out with a bbq grill or super conductive responsive sonar, oops color sonar reflector with a special attachment for weed less traversement. The fish just see the bait at the end of the line.

Do you think of yourself more highly then you ought to think? Are you looking at your boat and going man I am good, man I got the training and the know how to catch the fish. BALDERDASH then tell me why your boat still sits on the rack and hasn't touched water in a month. We sometimes get full of ourselves and sit looking at the tools we have been given instead of applying them in our lives.

Don't sit in the driveway or on the dock but push away weather you are in a bass boat, john boat, canoe or even with floatties.

Your Guide

Luke 1:79 To give light to those who sit in darkness and the shadow of death, To guide our feet into the way of peace."

Have you ever been on a tour of some historical site? When I was in Germany we went on a tour of the castle at Heidelberg, we went on the English tour and walked around the grounds and cellars looking at chapels and wine barrels. Seeing where the armament and defensive positions were along the walls and stuff like that. The guide did a good job of explaining the history of the castle and stories of events that happened. I had been to this castle a couple of times before that visit with Tammy but this was the first time I actually spent money on the tour (maybe I was trying to impress her). Sometimes we can't figure it out for ourselves but we need a guide in life, do you listen to the Guide or are ya trying to do it by yourself.

Christians are a funny lot, oh you know we are so don't get all huffy, we say we are going to vote on this or that to see what to do then if the vote doesn't go the way we want we act like the chadds didn't get counted and huff about it even more. Why oh why do we split for others just because they want orange and blue shag carpet instead of the crimson and white shag or because they want to use the rooms for classes instead of storage units. Of course we are using our own guide our own desires to guide us instead of allowing ourselves to be guided by Christ.

Can I ask you something, have you ever gotten your hackles in a bunch at church because some one wanted to do something a different way then you did? Did that help the situation out any or did you just end up holding onto that as well almost as if it was a personnel affront to you. No wonder we argue about how to spend a dollar when there isn't even peace about how to paint the room.

I know this guy who when you ask him something he nods his head and acts like he listens to you about this or that but then just well blows you off as he walks away. Sure I have been accused of that very thing but well this isn't me (nudge-nudge). Have you ever thought pastor or associate pastor or you deacon or WMU director that God uses those folks whom He has sent to you to convey a message. When you or I blow them off we are on the tour ourselves and well we go thru the motions but we miss the important stuff.

The Holy Spirit moves on this day just as He did back in the day, Christ's words are in red in many a bible today. We in our life must be the light reflectors as Christ shines thru us. Ya want peace well what are you going to do to gain peace sit on your can or be led and follow the guide.

Comfort

John 14:23
Jesus answered and said to him, "If anyone loves Me, he will keep My word; and My Father will love him, and We will come to him and make Our home with him.

Is home where you hang your hat or where you plant your flag? Back in the Oklahoma expansion they had a land grab first come first to plant their flag proved ownership over that plot of ground. Did this flag make it home or did it just say this is where you are, for where you are there you are at. (not supposed to make sense) What do you call home is it Birmingham, Nashville, Louisville, Valley, Lineville, Clay County (the entire county), or is home heaven. Now if you are reading this you haven't gotten to heaven yet so home is some place where you have yet to be, but it is with Christ and God that we long to reside.

When one travels or is transferred to different places you have a wonder of learning that has to be done. Yes I say a wonder because if you are not from that area you must learn the local language and customs. Look I have lived in Alabama for 10 years now and each day there is something new that I have learned, a new phrase a new variety of cuisine (food) just a myriad of things. Even thou I drive the roads and read the map I am still a Midwesterner and most love me despite myself.

When you live for Christ and learn from Him He is with you guiding you home, not to a white picket fence but an eternal mansion. God and Christ's home is in the life of those who love Him and those who keep His word and God loves him who loves His Son and keeps His word. So as you and I look to see where we stay, where we hang our hat so to speak God seeks those whom love Christ to be at home with them.

Time and distance has no relevance to being where God is if God lives with you. You can find comfort by holding Him near. By keeping His commands by glorifying the Son one can come closer Home. Sure we may miss those whom we do not see everyday or every once and awhile but we know they are but a phone call away. Abba is with you; we have but to reach out to Him. It doesn't matter if you plant a flag on this earth your true home is with God and Christ, this home can be where you are now and will be tomorrow.

Take comfort in knowing God and Christ let the Holy Spirit surround you with the Love that comes from the Father. Home is not the hat but faith in Christ and obedience to His word. Shhhhh be still in comfort.... Selah. Take a moment to be at home with God. Selah

Prep for worship

Oh Lord My God I sit in your quiet, in your stillness and prepare my heart for worship

Most heavenly Father I sit here with hands folded upon my lap and head bowed at the proper angle

Abba I cry out to You lead me, guide me, let me do the right things

But um God could you do it quickly because it is a minute before church is going to start and ya only got an hour to touch me and change me so well basically good luck.

Does it sound extreme or even a bit critical that we only start to prepare for worship at 10:58 a.m. instead of spending the week yes that is 24-7 to prepare for worship. But Fran, look you are saying that we should be holy all that time, it is impossible, no way can I do that, look here boy-o I am just as good as you are. I am not the measure but Christ is, so as Br. Robert said "if your worship service was graded what grade would you get," well how about it Joe, Doug, Leigh, Cathy and James how would your worship service be worship or will Sunday just be an hour where you half heartedly even sing the songs, listen to the message, trying desperately to get something out of it and yet falling short because well lets face it you really didn't come to worship.

Isaiah 6:²Above it stood seraphim; each one had six wings: with two he covered his face, with two he covered his feet, and with two he flew. ³And one cried to another and said:
   "Holy, holy, holy is the LORD of hosts;
   The whole earth is full of His glory!"

⁴And the posts of the door were shaken by the voice of him who cried out, and the house was filled with smoke.

IS HOLY HOLY HOLY upon your lips crying out from your toes or do we just say holy holy holy, yep God is Holy okay got it now what?

I know it is Friday and that we have been looking forward to the weekend with anticipation oh I don't know what since Monday maybe. Tell me this Joann are you looking forward to Sunday morning with anticipation of coming into contact with God in His house. I fear that the altar will remain vacant in many of our churches this Sunday because people haven't prepared themselves to come in contact with God. They have allowed sin in their life to be comfortable and even acceptable they do not see that God is HOLY and cannot come in contact with sin, even if you accept sin God doesn't.

Look you have an opportunity Tim on Sunday to Worship freely the Great I Am, doesn't that mean something do you, really on Sunday you have the opportunity to come before the Kin of Kings and yet we worry about the clothes on our back instead of the monkey called sin on our back.

It is time to shake the doorposts with Worship, prepare today this hour and take some one with you to God's House.

Nourishment

Matthew 4:4
But He answered and said, "It is written, "Man shall not live by bread alone, but by every word that proceeds from the mouth of God.""

Are ya eating your vegetables?
Eat poopsie be big and strong like your older brother, eat poopsie eat.

Are you being a picky eater or are you taking it all in, daily reading God's word and applying it all to your life instead of picking the good stuff out and leaving the things that balance your intake out. Sure it is fun just to go straight to the dessert, the apple pie with homemade vanilla ice cream. Then going back and eating the steak and then the rice then the broccoli (if there is room) then maybe eating to the salad. You betcha it is nice to start with the dessert, unfortunately our dessert often makes us a desert leaving us empty and parched for something real.

We live by the word of God or rather we try to live by the word of God, sometimes not every word but just those that we cling to, those that make us feel either important or safe. Yes God's word is there for us to cling to; yes it is there also for us to be encouraged by it is also there for us to be disciplined by. We must balance all of these and many more in our life our Christian walk if we want to have the energy to make it across the plains make it up the hill or mountains and yes at time even across the deserts in the valley.

Marathon runners have fluid "refreshment," stands set up along the way to replenish their bodies of duh fluid and calories that have been burned off and to give them fuel for the next leg of the race. If they don't pause long enough to grab a bottle they run the risk of cramping up into a ball or collapsing for lack of energy the never reach the end of the race but lay along the track in a heap.

Do you think you can make it along the trail, do you think you got enough to make it to cross the finish line, far to many folks end up discouraged and curled up into a ball because they have not paused to study and learn from God's word they just figure they got it all because they ate the dessert first and that will be enough.

Every word is exactly that every word, not just the new testament but also the old testament, it is also stopping to listen daily what God says to you when you pray do you listen for the answer.

Eat your veggies boy-oh, balance out your reading and learning applying it all to the race.

How He Opened your eyes -

John 9:26
Then they said to him again, "What did He do to you? How did He open your eyes?"

When questioned about why you believe, trust, have faith in Jesus Christ how do you answer that question, How has Christ opened your eyes?

Selah

This man who was blind and now he could see knew who it was who had healed him. He knew that he was once blind but now can see, do you realize how blind you were in your sight and now you have abundant sight. Can you see who it was who gave you new sight and will you when questioned answer the call and tell some one about Christ?

Selah

There are things in each of our lives that I could share with you about how Christ has been there with you, helping you out of the valley, guiding you along the trail, who when you came to harm helped you thru it. Sometimes we only share these stories at church and at church is fine but outside of the walls of the building is even better. Sometimes even in church we find we discuss the things of this world instead of the things of Christ. Where do you see Christ at work in your life?

Selah

Those who asked the question were skeptical of what the answer would be, some might say even a bit intimidating to this fellow after all they had the power he did not. Still he didn't relent and deny what had happened but gave credit where credit was doe. Can you say the same, will you say the same, but we sometimes feel more intimidated by the one who is questioning us then we do fear of the One who healed us. If you are asked, Ya know what Doug you are crazy if you think God actually knows how many hairs you got on your head, Joann if you think God can heal you are out of your mind, Joe are you telling me that you actually think God answers prayer then tell me ya'll why is there so much death, so many who are hurting tell me you believe in this God tell me why? Can you answer that or will we just walk away?

There is pain and loss in this life; there are times when bad things happen to good people. These things would happen and even worse if there wasn't God. Just look at our schools after God was told He wasn't welcome in there anymore. God is the One who extends the hand, who picks you and I up when we are down, God is the One who heals when we are sick, and yes God is the One who answers prayers. I have no answer that is complete of why bad things happen to good people but this is what I do know, when bad things have happened to this sinner God was there to forgive and reconcile with and who lifted me up out of the mire and cured my sight.

Which Path

Matthew 7:[13]"Enter by the narrow gate; for wide is the gate and broad is the way that leads to destruction, and there are many who go in by it. [14]Because narrow is the gate and difficult is the way which leads to life, and there are few who find it.

I have a question that ya'll need to ask yourself, respond if you like but answer it if only for yourself.

Is it easy to be a Christian?

Such a double sided question, what you say double sided seems straightforward to me. Then you answer it. Is it easy to "be," a Christian, you can't answer this one without looking at what path you are on today. Is it the wide path where everyone else is on cause hey we like being in a crowd/herd or is it on the narrow path where you will actually have to stand for something.

There may be less obstacles on the wide path because you are not a target, you are already where Satan wants you. So just as a cow in a herd ya just gotta stay happy eating your cud and moving along to your end destruction as a grass fed steak on the plate of hell. Is that to harsh, really tell me is there anyway to make hell sound like a place you want to be? But alas there are many who traverse this path blindly going along to their ultimate destruction.

There are obstacles on the narrow path, things that stub your toe and test your desire at times even tripping you up and making you stumble. How difficult this path is to go along on at times you may think you are by yourself as you stand up with eyes wide open and see the stones that lay there, many you avoid but some you don't. Christ said "difficult is the way," He didn't say it was impossible.

When I was a kid we would pick up rocks out of the fields because they would damage farm implements. No not the most exciting job in the world, you would walk along rows looking at the ground to see if you saw a rock that was fist sized then pick it up and toss it in the loader. Every once and a while you would pick up your head to see that there was an end to the row and a water break waiting for you. The best way to pick up rocks is not to stare at your feet but to look ahead of you so you can see the stones before you bash your foot on them.

You cannot ride the fence and try to keep one foot on the narrow path and one foot on the wide path. Is it easy to be a Christian at times no it is not, because of the stones that are thrown into your path, look up and see that at the end, there is an eternal break in heaven. Follow the footsteps of Christ, He has walked this path already for you and walks with you.

How are you known?

1 Corinthians 13:12-13 For now we see in a mirror, dimly, but then face to face. Now I know in part, but then I shall know just as I also am known.

And now abide faith, hope, love, these three; but the greatest of these is love.

When you looked in the mirror this morning, whether shaving or putting on make-up did you like what you saw, did the face in the mirror make you pause and wonder what has become of the child that was once there? No Ricardo I am not talking about how your hair was cut or the general appearance of age and what weather had done to one's face but rather the man or woman that stared back from the silver-platted glass. Do you have love, and is this how you are known or are you only known by the reflection in the mirror.

I have been accused at times of being closed off that I don't let people in very often, what is funny is that I have also been accused of the opposite of that. What is real thou is hidden to many of you, and it is something we all do, there are those who know me well and those who know just the reflection on the mirror. I am sure that some head-doc has some sort of term for this, defensive nature, but I call it trust. We pick and choose whom we trust but we fail to love because love is not trust, rather trust is a by-product of love, so I don't love as I should instead I put up a wall, and I am wrong because of it.

You must first love the one in the mirror, not the image of a clean shaven face or the Mary Kay product line, we must love who we are to be able to love others as we should. Does that make sense Russell and David, makes sense but Pat and Julie do you love yourself and you Ricardo do your really love yourself? Lou and Jeff how can we abide in faith hope and love if we first don't love ourselves? Not a wow what a model of humanity and vitality I am prideful kind of love, but love as I am a child of God kind of love.

The greatest of these is Love, everything starts with love, even you started with love and no I am not talking about conception of man and woman but conception of God's love and authority. You are here right now because your Abba Father Loves you, you are saved because the Great I am sent His only begotten Son to die for you because of His Love for you.

We can have faith we can have hope but without love what are they really but empty cans waiting to be filled with love. You see if you Doug don't love then what you do will seem empty and lead you to question why. It is only love Joanne that keeps you from getting out of bed in the morning.

I know at times we find others hard to love but they probably feel the same about us, so put that to the side. How will you Kevin and Hugh, and you Joe and Joe and Charles and Jan, and you Clara and Tammy and you Tim and Lynn and Nancy and Beth and YOU how will you love first today?

Swallowed Up

Psalm 124 [8]Our help is in the name of the LORD, Who made heaven and earth.

Do you have a cup of coffee in your hand or next to your computer this morning; oh I'm sorry IT says not to drink around your computer so that isn't happening is it. Anyway we sometimes need that extra boost of caffeine and sugar to get started and yet some continue to drink it all day long, as for me can you imagine me on a caffeine high all day long scary I know. Now some drink it all day long because they just like the taste of burnt bark while others drink it cause they need the caffeine all day long. So if He is our help who made the heaven and earth then how many times a day do you drink in His name?

Most of Psalm 124 is praising God because He has kept us out of the fowler's net, He has protected us from being destroyed and we must-should-wantta praise Him for being with us all day long. Not just putting a cross around your neck or a fish on the bumper of your car or a "WWJD," bracelet on your wrist. These are all fine things they are and can be reminders not only to those who see them but also for the one who placed them there. More than that thou His word should be our comfort and should be placed in our heart so we can take a shot when we need it.

What does the word of God mean to you, what is in His name that makes you want-desire-need it every day and every part of the day? Is it sufficient for you only to get a devotional in the morning along with your cup of coffee? Ya know what would make me happy, if you would say "I haven't had time to read your devotional today because I started my own bible study today." When you grow personally that is when we will see change.

It isn't black tar in a cup that should give you a shot of energy today, sure my eyelids need to be more open also, and rather it is God who will keep you close today. He who will cover you and I with His arms and hold us dearly close to protect us from the woe of this day and even when stuff happens we can turn to Him and look upon His glory and know we will not be destroyed.

I know this lady who lost a child who probably could have suffered endlessly thru her days and never to feel joy ever again and we would understand. She instead holds the memory of this child dear and with God, she doesn't need to be reminded of God's power and authority she is assured that one day she will be able to rock her child again and the thought may bring a tear but also brings great joy.

We all have hope for each and everyday, hope is not idle it doesn't fall in your lap you must seek after it. Let hope be your caffeine the thing that keeps you going for we also one day will be rocked in the arms of our Abba Father. Who will keep you out of the snare, Him who created the heavens and the earth.

Do Ya

Psalm 111: [1] Praise the LORD! I will praise the LORD with my whole heart, In the assembly of the upright and in the congregation. [2]The works of the LORD are great, Studied by all who have pleasure in them.

Did ya have a good day at church yesterday, or did ya just go thru the motions –

Did ya have a good Sunday school class yesterday, or did ya just see acquaintances –

Did ya praise God with your whole heart and study the works of the Lord or did ya just flibble-flabble-dribble-drabble-

The first word in this psalm should be the first word in our lives, each day we should wake with Praise for the Lord. Now I know that no one wakes up bouncing giddy happy but that it sometimes takes time for people to get motivated to even put their feet on the carpet (floor) to even get the day started. So that being said why should our praise be hindered by how awake we are? Some people may just have well stayed in the bed for all the effort they put into praising God corporately or individually.

Can you tell me, yes that is you right there when was the last time you praised God with your whole heart? Seems to much to ask sometimes doesn't it Jeff that you would ask people to worship God with their whole heart, well ya'll it isn't your pastor, teacher, parent, uncle or writer that is asking you to praise God with your whole heart rather it is God asking you to open your heart to HIM and PRAISE HIM. After all hasn't God done some marvelous things for you, not to ya but for you?

Do ya really realize that God has been watching you all night long, that He never once took His eyes off of you? Not to condemn you or to see what you are up to but rather because of His love for you. Do you also know that God wants to be a part of your life to lead you to be with you and when you deny Him and place other things like your time, possessions or desires in front of Him He is jealous?

Look if you don't believe that God wants to be a part of every aspect of your life look into His word there are plenty of examples of not just healing the sick but also of encouraging the poor and giving them justice, there are plenty of examples of God in the lives of ordinary folks. Moses, Job, Ruth, Joseph, and Paul were just ordinary folks and yes-even Peter was ordinary after all alls he did was fish before how ordinary can you get.

Did ya praise God this morning or do you still have to even invite God to be with you today? Did ya can you will ya would it help if I said please, well then please.

Make it thru…

Psalm 16:11
You will show me the path of life; In Your presence is fullness of joy; At Your right hand are pleasures forevermore.

If this devo today is a bit on the mushy side well, so be it Amen. What is something that truly brings you joy? Is it something that you can do is it being out on a boat in the middle of the lake, or looking out at a pasture from the tree line, is it striking the ball and watching it actually fly towards the whole/green are these some of the things that bring you joy? We can close our eyes and have joy, not in sleep but in just the stillness of our hearts because we have turned our life to the Lord.

Is it to un-conceivable Bob to be able to just sit in your office and close your eyes and think of Christ and just the thought of Him can bring you joy. We look sometimes at events in our lives that have brought us joy like meeting our spouse, the birth of our children, but these are events in history that are memories of joyful times where is your joy today. Sometimes we get so wowed up with ourselves and wound up with what we must do that we miss seeing where daily joy is and where it comes from.

Where is Christ in your life today Helen, is He there next to you or is He at a distance just out of reach? Today Christ sits at the right hand of the Father; His body has not been corrupted by death but rather glorified in life. Just the thought of Christ should bring us joy for He is alive, He is not buried in a tomb or lie in state in some crypt. That He is not at a distance but by the power of the Holy Spirit He is also next to you to be with you, helping you, leading you, encouraging you and these things do they bring you joy.

A couple of months ago I let some one who is very dear to me and who still is, steal my joy because they were disappointed in who I am and who I have become. Since then I have been trying to get it back, this joy I mean. Trying desperately to try to understand but failing just as desperately, until I realized that I need to get my joy from God first because He has always been there for me always. People will let you down and it may be disappointing but it is not life ending but how sad it would be if I didn't have God to help me thru.

Is where you have been brought you joy or is your joy based on Who you know? If you understand that God blesses you and that those moments of joy are just brief glimpses of what blessings God has in store for you. If you understand where your joy comes from no one can take it away from you. Share the Joy in the Lord with someone today, let some one know where that seated at the right Hand of God is Christ.

Its up to you

Isaiah 1:16-17 (New King James Version)
[16]"Wash yourselves, make yourselves clean;
Put away the evil of your doings from before My eyes.
Cease to do evil,
[17]Learn to do good; Seek justice, Rebuke the oppressor;
Defend the fatherless,
Plead for the widow.

When was the last time you defended the fatherless, or pleaded for the widow, or sought justice or are you still waiting to do these things for the first time?

God is so cool you know if I would have wrote these verses on my own a while back I would have put 17 where 16 is or 16 where 17 is okay basically I would have just flipped these two verses around. Yep that is right I would have said work and be good and do good things and God will recognize the good things, but that is not the way of it at all for all God can see is the sin that remains on you, that keeps you stanky.

We can do good things and help people out but a lot of the time we expect something in return instead of doing good things as fruits of our faith. There is an expectation of hearing what thank-you or gaining points in favor of some one, tisk-tisk-tisk. I know sometimes I still find myself like that. You are not evil because you want to hear thank-you. It is just that sometimes we get these two verses flipped over.

SO ya need to ask you self one thing are you washed, scrubbed, shower sponged off or have you just let the water roll off your head and down the drain. What evil thing do you need to put away, and please don't sit there and justify something that you know because God's words says it is sin but let it go. Don't go on Sunday and worship God then on Wednesday go ahead and pick up that sin again. The stain of sin needs to be washed in the blood of the lamb and rinsed down the drain not placed on a shelf to be used later.

Four words that each of us must do but so often fail at "Cease to do evil," do you cease or is it just a matter of maybe not now or the situation hasn't presented itself for you to sin. CEASE to do evil is an everyday gotta do.

Learn to do good, sometimes maybe doing good has to be learned which means you are going to have to put an effort towards it. Roll the sleeves up and learn to do good. Rebuke the oppressor instead of crawling onto their bandwagon, defend the fatherless and in this day and age of single parents there are plenty of fatherless to defend, are you defending them or just by saying this rule and that rule you have really oppressed the fatherless. Plead for the widow, be their voice help them in their life to know that they are still loved

Don't walk out the door today with out your shower, and in the freshness of the shower Learn to do good and give the glory to God.

Don't pick or choose

Mark 13:31
Heaven and earth will pass away, but My words will by no means pass away.

We cleaned out the garage (again) the other day and we added more boxes, boards, junk and trash to the landfill, I think we are getting to the 1 ton mark and a free t-shirt. They don't even ask me anymore if I know which way to go they just say okay they have the weight so when I return they can weigh the truck again to see how much we chucked into the dump. If ever there has been a place that one man's junk is another man's treasure could be said it is out at the dump, well there are garage sales also but I aint going to go there or some one will beat me again. Now there aren't people standing out there going thru the dump to see what is worthless and what they can use but sometimes some one will ask ya, are you really going to throw that away so you let them take it, but hey that just helped them when it comes to weight – oh well. Look it doesn't matter how many books you have on your self if you don't read God's word then you have already placed it in the junk pile. You see if we value something we use it daily, we don't place it somewhere where we have to dust it off to read it.

There are something's that people do that well I just don't understand, those who take the Old Testament and say it is worthless and cast it into the pile, those who study and don't apply what they learned, and those who want to say well that was fine for back then but we are more evolved then that now. When really have we advanced more than those who James was speaking about when he spoke of taming the tongue, have we really advanced more than those who Christ had called a brood of vipers, have we become the Pharisee with our hands lifted praying to our glory instead of God's.

God's words will not pass away anytime in the near future, His words, which are contained in the binder of the book, called the Holy Bible. But even if every bible was placed on a heap God's word would still remain, you can destroy the paper but you cannot destroy the words. If we choose to pick over what we want to live by and toss out the stuff that we consider archaic our view of archaic is wrong because it is all His word.

IF you really want a life with a deeper relationship with the Lord then study His words, get to know what He has for you, which is revealed in the Scriptures He inspired. Don't pick out and place on the pile those things that you well basically that you and I don't want to deal with because they don't fit into our pattern of life. Rather learn from all of those verses even more, if it challenges you it will change you for you will have to respond to it. Pick it up!

Fight

1 Timothy 6:12
Fight the good fight of faith, lay hold on eternal life, to which
you were also called and have confessed the good confession
in the presence of many witnesses.

A re ya fighting the good fight or are you still in the corner, the
bell has wrung we must go into the fight. What keeps us from
stepping into the ring and why do we not let go of the ropes? Fear,
shame, pride or doubt probably for each we have our own reasons
and it is this reason that keeps our dairy air (that isn't Latin) on the
stool, but we call it a pew.

Can you think back to when you first were saved, when you
knew beyond a shadow of a doubt that the Holy Spirit had rested
upon you and you were one with the Lord and you felt as if you
could take on the world. That day when you wanted to go out and
tell everyone that you came into contact with about Christ. Do you
remember when your head came out of the water at your baptism
and because of this public display of obedience people knew that
the first fruit was born. How you went to work or school on that next
Monday, you were ready to answer the bell. Now lets face it you
only knew one thing at that time and that was Christ. You had know
deep learned ingrain theology or religion, you hadn't gone thru any
40 day program or 16 week class on this that or the other thing you
had but one mission it was to tell others about Christ.

Ya know what I love about the first missionaries? Well for starters they had no idea of what they were doing as in they didn't sit around and plan out their 5 year mission statement or in 20 years we will be here or there. They just got up got out and took off on across the roads, sure with a bit of prompting. Another thing is these guys were just folks they didn't ascend up the racks of a governmental system of religion but rather could have cared less about who was who. I wonder when Paul took his course on church planting, the *Seminary of Life*. What would happen if you were like Paul and just heeded this same advise he gave to Timothy and fought the good fight of faith.

When you publicly confessed the Lord as your Savior you and I stepped into a ring that we would take some blows, we would get punched and jabbed at with the only thing to strike back with would be the word of God. Sure sometimes we retreat into the corner we take a break, we need at times a season of refreshing and renewal but a season is not life the season changes and it is time to get back into the fight. Recall the zeal you had from the Lord and for the Lord of the time of your confession of His as being the Christ. Take hold of that passion again, do it.

Take Up Your Mat

Luke 5: [23]Which is easier, to say, "Your sins are forgiven you,' or to say, "Rise up and walk'? [24]But that you may know that the Son of Man has power on earth to forgive sins"--He said to the man who was paralyzed, "I say to you, arise, take up your bed, and go to your house."

It is time to take up your mat and go home.

There have been many times in the past where I have been so unworthy, please note I didn't say felt unworthy, no but rather times where I have just been unworthy. Sin at times keeps us down, no not at times but all of the time. That sin weights heavy upon your person so much so that you don't do anything, you can't be used and well it is just pitiful when sin is not been confessed if it is not confessed it can not be forgiven. Then there is the time when you do confess your sin and God is faithful to forgive this sin and you still just lay there, pick up your mat and go home.

Which is more on a scale sin or forgiveness? If you were to place all of your sins on a scale and all the forgiveness on the other side would it be balanced or would one out weight the other? There is no balance ratio between sin and forgiveness nor should we seek to balance the scale but to be weighted on the side of forgiveness.

One drop of blood from Christ was shed for all of our sin, those sins of our past your present and our future.

Some who saw this man on the mat heard Christ say your sins are forgiven, and Christ knew what they ponder in their heart. They called it blasphemy for who could forgive sin but God. They still didn't accept Christ as the Son of God, healer sure, magician okay, teacher not denied but Savior Messiah nope.

So let me ask you who is Christ to you? I know some one who thinks that the bible is just a good story and Christ a good teacher right along with Mohammad or Gandhi, well who is Christ to you. We prove who Christ is to us by the way we live, by taking up our mat after we have stumbled and fallen. We ask for and receive forgiveness of those sins because who we believe in, the scale doesn't come into balance no rather it is weight down on the side of forgiveness.

We must always repent and actually turn from our sin, it is not only a given but it is also a necessity right along with getting up. Do you need to stand today, do you need to get up off of the floor? Well what are you going to do about it? Forgiveness is so much of a better feeling then guilt live with the forgiveness of your sin instead of the guilt of a forgiven sin.

Ask -

John 14:[12]"Most assuredly, I say to you, he who believes in Me, the works that I do he will do also; and greater works than these he will do, because I go to My Father. [13]And whatever you ask in My name, that I will do, that the Father may be glorified in the Son. [14]If you ask[c] anything in My name, I will do it.

Tell me something have you prayed today to ask God just to get you thru this day, to keep a watchful eye upon you and keep your loved ones under His protection and care. Have you prayed Doug just to make it to 5 o'clock? It does seem a bit of a predicament that we say that we long for the day to swoop on by yet don't ask God for specifics of today.

You can do it, just say the name of Jesus Joe, go ahead and just say Jesus Christ? Does it send goose bumps up your arms just by saying the name? No, is the name of Christ just a name like Bob or Tom or Fran? No assuredly it is much more than just a name and sadly we sometimes treat is as it is just name like David or James.

Do you believe in Him? If you do the works that He did you will do also, how are your works are they Christ-like or manlike? The things that we do should, no scratch that and put MUST instead of should, our actions must reflect our belief in Christ. In our daily life we have ups and downs, side-to-side and sometimes flat on our backs. We find that we or rather I don't do the things that reflect good on Christ all of the time, shocker I aint perfect. Is there enough evidence in your life to show you as a believer in Christ, or are you just relying on knowing how to say the name of Christ.

"What ever you ask in My Name, that I will do," but how often do we fail to ask in His name?

Let your works today bring glory to the Father, that today when the punch clock sounds that people can look at you and say that you are different that you had joy that you were Christ like today instead of man-like. Don't lash out don't strike back, open your heart and ask Christ to be with you in all that you do. "Ask and it will be given," "you don't have because you don't ask."

What Kingdom?

Mark 12:33
And to love Him with all the heart, with all the understanding, with all the soul, and with all the strength, and to love one's neighbor as oneself, is more than all the whole burnt offerings and sacrifices."

So tell me whose kingdom are you building, yours or His? Well look at these verses, I know they don't say anything directly about kingdom building (maybe) but in these verses is wrapped the whole of where our desire should be. The greatest commands, to do two things: 1) to love Him with all your heart, all of your understanding, with your very soul and with all of your strength and 2) to love that person who ticks you off, that person who insults you, that person who bewilders you, to love your neighbor as you love yourself. In doing these things it is better than all of the burnt offerings and sacrifices; i.e. the burnt offering of a ram that took the place of a son on a hill, the offering of the son of Adam that was pleasant to the Lord.

To Love Him with your heart, mind, soul and strength nope sorry that is wrong you see look again at the beginning I just said to Love Him with your heart where as it is to be <u>with all</u> of your heart, all of your mind, all of you strength, and with all your soul. We must place our everything into this relationship with the Lord, holding nothing back. If we are about Kingdom building then we should be placing all of our self into it. We should be putting more emphasis into God instead of self, we should be using all that we have to serve and love Him. But can I ask you, no this time not the person next to you or the person whom you may forward this to but you sitting right there. Are you holding back? Not what are you holding back but are you holding back what is rightly His. Who is more deserving than the Lord to be loved with your all in all?

Whom do you love more than yourself, well whom do you place on a pedestal. Look I love Tam and the kids with all, just as you place your spouse or moms your family above your needs and your desires/wants but what is the gain in that? Loving those who seem un-loveable is a reflection of God's presence in your life; I would say that it is fruit of a person whose faith is where it needs to be. So here we are facing the fact that we must love our neighbor as much as we love ourselves, this is not an excuse to say your humble by the way, "Oh, but I only love myself a little bit so I only have to love those buttheads just a little bit," Spare me the semantics and lies for you know you are just trying to excuse your behavior away. *Dr Wynn: an excuse is just a lie wrapped up in respectability.*

Ya want to build the kingdom of God, then love HIM with your all and all, trust in Him He will be your stronghold in times of storm, put your all and all into your daily walk with HIM. Love those around you, don't deny even the spiteful the shirt off of your back, use your position on earth to reveal God's Kingdom. Let your fruit be fruit of the spirit instead the fruit of selfishness.

Strength for today

Psalm 3:3
But You, O LORD, are a shield for me, My glory and the
One who lifts up my head.

If you read all of Psalm 3 you see that David poor David is under assault and that there as people who wish him harm and he consoles himself in knowing who is really in control. Did the situation end immediately, no but in knowing who was really in control gave David strength for the day. In your day today is God in control or are you trying to take control?

A shield is protection for a person, something that is a barrier between the onslaught of arrows, blades, stones, and other projectiles. This shield deflects the harm from the person holding the shield, oops there it is thou the person must hold onto the shield. What good would it do if you had some one else carry the shield for you, would they be able to get the shield into position, or how about if you just left the shield lying on a shelf some where to be used only on a lets say Sunday morning as a well here is my shield. We must take up the shield daily and hang onto it placing its word in front of us not behind us, it must be with us daily. Here is a question for you; do you know enough of God's word for it to be an adequate defense for you?

What kind of protection does God grant to those who trust in Him? He lifts their head, does your head need to be lifted? David isn't saying he is glorious but rather that God is his Glory, how it must have been for David to have people not just want to insult him but also to insult his flesh with spears and death. There was God with him every day, lifting him up preparing him for the day, being his shield as he ventured into the fray of life.

There are days when we would just like to stay in the bed, or at the house not to get up and go to work or even to go be around other people. Just to stay in the cave and skip out on life. We have forgotten that we must get ready for the day by leaning on the word of God. We must hang onto the shield and place it in front of us as we go to work and or play.

Let the Glory of God raise your head today, don't be down cast because junk happens but rather turn to the LORD and let go of the reins. Who is in control but God no matter how hard we sometimes fight against Him for the reins.

Press On!

Philippians 3:14 I press toward the goal for the prize of the upward call of God in Christ Jesus.

What is your end goal for your life, to be with God for eternity right, or something along that line? Then shouldn't this also be our daily goal, each day gaining ground on the ultimate goal. Today there are steps that you must take towards this very goal, will you or are you going to continue to be in coast mode. How many of us need to heed these words found in Philippians, spoken by just a guy a brother in Christ who is imploring us to look forward and continue on?

When I was just a wee yonker delivering papers in February in Iowa there were days when the snow seemed deep but it was the wind whipping wind-chill that caused me the froze me to my very core. Bundling up on the porch before going out thoughts of how can I get thru this quicker so I can get back with the least appendages frozen off. Then out on the route I would walk between buildings and yes the occasional tree to try to avoid the bitter cold of a –20 degree wind-chill. You would do anything to avoid the wind even walking backwards to keep the wind off of your face. But there was one thing you had to do and keep in mind, you had to start to get finished. Too many Christian's haven't even started; they are still on the porch trying to bundle up, and there are also those who have gotten out into the wind and need to find shelter.

It is your and my responsibility to help give protection and encouragement to those who have been assailed by the wind and arrows. We must press on together! To encourage those who don't want to leave the porch. Each of us must keep our heads up looking toward Christ not at the junk at our feet, the mire that tries to hold us down. Have you found that you look at the situation you are in, and instead of dealing with it you stand there exposed to it all. Then take a step forward towards the LORD, reach out to Him He is reaching out to you.

Are you pressing on or have you been pressed down, please oh please in God's holy name stand up, knock the dirt and debris off and continue on. That person whom you know who has been knocked down help them up, lock arms with them and get going. Isn't that person whom you know who has never accepted Christ as Savior and Lord worth you sharing the gospel with them and you being an example to them after all what is the alternative for them.

Press on, look forward, this is the day that the LORD has made will you rejoice in it?

But I...

Matthew 7:5
Hypocrite! First remove the plank from your own eye, and then you will see clearly to remove the speck from your brother's eye.

Church folks are a funny lot, ya know we spend so much time talking about how awful some people are, how they certainly have faults in their lives that they gotta deal with. How can we possibly see what their faults are when we have a building sticking out of our own eyes, yes a building because we don't ever deal with the plank it just keeps building up to a shed, one-story house, then two-stories hopefully we deal with it when it becomes a mansion.

Can you just imagine what a person looks like with a mansion attached to their face, now that is kind of funny, no not exactly theological but it is funny. Sure people don't see the building but rather they can hear the arrogance and pride when church folks look down their noses at people.

Hey you, (I won't use a name here because each of us need to be named) how many times in the past week, month or year have you heard church folks talk about how this or that is wrong yet they don' t ever get involved. You know those girls who get pregnant before wedlock how awful, but they don't spend anytime at Save A Life, or I have never needed drugs or alcohol those folks over there are just druggies and drunks but they have yet to spend time at a rehab. Here is something that we all don't do which if we did it would probably help, talk to them instead of shunning them.

It is funny we don't seem to have any problem with gossips or slanderer's; we don't seem to have any problems talking with liars and hypocrites. Tell me could it be because we have yet to even try to tame our tongue?

What a slap in the face it would be to be called a hypocrite from Christ, but that is what we are if we don't deal with sin in our lives. Not a blanket gee God I have sinned but rather dealing with that individual sin, that specific sin that we have committed, do you see yourself as a sinner today if so have you repented of the sin in your life. All to often we have no stone to throw so put the stone down let it fall on your own foot because that is truly where it belongs.

Repent and turn from the plank that sticks out of your face, don't look down on your fellow sinner but maybe they need your help and maybe you need theirs.

Kingdom Building

Matthew 28:20 teaching them to observe all things that I have commanded you; and lo, I am with you always, even to the end of the age." Amen.

Did Christ teach you what time to go to church, did Christ teach you where to sit and what to wear, did Christ teach you what songs only to sing? Did He teach you how to do church, right about here Douglas is saying yes He did teach us how to do church, well how faithful are we in doing church the way Christ taught us to do church.

We love numbers and volume, we fluff membership when did attendance stop being more important the membership on a role, is this what Christ taught. 'And ye go make sure ya at least got their name on a card,' okay that is a bit of a stretch but how true is it that this is what we promote. In days of increasing population we have decreasing attendance in our churches, people have been taught to play church without a commitment to Christ so what motivates someone to go to church?

Well what motivates you? What have you learned that is so different from that of what the person you know who stays home on Sunday was taught? Have you asked them, have you asked yourself that question?

Going to church is not what gets you saved, but it does show fruit of a relationship with God. No Tim I am not suggesting that everyone who graces the doors on Sunday is saved, nor am I saying that everyone who doesn't show up on Sunday is lost. Rather it is the more then a want-ta it is a need-ta, if you miss a Sunday do you miss it?

You and I have a commission to go out and share the gospel, we have the responsibility to make them disciples of Christ not of our brand of church. Tell me who is it that you need to go to and encourage to come to church, maybe it needs to start with asking them if they believe in Christ. We need to be about Kingdom building not role fluffing, we must be faithful to in witnessing to those who are lost without Christ in their life not because they are another denomination then we are, but rather seeking to share the gospel of life with all we come in contact with.

Shelly whom will you share the gospel with today, how about you Chuck who is it that needs you to tell them about Christ, and you Crystal who in Auburn not Thailand need you to be a witness in their life today? And YOU when will you talk to that person you have been hesitant to witness to, when will you accept the commission and witness to the end of the earth by starting in your own home in your own community in your own church in your state, your country and then to nations. When will we truly do Church God's way by worshiping in Spirit and in Truth, when will I when will you. Today is a good day. "And lo I am with you even to the end of the age. Amen" Christ is with you when you go, always.

Encourage the guy next to you.

Now me being whom I am please understand that in this sense guy means both ladies and gentlemen who are next to you. See Mike you can take the man out of Iowa but you can't take the Iowa out of the man. Any way my point to this is there is some one whom you know needs you to share the gospel with, to share your story with, or simply for you to open your heart to and listen to them. Each of us has a commission as we spoke about yesterday, but have you acted yet upon that commission. Some one replied that they will wait until Thursday and yes they were just kidding, but in their humor they really hit the nail on the head. You are going to put it off until you are put in a corner and have no choice.

Some one once asked well what verses do I use, what do I say, when do you know the right time is to share the gospel or to share your witness with someone. To be perfectly honest with you if you are waiting for your right set of circumstances to feel comfortable or to feel empowered or whatever, then you will have missed multiple chances to be the witness that you say you want to be.

What is the right time, situation, place to share the gospel well can you tell me how many times Christ witnessed to folks in church or how many times He shared the Light while on a street or on a hill? He went where the people were, not sitting in a classroom waiting for people to come in. Yes I know we are not Christ so it isn't fair to use Him as an example, even thou He is the example. Ya know what I was going to say "okay I'll let ya off of the hook this one time," but nope, He is the example so strive to be Christ like just as Paul, Peter, James, Timothy, Philip and many others did.

> *Luke 4:22*
> *So all bore witness to Him, and marveled at the gracious words which proceeded out of His mouth. And they said, "Is this not Joseph's son?"*

We have all seen the things that God has done for us. We have even read the things in the gospels of what Christ has done. Have you stopped marveling at what God can do or has done for you? Some will say the same thing of you, is this not Ruby's son, is this not Mr. Show's wife, isn't this Sarah's mom, isn't this Mr. Hackleburg 1986? This they will know that it won't be the old man that they see but a changed man.

A Psalm of life,

Psalm 23
The LORD is my shepherd;
I shall not want.
²He makes me to lie down in green pastures;
 He leads me beside the still waters.
 ³He restores my soul;
He leads me in the paths of righteousness
For His name's sake.
 ⁴Yea, though I walk through the valley of the shadow of
    death,
I will fear no evil;
For You are with me;
Your rod and Your staff, they comfort me.
⁵You prepare a table before me in the presence of my
    enemies;
You anoint my head with oil;
My cup runs over.
⁶Surely goodness and mercy shall follow me
All the days of my life;
And I will dwell[a] in the house of the LORD
Forever.

This is a Psalm of life not a reflection of death, a psalm for Thursday a psalm for today.

Catherine and Jenna is this a psalm that reassures you for today? I guess this psalm is used a lot at funerals and the like, times of mourning and hurt. Jeff is this psalm supposed to reassure us that everything will be okay after we have lost a loved one or can it possibly be a reflection a daily walk with GOD.

Will you fear evil today or will you be comforted because He is there keeping watch over you and guiding you. God has prepared a table before you, but have you sat up to it? If you look at these verses ask yourself something, three words only "HAVE I ASKED."

Do I want because I have not asked? Is my soul in need of being restored because I have not asked? Have you ever found yourself walking next to raging waters next to the rapid and that if you were to fall in certainly you would be dashed against the rocks, who led you to that predicament? God doesn't wish for you or I to suffer, before we took the path to the rapids there was a choice. Lets face it most of us make bad decisions everyday we find that the water churns and foams. We wonder where is the still water? Well have you asked, and after you asked did you listen, if you listened did you follow God or did you go on your own.

Today ask, listen and follow.

Simple

Matthew 10:7
And as you go, preach, saying, "The kingdom of heaven is at hand.'

What time do you have, what day is this, and oh where are you? To get the answer you look at your watch, a calendar, and or your feet simple huh. Simple isn't it! Then tell me something where will you be tomorrow or the day after, is this as simple to answer? Nope we don't know, we hope we will be here but we are not promised tomorrow, and for that matter you are not even promised the top of the hour. Where are you in the kingdom of heaven?

The instructions that Christ gave the 12 were simple, go to preach saying "The kingdom of heaven is at hand," He tells them to go only to the Jews, not to go to the Gentiles cities, or Samarian cities but to the Israelites. While there they were to heal, raise and preach. I can't find what happened when they went out or the report of when they returned. They were only to take limited supplies and provisions that they would have to trust those to whom they preached for their well-being.

So as you start the day today what have you been told, to go and preach saying that the kingdom of heaven is at hand, haven't you been told that very same thing or do you bow out and say well that's the pastor's job. Tell me who was the last person you shared the gospel with? Did they look like you, act like you, were they in your same social economic class. Can I bet ya something, you haven't even shared the gospel with those who look like you, act like you or those who are in your same social economic class.

Now I am not saying that Christ sent these out because they had to get used to sharing to those whom they knew and the Gentiles and Samaritans would come next, with that being said He did send them out to those whom it should have been more comfortable for the 12 to go to because of a common culture and understanding. Even in this Christ gave them warning that some would reject what they had to say about the approaching kingdom and how to knock the dust from their feet.

Are you changing the world or is the world changing you?

I plead with you today to not let the world change you, that maybe we must do some dust knocking off of our sandals' and reject what the world says. The kingdom is at hand, are you ready, if your not ready how can you tell some one else.

Carrying

1 Timothy 6:7 For we brought nothing into this world, and it
is certain we can carry nothing out.

Looking at my bank account it is assured that there won't be
anything left to take with me even if I could or for that matter
wanted to. Then again what do we bank up instead of banking on?
What did you come into this world with, lets face it you were as
naked as a jaybird without a banknote to your name. What was in
your hand, what was in your heart, what was your desire, other than
taking your first breath there wasn't a thing that you thought about.
Somewhere along the line we started working towards something,
for some that knew what they would be when they grew up for
others it was towards a cushy retirement. Can I ask you something
of you financial wizards out there Doug A. Doug D., Jesse, Rod and
Chuck oh you also Bob-oh. Can a person be 100% financially secure
without chance of it being taken away or being stolen? 100% mind
you is as thin as a cloud, it may look solid but it can be blown away
with the least breeze.

So now tell me ya'll what are you working to build, yep me I am
building the Fran Empire. Which is a scary thought, (no comment
out of the Ricardo section) but what is it that is our goal or should be
our goal. If we can carry nothing out with us what are we counting
on? Faith, it is as intangible as the breeze but it can also be as solid

as the mountain. Is your faith something you hold onto, not your church motto or action plan but your faith in … Christ?

I know we want to leave our children well off, we want to provide for them after we have entered the grave so that they can have what we never had. This could be the problem, maybe we leave them as empty as we are if we don't have faith in Christ. The one thing that you could give to your children is something you can't give them but something you can encourage them to have and that is faith in Christ.

Time Out: Jesus Christ, the Light, the Word, Emmanuel, the Son, JESUS CHRIST!!!

(I just had to take a moment)

When you were a child you depended upon your parents to provide for you, even if you didn't know it or really who they were. Only when you grew older did you grow in understanding to know who your parents were. Are you still a baby without understanding of who your Father is?

Look you there are no atms, swipe cards, or out of state checks in heaven. At the gate is not a punch key or speaker announcer. Heaven is the ultimate gated community and you do not gain entry from what is in your wallet or what you wear or who your friends are unless you know Christ as your Savior and Lord you don't know the right people.

If you went out today and left this world as you came in what would you leave with?

View

Genesis 1:1 In the beginning God created the heavens and the earth. ²The earth was without form, and void; and darkness was on the face of the deep. And the Spirit of God was hovering over the face of the waters.

³Then God said, "Let there be light"; and there was light. ⁴And God saw the light, that it was good; and God divided the light from the darkness. ⁵God called the light Day, and the darkness He called Night. So the evening and the morning were the first day.

Have you considered today that this is also a day that the Lord has made and that it is no different from the first day that God created?

"In the beginning God," can you add anything to that for the start of your day, have you started this day off with God. Even if God created the earth from a molten ball out of the sun it was God who did the creating not some random set of cosmic collisions. Tell me Jo Ann are you a random set of cosmic dust that just so happened to have taken the form you are now in, some of ya sure but most of you are God created, God designed and God breathed. God took His time and created those things that would sustain life first then created us. Look here Ricardo God has created you just as much as God created Jacob or Paul, and in the same way all of us have the opportunity today to live up to our creation and glorify the Lord by what we do today.

As the sun creeps over Georgia and across the plains to Nebraska it is a new day a day where the sun rises. "God saw the light, that it was good," that nothing will be hidden in the light for the light reveal everything and that light is life. There isn't a plant on the earth in the sea that doesn't respond to light, yes even in the deepest ocean floor there is life around the cracks in the earth where molten gives off its light. That if the earth were plunged into darkness it would grow cold and would die and everything upon the earth and in the sea would also perish.

Look around the world today, the Light is being pushed aside and the world grows cold. How about in your life, does the Light shine or does self shine, do your ambitions shine, do you walk more in the darkness where things maybe hidden from others. Understand that God can see both in the light and in the darkness, that there is nothing you nor I can hide from Him. This is our choice you see to walk in a way that is in the light as the first day for the Light who is Christ has come into the world.

View your life and see if you relish the darkness rather then the light, or if you are trying to skirt between darkness and light, just good enough but not giving up that what the world takes pleasure in.

I wonder if when the Spirit of the Lord hovered over the waters if today, that is this day passed thru His thoughts? How will you live today, really the choice is yours.

Have You A Hunger

Matthew 5:6 Blessed are those who hunger and thirst for righteousness, For they shall be filled.

Out in the field we would have to eat MREs that is a military way of saying meals ready to eat sorta. Marines always had it easier eating MREs because well basically they had knifes with them all of the time and could get thru the 1000 ply plastic that protected the MRE. After about a week of MREs one would almost get a hunger for Crusty's pizza (that is for another devotional). I know people debate on what is better the suki-yak-I or the beef-stay down-stew but to me the best was still the peanut butter and crackers, to you Doug the hot dogs would be a delicacy because they are more like Vienna sausages on steroids. There is only so much trading for peanut butter one can do in a week to stave off hunger, eventually you need something of substance.

Have you a hunger for righteousness, do you thirst for it do you even seek it at all? Breakfast is the most important meal of the day right, but most of us skip it or say well my third cup of coffee is my biscuits and gravy. In the same way people skip their relationship with the Lord in the morning. I know we love listening to the radio on the way to work and many of you bee-bop to the songs and worship right there behind the wheel. Tell me how much better are those days that you begin the day in worship from those where you just sip the cup?

Something that comes to mind is those guys in the movies who are out in the desert and are crawling on the sand, in tattered clothes and whispering "water-water," they may see the delusion or mirage of water up there ahead and pass right by the well. Can our thirst at times be so great that we may feel that we must plug on to some mirage instead of just looking around us?

I ask you when was the last time you opened up God's word and read it to learn from it, to apply what you read to your life? Is there in your heart a desire to seek that, which is righteous, and you are willing to crawl on your belly thru scorching sand to take a drink?

Lets face it most of us don't know what it is like to be hungry or thirsty for material food or drink, we live in a place where grocery stores are on every street corner and vending machines are in every building. Food for your body is plentiful, but tell me about your soul have you fed the hunger there have you filled the thirst that is in your heart or are you still waiting for tomorrow. Sad isn't it, that nourishment is available but we don't consume it.

Blessed are those who hunger and thirst for righteousness, for they will be filled. Has nothing to do with what is in your belly.

Rest

Psalm 37:7 Rest in the LORD, and wait patiently for Him; Do not fret because of him who prospers in his way, Because of the man who brings wicked schemes to pass.

Hey Jesse and Rod can I ask ya something, is everybody working for the weekend so they can get some rest? Aint we a bunch of ninnies only finding time to rest on the weekend, please give me a break look at your weekend you don't rest, many of us don't even "sleep in," on the weekend we got to much we gotta get caught up on. My point is we don't rest, we fill up our days with junk and stuff thinking this is the good life and then wonder why we gotta take medication to sleep, or lower our blood pressure. Rest what is rest?

Rest as defined by Webster's **(man look at how many definitions rest has, seems a bit busy)**

1 : REPOSE, SLEEP; *specifically* : a bodily state characterized by minimal functional and metabolic activities
2 a : freedom from activity or labor b : a state of motionlessness or inactivity c : the repose of death
3 : a place for resting or lodging
4 : peace of mind or spirit
5 a (1) : a rhythmic silence in music (2) : a character representing such a silence b : a brief pause in reading
6 : something used for support

- at rest 1 : resting or reposing especially in sleep or death 2
: QUIESCENT, MOTIONLESS 3 : free of anxieties

So now tell me do you rest? Can you rest in the LORD? Tell me
something Jenna and Deanna why is it folks don't rest in the LORD
who can actually do something about our ills and wants? For it is
our ills and wants that cause us not to rest. Our ills being our sick-
ness or illness or those of our loved ones who are not well, so we fret
over their health to the detriment of ours. Our wants, thinking that
the grass is greener in the other yard and struggling to get the bigger
widget becomes our desire. Is there rest?

The rest for you Hugh is in the LORD, and you Jeff is in the
LORD. We will not rest until we rely on the LORD instead of our
hands He waits for you and I to rely on Him.

Fish Or Catching

Luke 5:4-5 ⁴When He had stopped speaking, He said to Simon, "Launch out into the deep and let down your nets for a catch."

⁵But Simon answered and said to Him, "Master, we have toiled all night and caught nothing; nevertheless at Your word I will let down the net."

Let it be known that I am a fisherman not a catcher man, meaning I can go to the water and cast out a line but for all the casts that are made few is the return. Definitely when I am on the river the safest place for the fish is in the water. That's is okay cause I am only there to soak up nature, bull pucky, I would like to snag me a hog just once. A hog in this case for those of you from Iowa isn't a four-legged creature but rather a 9 Lb large mouth bass that jumps and slashes a fish that is worthy of going up on the wall. Know what I mean Doug and Richard. SO you can sit back and hook your thumb into a belt loop or pocket and go "yep that thar was one great fight, but there she is up on the wall."

Are we like Simon, we have fished and not gotten the results that we had desired so we are ready to call it a day and just go home? When Christ got into the boat and then taught from the boat and then after He was finished told Simon to push out into deeper water. Could it be that we shouldn't give up either that maybe Christ is also calling us to deeper water and to cast our nets out? We can be like

Simon and tell Christ that we have been at this for a while and don't have didly to show for it. Then we must also look at "nevertheless," and this is the hook.

Unfortunately we sometimes end with "I give up," instead of saying "nevertheless," because we are what; lazy, tired, ran out of time or whatever excuse we use to get out of the boat. We would rather go to the shore and shallow water rather than stay in the boat and go to deep water. We say we want people to hear about Christ but we stay in the shallow water and hope the fish will swim up to us, and yes on occasion they do, but rather just on occasion. But the fish live in deep water. To use a Dewberry expression "fish where the fish are."

So today as you push off from shore are you only willing to go so far for Christ or do you dare to go to deep water. If God leads you what is the worry, the worry is self and not the fish. Isn't it sad that the shore is full of bystanders where the deep water remains vacant, boats hug the coast but only a few venture to the deep water. We catch what we fish for, if we sit on the shore we will catch the occasional fish but if you truly want revival ya need to go to deep water.

Nevertheless, because He said to go and cast your net for the catch

True Worshipers

John 4:23
But the hour is coming, and now is, when the true worshipers
will worship the Father in spirit and truth; for the Father is
seeking such to worship Him.

A re we doing worship-service aerobics, stand up sit down, kneel
get up stand up sit down stand back up bow sit down sing this
song recite this prayer sing this song at this time only. Now I don't
claim to be the world's best writer or anything, basically I have been
rightfully accused of having to many run-on sentences, that I don't
use punctuation near enough or as much as I aught ta. So what? We
live our lives with such structure that it is truly amazing, each of
us go to work at a certain time, we go thru the routine with almost
mechanical un-awareness. We miss out on the little things because
we are on autopilot. Unfortunately this is how we also worship
GOD, just on autopilot going thru the motions, staying within the
boundaries of punctuation.

Now I know that structure is good, for pete sakes, I am the worst
about getting into a rut oops I mean routine. That there is reason
enough for proper punctuation is a fact, some one I wont mention
names but Lou we both know him (nudge-nudge wink-wink) would
probably say "punctuation conveys understanding." Still no argument with me on that but as yet this has nothing to do with worshiping
in spirit and truth and that is where the rubber meets the road.

Is our worship becoming so structured that we engage the auto-pilot as soon as we enter the doors or even before we crank up the car? If you look at attendance in your church that people are not coming to church like they did in the 60's or even 70's they have set a different course. It is one of those funny things to me that some denominations talk about how other denominations are so rigidly traditional but then turn around and say but only sing this song in this spot. How is this in spirit and truth? Or when some one comes into church with shorts on, of course what you wear is all about spirit and truth, isn't it?

I wonder if you would pause after this devo and close your eyes and picture the LORD in your hearts eye. IF you see GOD reaching out to you because of what you are wearing or who you are or what denomination you proclaim? All of that is bumpkiss to God it is as filthy rags. Does He care more about what is on your back then Who is in your heart, does He care about your title compared to His, give me a break. He reaches out to you, seeking for you to worship Him in Spirit and Truth, not because you have to or aught to but because you want to need to desire to just WORSHIP HIM.

Being Bold, or just thinking about it

1 Thessalonians 2:2
But even after we had suffered before and were spitefully treated at Philippi, as you know, we were bold in our God to speak to you the gospel of God in much conflict.

What was the last thing that you did that was bold, have you ever done anything that was bold?

First lets get something straight it isn't we just need to be brave, sure a certain about of that is good, rather we need to be bold putting our bravery into action. If you have ever seen the story of Sgt. York you would see that when the fire hit the fan that it came down to taking action instead of staying under cover. I am not sure how accurate the story was but there are two things that were bold about York that are un-questionable, 1) He did write a conscientious objector letter, and 2) He did step up to the plate and took action to silence the enemy to spare his fellow countrymen. Alvin York was a brave man. Paul stood up and stood his ground despite mistreatment by those around them, his bravery is also unquestionable and his boldness is an example to us all.

In this day and age of political pomposity we have cowed to what is so called diverse and open-minded by engaging in being politically correct because we have grown soft and feeble in our boldness to speak the word of God. We have come to be concerned more of what is in our wallets or what we drive because we mustn't make waves less these things could dissolve. By the way this isn't directed just at those from the pulpit, no – no my friends but it is directed at the Sunday School teacher, the men's ministry directors, the WMU directors and yes even the member who sits with folded hands in the pew. We all need to get up and be bold and stand bravely for the LORD.

We have but to share the gospel, we don't need to bell and whistle it or tweak it of dilute it to fit in a certain form. We must be bold to share it in its form. How many times we turn our heads and walk away from a situation because we want people to go to hell, oh that doesn't sound nice does it. Who will share the gospel with that person if you don't, how will they ever know but unless you stand up and call them on it. Lets not forget that they will end up in hell if you and I and the guy next to you or the person you may forward this to, if we don't share the gospel of Christ with them.

The price has already been paid for your salvation; the blood on the cross is still fresh, yes even after all of these years. We don't have to be bold to tell people about ourselves and where we are from, not at all, we must be bold to tell people about Christ. Who He is, what He has done, and Why He did what He did. Can we even answer those simple who, what and why statements. YES WE CAN AND YES WE SHOULD. This is not a space odyssey but rather an eternal destination for you and for the person whom you really don't want to see go to hell.

Don't just nod your head and say sure that is what we need to do, rather stand up and get out from behind cover and meet the enemy in the fray. Be armed with the Word of God, Put on His armor.

Written Name

Revelation 3:5
He who overcomes shall be clothed in white garments, and
I will not blot out his name from the Book of Life; but I will
confess his name before My Father and before His angels.

Okay, Doug – Doug, Jo Ann, Tammy, Hugh, Walter, David, Tom, Jesse, Joe, Linda, Pat, David, Rod, Deborah, Crystal, Lou, Tim, Lynn, Ricardo, Chuck, Matt, Deanna, Rachel, Rusty, Etta, Danita, and every one else your names are on the address list to receive this devotional but are your names where it counts? You know in the Book of Life I don't have to worry about if God is going to say Fran well I thought you were a _ _ _ _ _, for He will have Christ confessing my name to the Father and before His angels.

It was funny out of the three events over the past few days people had come up to me asking when their names would be in a devotional while others just joked about it. Ya know Joel that is kind of funny isn't it? Some people have said that I shouldn't put peoples name in the devotionals but I still do not to point to anyone in particular because in Fran's book of psychology I have noticed that everyone places more attention on a name and will put their name in place of the name that was written on the page. Now if your name does appear in a devo it is not because I saw you doing anything wrong but rather it is just because I happen to put your name in the devotional. Now if your name is not listed don't be upset with me either okay Alison cause ya know that you are my sister in Christ and yes you too Nancy and Leigh.

I wonder though how many of us have our name in the book that counts, and if we show as much curiosity about having our name in that book. Hmm I wonder, if we will hear Christ confess the names of those people reading this devo or the friends of those reading this devo, or the family of those reading this? Is your name in the book?

Ya know Charles that those who overcome shall be clothed in white garments, that those who endure to the end will have the reward of life. Does it say that those who have lived a perfect life Jeanne, does it say that only those who have never sinned will overcome, no it doesn't for only Christ lived a perfect sinless life, only Christ. There are is something special about the word "overcome," it implies struggle and victory. There is a battle out there Joel that we must or rather that we go thru, we don't go into that struggle without weapons or a defense. We only overcome when the blood of Christ has washed us clean and the victory is ours because of Who HE is.

I pray that today you overcome that you look at where your name is or isn't written. That you look at one thing; do you know the Name of the One who is doing the writing or do you just know about who He is. It won't really matter in the end if I do or don't use your name in one of these devotionals, make sure God knows you and that you know Him and He will write your name in His Book.

Acceptable

Psalm 19:14
Let the words of my mouth and the meditation of my heart
Be acceptable in Your sight, O LORD, my strength and my
Redeemer.

Have you ever tried to please someone, husband – wife – child-boss – friend – stranger? How do you please these people, by doing what they ask, by doing what you know they like, how do you go about making them happy? We please our spouse, most of the time I hope, because we love them and respect them and cherish that relationship, our desire is to make them happy, you could apply that to your child (ren) also. So how do you please your friend or boss, I have to say this carefully because my bosses are reading this and it could reflect positively or negatively. That in and of itself is what we do, we try to please our bosses and friends by doing what is safe and not causing a rift in the lake/pond. You and I don't want to call our friends on something they did that is wrong nor do you want to tell your boss that things have crashed and burned. But can you tell me who's statutes are right, who's law is good and is there to keep you from harm, the Lords ways are right and His statutes are just. We should concern ourselves with living by the LORD's ways and if it doesn't please our friends then are they truly our friends, and the statutes or policy's and procedures of work conflict with God's law then who will redeem you instead of just fire you?

I highly encourage you to read the entire Psalm and then to meditate upon it. Open your heart to it and ask yourself if you can live up to it. If you say you can't live up to it then what is it that is keeping you from it. Tell me this are there words from your mouth that are un-acceptable to the LORD, are some of the things you dwell on are they contrary to God wish for your life. In today's society there are many things that are contrary to God's design for our life. Have we steeped ourselves in the things of this world instead of the things of God?

Profanity, depraved sexual relationships, slander, gossip, are just some examples of things that have become more acceptable in the world and also in the church and it is our fault because we don't stand up and call anyone on it. Sure we may not hear these things in the sanctuary but how about in the stairwell or Sunday school class-room or in the parking lot. These things are reflections of a lack of meditating in God's word, they are a reflection of being transformed by the world instead of by the LORD.

Tell me something, have you ever heard of anyone taking shots at someone else at church or talking ill of some other race or group, show me in God's word that this is right to do. Have we accepted adultery and marital infidelity in our churches? It may not be as open as gossip or slander but we can all probably sit back and think of a time when we have see it go on. We should love the sinner not accept the sin, well to often we love the sinner and look over the sin because of the size of the wallet the sinner has. Show me in God's commandments that this is right to do?

What will you read and meditate on today, will the things that you meditate upon be pleasing to the LORD?

Have You Turned

Ezekiel 14:6
"Therefore say to the house of Israel, "Thus says the Lord GOD: "Repent, turn away from your idols, and turn your faces away from all your abominations.

There is a sign at a church here in the Valley that reads, "America Needs Revival," and all of you, okay most of you said yes to that, but true revival will start when the local body of believers stops playing church and starts being Christ like and serving God instead of themselves. Ya know I wonder how in the world the Jews ever turned from God, I mean the time from Abraham to Moses wasn't all that long, the time from Moses to Daniel wasn't that long, how soon they forgot who brought them out of Egypt. I guess they started to think it was Moses who brought them out and turning from a man is not that difficult.

The time from Christ till today is really not all that long either, because unlike Moses, Abraham, Daniel and David Christ is alive and the Holy Spirit works even to this day. How can we forget who is still alive and doing miracles today, but we do forget. How many folks do you know who worship their idols of work – play – money – whatever it is that they have placed before God is their idol? I wonder if we have truly turned away from the old self and our old ways.

Could God say to you "Thus says the Lord GOD;" Repent, turn away from your idols, and turn you faces away from all your abominations. Sure He could and certainly He does. Why do the local churches need revival, could be for a lot of reasons. Each person needs revival, in Webster's it defines revival as a spiritual awakening. That doesn't sound like something we should put on the calendar to me, we need to have 2 revivals a year one in the spring and one in the summer. Each day we must have a spiritual awakening, learning something from God each day.

You see if we place work – money – play – or whatever in front of God then they become our focus and we learn from them and grow in them instead of God. Look Doug A. don't you think it would be a good idea to have God with you at work, instead of just checking in with God once a week or month or twice a year (Easter and Christmas). Sure we think it is a good idea, but do we do it? More often then not maybe huh.

Right and wrong are miles away from each other, you know what is right and what is wrong, but do we know what is sin and what is not? If we don't know what is sin then that is a BIG problem, maybe just maybe we need to have a relationship with God and turn from the our old ways and turn to His Eternal Way.

Fell

Matthew 26:41 Watch and pray, lest you enter into temptation. The spirit indeed is willing, but the flesh is weak."

How long have you waited, how long have you watched, how
long have you prayed or have you stopped looking, stopped
watching and just fell into temptation. While in the garden Christ
asked His apostles to pray and keep watch before He went off sepa-
rately from them to pray alone, by the time He returned they had
fallen asleep. Not an hour passed and these guys zonked out, bless
their heart. Then again what were they thinking, this was after the
last supper where Christ even pointed out that He would be turned
over. Why were they not more on alert, after all Peter went armed?
Simply that in their heart they wanted to but in their flesh they needed
sleep and the flesh won out.

Are we any different from they who fell asleep, haven't we fallen
asleep because we want to do things that are of the flesh instead of
doing things of the Spirit. After all Christians can't have fun they
have to be holy pious and blah blah blah spare me. There are too
many Christians with down turned mouths, somber in appearance
and dull in disposition because what cracking a smile would crack
their face, please. The reverse of that is also true that there are
Christians that are so into the world that you can't tell them from
the world; they have forgotten that being holy is to be separate from
the world. About here one would say that there is a fine line between

piety and worldly but I won't say that at all, but rather it is a matter of prayer and watchfulness and obedience.

You see, when I look across the things that God has created from the hills and mountains to the creeks (cricks) and rivers from the lakes and ponds to even more human things of marriage relationships to dating from friends and family that all of these things are creations of the LORD GOD. It is the abuse of what He has created that brings about sin, not the use of the things for what their intentional use is that is sinful. God is not against having fun after all He created it. Some people look at me and go you're a pastor but you're so full of personality (I like that one) then there are some people who say you're a pastor you're supposed to act like... Sometimes that just makes me cringe down to my heals, if I have to act like something I am not then I am not doing what God has called me to do, I do keep watch and pray for God to lead me.

Our Christian walk is supposed to be about our relationship with God not how we feel we are supposed to act like to others. If you keep watch and pray God will be there with you leading you guiding you, it is when we succumb to the flesh that is not God's leading or guiding and we have far to many folks sleeping in this day and age. WAKE UP, KEEP WATCH that you may not fall into the temptations of the flesh, PRAY in your watchfulness and live for God and not for man.

Enduring

Psalm 22:26 The poor shall eat and be satisfied; Those who seek Him will praise the LORD. Let your heart live forever!

Christ has died, Christ has risen and Christ will come again – do you believe?

What have you endured in the name of God? Over there at West Point what really have people done to you because you profess the name of Christ as the way the truth and the light. How about over there in Lanett, who ridicules you and harms you because you confess that No man comes to the Father but by Christ. Do we think that because we do good community events that this is cause for patting ourselves on the back, or that we give money so missionaries like Paul and Barnabus have the resources to go out that this things are as good as we can do but that isn't even suffering for us. If you were to read Psalm 22 you will find that it talks about the suffering that Christ will endure, and suffer He did but in the end the victory was His. Just as one day you may have to suffer for the Lord because of what you believe because of where your faith lays, will you endure?

There is a term that is creeping its way into popular culture that is semantically fine but in the application of this word it is one sided or slanted against certain groups. Diversity is a fine word but diverse is not all that it implies. Rather there is a group that calls their lifestyle okay and right and if you speak out against that lifestyle you are phobic. Diversity is being used as a guise of acceptance and tolerance oh but if you don't agree with a particular group then you are closed-minded. Sticks and stones you may say but there are laws on the books that you could receive fines for by just speaking out against the groups, hate crime. So much for your freedom of speech if you are a Christian who takes the word of God as the Word of God because your freedom is not as valid as others freedom of speech.

Will you have to suffer on a cross of wood and nails, will all of your bones be exposed, will they cast lots for your clothing? Will you suffer a demotion, will you loose out financially, will you endure being fired all because you will not back off of your position of Faith. Maybe it is years down the road, you know in your grandchildren's age, that we will see active assaults on the church that are more than just words. Tell me who will you give money to when it comes down to that, tell me where will your voice be when things start to unravel?

What are you waiting for to get more involved, are you waiting to pass the plate or are you strapping on your shoes?

Teacher

Matthew 10:25 It is enough for a disciple that he be like his teacher, and a servant like his master. If they have called the master of the house Beelzebub,[a] how much more will they call those of his household!

I was out at the river yesterday, again its close by and there are fish there in need of catching, and when the sun came out time-to-time and the waters reflected the trees and shrubbery that line the banks. I noticed that the reflection was imperfect because of the flow of the water and it dawned on me that sometimes we are an imperfect reflection of Christ or at times when the Son is blotted out by the clouds, that we don't even reflect Christ at all. We haven't learned from the master or the teacher because at times we refuse to be the servant or the student.

There are many things that keep us from being and doing what we are supposed to do, many excuses to not reflect the light. Then again for each excuse there is a reason to reflect the light, we just choose the path of least resistance. Some one asked yesterday why we sin, is it because of original sin or is it because well we choose the easy way and the easy way is often sin.

Each day that we wake we must strive to live as Christ lived, sure some days are better than others and sure sometimes we fall on our cans' but in a way whether you are on you backside or on your feet what is the lesson that you have learned? Well gee I can never do the things that Christ did, I can never even come close. So what that gives us the right to throw up our hands in defeat, great so then what will happen, what God can just call you home. But He hasn't called you home, so that means that you are still a part of His plan here on earth so get up and stop thinking about what you can't do and start thinking about what He can do thru you.

Do you live up to your favorite verse in the bible; do you everyday live up to it? I know I don't every day live up to it but I shall not stop trying will you or am I just that much better than you are? That should just tick you off because you know that I am no better than you are, hey I know that. To many people have stopped even trying to live up to God's word and just settle to live up to a pastor or deacon or family friend or mentor but they are not the Master they are not the Teacher.

What would happen this week if you and I tried to live up to God's word each day, thoughtfully and deliberately going about our day living up to what God has said and what Christ has taught? Can you imagine Helen and Julie if we all walked as Christ walked, loved as Christ loved, lived as Christ lived? One thing is for sure today Doug and David today you will reflect something that you have learned, will it be something of God or something of man?

Guided

Psalm 73:23
Nevertheless I am continually with You; You hold me by my right hand. 24You will guide me with Your counsel, And afterward receive me to glory.

Have you ever walked with your child or a child thru a shopping center or mall? You take them by the hand to keep them close and to keep them from harm. You guide their steps as God try's to guide your steps. I saw kids who would pull on their parent's arm to pull them toward the toys or the candy or try to twist away so they could take off. The parent would let the kids guide them and when the kid would get away they would say "now Johnny no-no," man if I did that when I was a kid it would have been now-now then duck cause there was going to be repercussion off of my backside for disobeying. People have lost their fear of punishment, how about you?

Sometimes we don't know which way to go, okay fur me a lot of the time I wonder which way to go. We for some reason have let go of God's hand and try to go it alone. When if we would just hang on He would guide our steps along the right path. Have you ever struggled with which fork in the road to take and sit there and scratch your head and hmm a lot debating the correct path? Then after you find out that you chose the wrong road you try to back track or get out of the way of that decision that has caused the discomfort of moment. Sometimes when we do these things we just need to stop and drop and fall on our knees and reach up and remember that God is there to guide us. That He will guide us out of the mess we have created, and even thou there maybe repercussions for messing up that God will be there with you even then.

We are not children any longer but still we try to pull and twist to go after what is pleasing to the eye instead of what God has in store for us. Maybe it is the grass is greener thing and we desire that which we don't have. Have you ever figured that the grass is greener because the sewer line is busted and that the grass may look lush and fine but it stains your feet with filth. How many times do we pull at God's hand and then let go to get what we want?

Ya know today recall that God is in control, that you must just hang on and He will guide your steps. That if you feel as if you are slipping to hang on even tighter, He will not let go of you. We are the ones who let go. We have a choice today to hang onto God's hand or let go. Whom would you rather be the guide of your life, God or you? Give me God over myself any day. Rationally speaking He has never messed up or miss stepped where as I have the uncanny knack of falling face first while I run after the toys.

Hold hands with God, take His guidance with love and grace and follow where He guides you.

In Your Heart

Romans 10:9 that if you confess with your mouth the Lord
Jesus and believe in your heart that God has raised Him from
the dead, you will be saved.

Okay first of all I just gotta say that I wish to offend no one with
this devo, that being said let me share with you the zealous
nature of Alabama vs. Auburn well just go ahead and throw in the
entire SEC. I think at birth most children are given two options in
Bama, that is to either be a Alabama Crimson Tide Fan or a War
Eagle Auburn Tiger's Fan. This is nurtured thro out their entire life
and I am relatively sure that there are Tide or Tiger fans that have
been buried in either Crimson and White or Blue and Orange. That
isn't much of a stretch is it Doug can ya see that, I mean Rod do you
even own any cloths that could possible be taken as Tiger colors?
This is as you can plainly see has been one of my biggest hurdles
down here in Bama since I am not native born.

You see I have not declared elegance with either team or any in
the SEC. Even thou I know the history of the Crimson tide from a
thunderstorm that created a mess of Alabama clay on the field and
their front line look like a line of elephants, that they have all these
national championships, and yes I know the history of the battle cry
of the War Eagle dating back to the Civil War and the SEC championships. Sure I know all about it aint over till the short man kicks.
Still knowing the facts and stats and history and about these teams

doesn't make you a fan, only until you live a live of dedication of Auburn or Alabama does one really get accepted as a fan.

So using this as an example do you know Christ as well as you think you do? Rather have you learned the stats, facts and stories but yet have never declared your commitment to Him? Look here you can know the stories and can even recite the bible verse to verse chapter to chapter but if you have never confessed Him for who He is and what He has done for you then you are just an outsider looking in. It is when you acknowledge that He is the Christ, the one who came from God, the one who died upon a cross for our sins, for your sins and that He was buried and that God raised Him from the dead will one then become a fan.

Sure sports analogies seem a bit weird at times but there is a lot of truth in just knowing about Christ instead of living for Christ. A child seeks to be like his Father, are you striving to become more like your Father. IF you confess with your mouth and believe in your heart, just saying you believe in Christ is just one part. Taking to heart His message is where the rubber meets the road. Where your heart is, there you will live.

How does one have God's forgiveness, heaven, and eternal life, and Jesus as personal Savior and Lord? By trusting in Christ and asking Him for forgiveness. Do want a personal relationship with the Lord or are you fine just being on the outside? If your want to be a child of God, a fan, an adopted son or daughter say these words not as calling out a recipe but cry them out from your heart. "Dear Lord Jesus, I believe that You died on the cross for my sins and that You arose from the grave. I now ask You to forgive me of my sins and to save my soul. Amen (so be it)" Tell some one if you meant this prayer.

Bearing the Cross

John 19:17 And He, bearing His cross, went out to a place called the Place of a Skull, which is called in Hebrew, Golgotha,

Was this man who walked up a hill bearing a cross of wood weak or meek, was this man who stumbled and fell from exhaustion longsuffering or a quitter, or was this man walking to His death to make a name for himself or salvation for us? Can you imagine with me today as a member of the crowd glaring at this man and wondering why He is going thru this.

As He comes out of the Roman jail already beaten and bleeding you wonder why didn't he just say something anything to get out of this situation. All He had to do was tell Ciaphus that it was just a big mistake and that well hey let me go about my way I won't do anything anymore. Sure that would have been the sensible thing to do, its what we would do. Deny our call when things get rough. The weight and strain of the wood as it bears down on Him, you wonder if He will even make it up the hill. Deciding to follow along, but not too close, you want to see how this will all pan out.

The heat builds in the morning, the dust from the crowd that has gathered and walking along with you has caked your garments. You look at this Jesus of Nazareth and see that the sweat, blood and dust have mingled to bloody clots upon His skin. Mostly you notice His eyes, the anguish that is there but even more the determination as each step is a focus of obedience to a mission. But why, why is there such determination, doesn't He know that He is walking to His doom. All He had to do was plead before Pilate that this was all some sort of mistake but He said nothing, He didn't make an argument or plea to save His life. Now you looked so intently as Christ that He turns to look at you and as your eyes meet you turn in shame. But why, could it be that the first twinkling of a seed has come to you, that when your eyes met you could see that it was for you He was determined to walk this trail and endure this cross and yes to die.

He stumbles yet again, certainly now He will give up and the only way He will make it to the top of Golgotha will be if some one else carries Him. Then once again you stare as He gathers His feet underneath Him and the wobbling legs as they push Him erect and take another step forward. How many times have you stumbled and just wanted to stay down, to give up because the weight of your mission may have been heavy. No – No it is not the same as you shake your head. The memory of looking into the very eyes of Christ shakes you to the core, He does this for you and He will continue on and endure to the end.

You stop, now and follow only with your eyes as the crowd and Christ finish the last few steps up the hill. Soon the ringing of a hammer upon nails echoes thru the valley and across time itself. Where are you now? Fallen to your knees saying I am not worthy of such a sacrifice, each strike of the hammer stretching into your heart. Why Oh Lord? For you, because this is why He was sent as a sacrifice for our transgressions, our sin. Willingly He bore the cross, determination and love carried Him thru till finally you hear "It is Finished," and the sky grew dark.

Crowd – Congregation

Acts 13:43 Now when the congregation had broken up, many of the Jews and devout proselytes followed Paul and Barnabas, who, speaking to them, persuaded them to continue in the grace of God.

Mark 15:11
But the chief priests stirred up the crowd, so that he should rather release Barabbas to them.

What is the difference between a crowd and a congregation? Is a congregation really just the same as a crowd? Are those who fill the pews of the church on any given Sunday a crowd or a congregation or are they a crowd that acts as if they are a congregation. Don't shrug your shoulders and say you have no idea, look and see but first look at yourself. If your congregations sit in different crowds based upon the who and the what then you are sitting as a crowd. You find in crowds that there is always some one stirring things up but in congregations everyone has come together for one purpose.

Doug as your relayed the joyfulness of your congregation, and how ya'll seem to be having worship was an awesome story. I thought about that a lot of the time on the way home and it was a long drive from Pickwick to the Valley. Why do some get it and others don't, why do some understand the joy of a relationship with

Christ and with others like-minded Christians. While others sad to say don't get it, but they think the relationship is all about them and the services should be what and how they want them.

Ya ever think Charles when you look out on a congregation after signing a special or speaking and wonder why you have to ask people to smile? For those of you in a choir have you looked out on the crowd to see if there is joy out there? Have you ever looked at your choir and seen if there is joy there? Correct me if I am wrong Doug and Charles but joy is not reflected in the words of a song but in the way in which the song is sung.

Another word for crowd could be mob; another word for congregation could be family. Tell me which do you want to be a part of; this is the simple part isn't it? We would all rather be a part of a family than a mob; well the choice truly is ours. On Sunday when you enter the sanctuary will you say hello to the crowd that you sit with or will you spread joy to the congregation?

Example

John 13:15
For I have given you an example, that you should do as I have done to you.

Y a know what I was going to type this story of what a bad example I have been to many people when I was younger, and how I try to be a good example now while I am neither young nor old but I aint going to do it. I however am going to embarrass some of you and ask others of you if you are being the example that you should be.

- Jeffery Hemmings is an example of how Christ washes feet today by taking the talent that he has been given (sound familiar) to fix things and helps those who are in need. Pay is not top on the list, he doesn't say it will cost ya this or what is in it for me. No rather he just girds himself with a tool belt and lends a hand. If we were all more like Jeff how well could we show that we love folks, as a servant?
- Julie Dewberry is an example of how Christ washes feet today by taking care of her family when her hubby is out in the mission field. How he doesn't have to worry about things at the house or with the kids because he knows that she is there minding the store so to speak. She quietly girds herself with family and loves them all the more.

- Tammy Irmiter is an example of how Christ washes feet today by how she has compassion on everyone and ya know what I mean EVERYONE. When she hears the stories of loss and hurt how if she could she would take care of the hurts and loss. She girds on compassion and love and serves those whom she comes into contact.
- Joc Duralde is an example of how Christ washes feet, this one will shock him more than anyone else cause he may think that since he doesn't go to church as much as even he thinks he should how could he be an example of Christ washing feet. It is because he listens and cares even to those who were once his subordinate(s) he doesn't judge he just listens and tries to help the best he can.

Now you know Rod and Jesse that I could go on to talk about each of you and yes you also Randy, Lisa, Tom, Jo Ann, Jeanne, Catherine, James and well all of you! But I have not the time nor space to give you each individual accolades so please accept my thanks for being examples of Christ-like actions.

Okay that being said what are you going to do today? Yes buddy, today, not just a one thing a one-time event but each day we must gird on our towels and wash some feet. I know it gets a bit hard at times because being human we some times wonder why, they never seem to understand, they never even say thanks, they blah-blah-blah. Look ya'll it is not for their gratitude that we must, note not should, be washing feet but because Christ did and by humbling Himself and washing the feet He showed that we must serve all.

Place and place

Matthew 28:6
He is not here; for He is risen, as He said. Come, see the place where the Lord lay.

Where is it you place your faith or rather what is it you place your faith in or how about who is it you place your faith? This morning as with every morning except for 2-3 mornings the tomb is empty, "He is risen." You and I have a choice today, to believe in the risen Lord. The reverse of that is that every Christian from the first Easter till this day has all believed in a lie. It is no lie, for there is far too much evidence in the reality that Christ lives. We do not have faith in an empty slab of stone, an empty cave/tomb but in a God who now as in times past and times yet to be sits upon His throne and that when He looks over to His right there Christ is.

Now that being said is this how you live your life? With the faith in knowing that God is on His throne and that He raised His Son on the third day. The victory of life is not just knowing that the tomb is empty but in living a life worthy of an empty tomb. I am the worst at taking everything personally, look Jesse I will admit that. Thou every day we know that the tomb is empty we at times need to be reminded about the Sovereignty of God. Nothing surprises God, we can be swept up in the rollercoaster of life but as for God He knows what is down the valley and back up on to the peak.

He is risen, and if He is risen there would be evidence of it and that evidence is it in your life? People will and can debate the things of God that are written on pages, in black and white or in red-letter bibles. People will try to debunk these words because hey they may lack faith or they may just be like Thomas and will only believe what they see and touch. One thing Mike that people cannot argue against is the evidence of Christ in your life, about how God has worked in your life.

People can see that the tomb is empty thru you Tom, thru you David they have witness that your faith is not in a corpse on a slab. How you approach the day, instead of just surviving it but dwelling in it is a witness of Christ. See He is not here; He is not in the place where He was laid to rest. Hmm rested for three days but risen for eternity.

How will you approach your day today? How is your faith doing? Smile HE IS RISEN!!!

Listen

Matt 20:29-34 (NKJV) [29] Now as they went out of Jericho, a great multitude followed Him. [30] And behold, two blind men sitting by the road, when they heard that Jesus was passing by, cried out, saying, "Have mercy on us, O Lord, Son of David!" [31] Then the multitude warned them that they should be quiet; but they cried out all the more, saying, "Have mercy on us, O Lord, Son of David!" [32] So Jesus stood still and called them, and said, "What do you want Me to do for you?" [33] They said to Him, "Lord, that our eyes may be opened." [34] So Jesus had compassion and touched their eyes. And immediately their eyes received sight, and they followed Him.

Is your life way to busy today, do you have to go some where got to go do something always on the go? Tell me how can you hear and listen if you don't stand still.

There is a miss conceptions about people from the South, okay there are a lot of miss conceptions, one of them is that those from the South are laid back slow and easy going. If you buy into that one I have a mountain villa in Iowa that I want to sell ya. These guys have personnel data devices (PDA) as a matter of fact their PDA's have PDA's, they got baseball, soccer, PTA, PTO, Band, Band Boosters, Kawana's, Pilot's Club, Football, dance and well just a linty of things. Oh! Did I fail to mention work-home and church, nope I didn't fail to mention it but sometimes home and church are a distant second and third to work.

Have you wondered why divorce is on the rise or why kids don't feel loved. Could it be that we have become so busy so wrapped up in our own lives that we don't take time to stand still. Tell me when was the last time you listened to the wife, put the remote down, turned off the computer and looked her straight in the eye opened your ears and just listened? When was the last time you made your husband feel like you were on the edge of your seat for every word about how their day went? Well how about your child, when have you just taken them and sat down on your back porch and told them how proud of them you are and how much you love them? I know that some of these things sound a bit corny but my point is this. In order for Christ to convey to the blind that He was listening Christ had to stop and stand still.

Standing still and being a part of the conversation is a large investment into all manner of relationships. From family to friends all want that precious time of yours and at times you and I don't want to give it, we would rather go off. Tell me is it that you are tired and don't want to hear the woe's of those who come to you? Do you have no more compassion to give so you avoid the story, the plea?

Why is divorce on the rise, why do children grow up split between mother and father, why is there so much hurt. Stand still and listen, and after listening act. Compassion is one of those things that if it isn't a fruit of the Spirit it aught to be. How many times did Christ take compassion on individual, He healed the leaper, the blind, the lame, and the sick, He fed the crowds and gave hope to the sinner. Maybe we don't show Christ-like compassion in our daily lives. When was the last time your heart was broken because of a story your heard, when was the last time you put down the remote and inclined your ear to hear? Maybe you should invest your time and stand still.

It Aint Easy

Jeremiah 1:19 They will fight against you, But they shall not prevail against you. For I am with you," says the LORD, "to deliver you."

Once a Marine always a Marine, to most of us that is just a saying but to a Marine you are never and ex-Marine. I say that with knowing I spent 8 years in the Air Force and as often as I think back on those days I know that I am not going to be called back any day soon into service. Now these Marines it is almost as if they seek or maybe long for another day in green where they can tote a M-16 again. They are prepared if not physically for battle they at least have their head in the game. Jerome and Hugh can you guys show me where in God's word it says that following God's will endeavoring to be Christ like in your daily walk will be easy?

Jeremiah was called at a critical time in the history of Judah and Israel, a time where the nations had turned away from the Lord, had forgotten His ways and well just basically lived like a lot of our nation does right now. Jeremiah was just a young man when he was called to do what God directed him to do. There is a funny exchange between God and Jeremiah; well I think it is kind of funny. Jeremiah told God "I am but a youth," like God didn't know that.

What is your excuse that you used yesterday when some one was not acting Christ like? Why didn't you say anything? But I am not equipped, I don't know enough, I am not a pastor, I am not BLAH-

BLAH. God knows whom you and where you are, He knows that you and I are weak, that is why He asks us to rely on Him for HE will deliver us. Do you believe that, do your actions believe that?

There are far to many folks who say they faithfully go to church on Sunday but act like the world on Monday. The thought that as a child of God we should be living our lives to the Lord instead of for our gratification has no thought between their ears on Tuesday. I guess could it be that people don't see themselves as called of God or are they yet lost?

If you hear nothing else hear this, God has called each of us. He has called you Jo Ann and Joe, He has called you Doug, David, Jesse, Rod and Paul and you. Are you living up to His call? Yet we often say "But I am _____." Take courage because of what you have between your ears, nahhhh instead take courage and strength in knowing that just as God told Jeremiah He also will for you when you do His will.

> [7]But the LORD said to me:
>   "Do not say, 'I am a youth,'
>   For you shall go to all to whom I send you,
>   And whatever I command you, you shall speak.
> [8]Do not be afraid of their faces,
>   For I am with you to deliver you," says the LORD.

Mighty Things

Luke 1:49 For He who is mighty has done great things for me, And holy is His name.

The song of Mary is what the title of this section in my bible is what this is taken from

How many times have I asked you about your psalm for the Lord your way of expressing joy if you will Doug? Please don't say freight trains sound better than I do when I sing, because I don't think that really matters now does it. After all do you recall when your kids were young and they would sing a song it may not have sounded the best but you still smiled and it filled you with such joy, please note that I didn't say you endured it till it was over and scratched your ear and were just glad it was over.

Anyway who is mighty? He is Who has done great things? He has

Whom has He done these great things for? You Whose name is holy? His

How many mighty things has He done for you? To answer this is the age-old question: is your cup half empty or half full? We don't keep a tally sheet on the mighty things that God has done but everyday He does do mighty things for us and we have just come to expect it. The term God Thing is when we catch those things that we recognize as being from God. Not the perfect alignment of the starts but as only God could have done that, a glimpse is you will of God's plan.

Mighty things indeed I tell you this, your life is a God thing you are a part of His plan. He knew you before birth and has in store for you mighty things. When you and I heed the direction that He is leading as Mary did then we will see the God Things everyday. Now I don't claim to be the worlds best theologian or that my steps are always measured, those of you who know me know that messing up is not a stranger to me. Now that being said this I also know that on those occasions when I recognize and obey God's Plan, then I see His mighty work His hand so to speak.

How has God done mighty things for you? You have been created in the image of God, you have worth and you are once again a mighty work and with God you can do mighty works. Sometimes you gotta get up and go instead of sitting back on you dairy air thinking that God will meet you where you are at. Tell me smart guy how many mighty works have you seen from your lounge chair? NO I am not saying God can't work there in the living room, but get up go out and look for them, these mighty works. He will be there keeping you safe, look Mary gave birth to Jesus but first she had to be available. Was it easy to raise Jesus? But each day she nurtured Jesus as a baby, thoughts of what lay a head had to come into her imagination but yet she endured.

Each of us can learn some things from Mary, how obedient are you, how much faith do you have in God that He will deliver you.

Re-New

Romans 12:2
And do not be conformed to this world, but be transformed by the renewing of your mind, that you may prove what is that good and acceptable and perfect will of God.

Are you in a state of transformation? Does God stand still? Are you more like the world today then you were yesterday? When was the last time you had one clear thought that was fresh, anew?

We promote walking an isle and getting dunked, and that is as far as we really expect people to go. Sure we would like it if that after a person was baptized that they would want to do, to serve, to give but we just accept that if they attend regularly that is good enough. What we don't do is hold people accountable for discipleship for growing for maturing in their faith. Far too many Christians haven't gotten off the milk of a bottle and matured to meat and it is partially our fault, yes as well as theirs.

Can I ask you something, when was the last time that after a Sunday morning service have you gone home and looked up the verses that the pastor spoke from. Studying those verses to glean for yourself the truth that is there. I wonder what would happen if we took Sunday School and Morning Worship and switched the two, so that the class could look at the message again as a group.

How about this, how about after you have read and studied God's word did you then change you actions to be more in God's will? I liked reading Louis Lamour books, they were wonderful stories of the west and eastern settlers, and basically they were good stories. Is that how we treat God's word, we read them as good stories but after placing the book down we walk away and live opposite to the words we have just read.

God's words do not stand still but they have life in them, they are to move us to grow us to lead us. We can learn from them, and live by them. You can turn to the Lord and He will guide you in His ways. Many people will stumble okay all of us will stumble it is with the power of His word that we can get back up and back on track. Our minds should be in a constant state of renewing it is called maturing.

Be separate from the world buy living by the Word.

Worship is Thanksgiving

1 Chronicles 16:7-8
⁷On that day David first delivered this psalm into the hand of Asaph and his brethren, to thank the LORD:
   ⁸Oh, give thanks to the LORD!
   Call upon His name;
   Make known His deeds among the peoples!

What has God done for you lately? Has He kept you from harm? Has He blessed you? Has He been with you in a time of trial? Has He been there in your quiet moments? Have you felt His arms around you? Tell me what has God done for you lately, and if you have to think about that too hard then how close to Him are you?

It is no small wonder to me that the latest Hurricane diminished so quickly and wasn't as devastating as it could have been. Yes for those who were in the direct path as it came ashore there was destruction that happened. Tell me did you and your Sunday school and worship services pray for God to reveal Himself as having Authority over Creation and to be with those in the storm. You biblical scholars what does it mean that "the prayer of a righteous man avails much," or "Thy will be done." In our prayer life we must never loose faith that God hears and answers prayers.

Oh, give thanks to the LORD? Call upon His name;

These are not just words like a recipe to make a cake or to make gumbo, certainly not. That doesn't characterize your prayer life does it; say this and that in this way checking off your list as you go? If

121

so then how many of our prayers start with Thanksgiving instead of petitions? Oh Doug and Walter give thanks for the LORD who hears you, Oh Bob and Sky don't be silent but rejoice because your GOD hears you. How many times Jerome and Rescue Ranger has God answered your prayer even before you prayed it. Worship starts with you, why not worship the one who hears you and answers you and fills your needs and cares. Worship the Lord because He is LORD.

Call upon His name, don't be shy but Tim and Nancy call upon His name for whatever you do or are going thru. Cry out to the LORD who has blessed you before in other situations and in other days He will hear you today. Why Joe do we wait until we are neck deep in the muck to call out, could it be that we have stopped being Thankful for the blessing of each day. We have grown used to God being there so we over look at times those blessing which have been given to us.

Make known His deeds among the peoples!

Ya know what I will just stop there, that as they say preaches.

Make known His deed among the peoples!

Oh God!

1 Chronicles 16
⁹Sing to Him, sing psalms to Him;
   Talk of all His wondrous works!
   ¹⁰Glory in His holy name;
   Let the hearts of those rejoice who seek the LORD!
   ¹¹Seek the LORD and His strength;
   Seek His face evermore!

"You are awesome in this place Mighty God, You are awesome in this place Abba Father"
With these words I opened my eyes this morning, strange but these words were not being sung in a church or in a choir room but in my heart. I know some will think this weird but hey when has that ever stopped me. These were being sung to wake me, from God reminding me that where ever He is with me and with you that is the place that He is awesome at. SO HE IS AWESOME IN THIS PLACE – Alabama, Georgia, Tennessee, Mississippi, Nebraska, and Iowa HE IS AWESOME IN THIS PLACE – Nashville, Elkhorn, Valley, Scuba, Birmingham, West Point, Tuscaloosa, Auburn, HE IS MIGHTY GOD in the USA, UK, Germany, Australia, Thailand, HE IS ABBA FATHER to – Tom, Russell, Russell, Kevin, Nathan, Tim, Tammy, Jan, Doug, Doug, Rod, Jesse, Jo Ann, Jeanne, Catherine, Leigh, Sky, Pat, Joe, David, Hugh, Jeff, Melissa, Ricardo, Gina, Richard and everyone you cast your eyes upon.

Ya'll let your hearts rejoice when you seek the Lord, the LORD. Don't be still today but lift up your heart and rejoice in the fullness of the LORD. How mighty is He, How awesome is He, Let you cup run over with the JOY of the LORD. Glory in His holy name for He is the LORD, the God who looks upon you now is the God who spoke the world into existence. Hang onto your joy with both hands and hang on to the LORD.

Seek the LORD in all you do today, Seek His strength Seek His face evermore! Evermore can start today if you are down, but evermore is everyday. Ya gotta wantta for evermore, each day waking with the attitude of worship and praise, lift up some one else who may be down, encourage those who's joy may be slipping. We are counting on you.

Tell me isn't the LORD worthy of your attention, in your passion and zeal, then seek HIM in His heavenly place with every fiber of your being. Put as much passion and zeal into your relationship with the LORD as you do with any other relationship you may have then double it.

He is awesome in the place where you read this! Seek Him there.

Give it up

1 Chronicles 16
²⁸Give to the LORD, O families of the peoples,
   Give to the LORD glory and strength.
   ²⁹Give to the LORD the glory due His name;
   Bring an offering, and come before Him.
   Oh, worship the LORD in the beauty of holiness!

What will you give today and to whom will you give? They say it is better to give then it is to receive, but is this how our relationship with God could be characterized. What can you give God? Look He don't need you money, He don't need you stuff, all of that is but bunk. Give to the LORD your - you.

Thankfulness, gratitude, praise, worship, love, respect, adoration, maybe these would be a good start to give the Lord. Give to Him out of your wealth of these things. I know it may seem a bit simple but it is these things that we should give. Yes you could give your local church a check for a thousand dollars or a million dollars and it would be nice it may even be worship that you give this, but it is solely based on what is the WHY in which you give.

As you look at your hands and consider your talents you may do as I do, wonder what can I possibly give to the LORD. Have ya ever done that? What can I just a mere lump of flesh and bone give to the GOD who is and was and will ever be? After all we are just basically carbon units aren't we. Oh you so sad man, you have you to give so give Him you.

Today as you go about your day you can give to Him when you see some one hurting or naked, you can give when you see someone hungry or in mourning. Bring your offering to Him as you come before Him. Lets not forget that He is everywhere not just locked away behind your church walls. He will be there when you give the shirt off of your back to the person who is naked, He will be there when you put your arm around the person who is hurting. Give to Him your obedience and love.

"Oh, worship the LORD in the beauty of holiness!"

There has never been a time when one has given and done for the least of these that it hasn't been a wonderful experience. In the beauty of holiness because it was given for the right reason that is when you know that GOD has turned His eyes upon you and we should hunger for that feeling it should possess our lives.

John 1:17
For the law was given through Moses, but grace and truth
came through Jesus Christ.

Grace: **1 a :** unmerited divine assistance given humans for
their regeneration or sanctification **b :** a virtue coming from
God **c :** a state of sanctification enjoyed through divine grace

Do you hold grace cheaply? How about truth is truth a cornerstone of your life? So if we don't hold grace and truth is not
the cornerstone of our life then are we more about the law? Maybe
you are scratching your head right now, good then tell me when
was the last time you thought about the grace you hopefully have
received, was it the last time you read a devotional about it? When
was the last time you thought about the truth instead of telling the
truth as you see it?

Grace abounds, as does truth, yet do we live by grace and in
truth?

Every once in a while I get it in my head that hey I am doing
pretty good, I compare myself to some of those around me and say
well I aint like that. As long as I look at those who are worse then
I then I can say what a good Christian I must be. This attitude is
dangerous and detrimental; it forgets grace and is not in truth. How
easy it is for us to slip-up and look down our noses on those who sin

in a worse way then we. Yet we are all sinners saved by grace and really sin is sin.

The laws of Moses were meant for good but then they got to be more like church by-laws and were only applied to the masses and not the few who ruled. Man made rules and laws are just that man made, hence with them come the failings of a corrupt attitude and heart. So what have we to combat the law but Grace and Truth, which come thru Jesus Christ.

What kind of an example are you of Grace and Truth? Lord knows we try to do the best we can, doesn't He. We must do more than just our best but live as Christ like as we can, striving each day to bear fruit of the Spirit, putting on the new self and abiding in truth.

The good news is that thru Christ all things are possible, grace abounds and truth abounds where Christ is. We as examples of Christ must reflect His grace and truth. It is not easy because of our deprived human nature but this is why we must stay in continual contact with God. We must be different from the world and reflect the Word, for the Word is Christ and in Christ there is grace and truth.

Goal for today

Philippians 3:13
Brethren, I do not count myself to have apprehended; but one thing I do, forgetting those things which are behind and reaching forward to those things which are ahead,-

What is your goal for today, is it to get to the end of the day? What a bland un-caring wasted goal that would be, just to make it to the end of the day, put in your time at work and make it to you chair tonight. Is that a goal at all, I don't think so.

Is your goal to learn something new today, to apply what you have learned and maybe even to share what you have learned with some one else? Maybe your goal is lofty and your desire is just to help some one today, looking for opportunity to lend a hand, a shoulder, something someway to comfort some one. Good goals and worthy of your time aren't they?

Now these things both being said what is your goal for today, how about to keep reaching forward to the things of God. Today will you bring glory to God thru your actions today because people will know that you do these things all to His glory and not your own. It may sound lofty but each day we must reach to be more mature than the next to keep reaching until we are with God in His Glory.

Enoch was a man who didn't die but was taken up to be with God. I have been wondering lately what kind of a guy Enoch was.

and was not found, because God had taken him"; [Genesis 5:24]
Moses died and he led God's people out of Egypt, Abraham died and
he left everything and followed God, David died and he was a man
after God's own heart. Exactly how good of a guy this Enoch was
that he was taken up, there are only a couple of lines even in Genesis
about Enoch, just a lineage report and "He walked with God," but
what did he do to walk with GOD, we need a list so we can mark the
things off of it as goals accomplished.

There is no list so to speak but a book, its called the bible and
with it we can learn and grow and walk with God. Without it we
shoot in the dark and try to do things our way. Bully for us. I guess
Enoch and God walked so close that God didn't want Enoch to suffer
from age or illness didn't want His buddy to suffer death so He took
Enoch home.

Is your goal today to walk with God? Not just along His path but
actually with Him during your day. It is a goal for the day that may
seem a bit outside of your or my realm of ability but it isn't that what
goals should be, something to reach for.

Approach

Psalm 65:4
Blessed is the man You choose, And cause to approach You,
That he may dwell in Your courts. We shall be satisfied with
the goodness of Your house, Of Your holy temple.

Where is it that you are dwelling? Since getting out of the Air Force Tammy and I plus the kids have lived in apartments and rented houses, with each move the house or apartment has gotten a little bigger, along with the yard to mow but I digress. We have lived in a two-bedroom apartment and a three-bedroom apartment, cramped kitchens and living rooms and all of that. Each felt like home once you got your stuff unpacked, Tam did the unpacking, Thanks Lady! With all of these moves and homes there is still one that we endeavor towards and it is in His courts, and we gotta unpack before we get there.

Blessed is the man God chooses, has He chosen you and caused you to approach Him? It is funny that we feel like we can't approach Him, that we at times find ourselves unworthy of approaching Him. Have you ever felt yourself being drawn towards God but you planted your heals in the ground and refused to go, refused if it were to be drawn towards God. Yet there are many who want to hang onto their life as it is and don't want to go to God, why is that? Disobedient rebellious depraved man.

Tell me Rod and Doug does God want you to walk with Him so He can point out your faults to make you feel bad? How about this one Sky and Leigh does God want you in His house so He can jump down your throat when you mess up? The answer to both of these questions is NO, an emphatic NO. Do you invite folks to your house so you can put them down and demean them, once again no. God wants you in the Holy Place because He LOVES YOU!

We find that we move around and try different bigger things, different perks and gadgets trying to make our lives more satisfactory when all along these things don't bring satisfaction because there is always a bigger widget to get the next time. It's like keeping up with the Hemmings' instead of being satisfied with what God has provided. How could we not be satisfied with what God has provided, could it be Tim that we don't at times dwell in our Father's house but rather we are just beyond the picket fence.

Can you be satisfied in your Fathers House in His Courts; are you satisfied in your Fathers House in His Courts? God is not inviting you and I in, drawing us near so that He can smack us in the back of the head when we mess up, He can do that where we are right now we don't need to be in His house to feel His authority. If you are satisfied you are what at peace, secure, loved, relaxed, or what? If you are satisfied in His house you are all of the above things in a mighty way.

Come to His Holy place don't dig your heals in thinking you already got everything you need and are just kind of happy with the life you got now. Let go and reach for God who is reaching out for you, inviting you in drawing you close. Approach Him in His Courts.

Wandered Away

Matthew 18:13
And if so be that he find it, verily I say unto you, he rejoiceth more of that sheep, than of the ninety and nine which went not astray.

One of the perplexing questions facing many churches today is where have the people gone? Where have they disappeared too? They are still here but they just may not be coming to church anymore for one reason or the other. Tell me do you see the same faces every Sunday and if by chance you don't see those faces what do you do, sit back and wonder where they have gone, then pretty soon it is even worse than that it is a well I guess they stopped coming. Yet no one asks them, no one goes to seek and speak with them about what is up.

The one who has left the flock, who has wondered away because: the grass was greener over the hill, some of the ninety nine made fun of the color of the one's wool, the one didn't connect with a class, the one didn't feel like it could baa-baa well enough, so the one stayed away longer and longer until it was out of sight. Many reasons to stay away what is the reason to stay, could it be who the shepherd is the Good Shepherd. A reason to stay is not the music, not the clique's, not the name on the church building but solely because of the Shepherd who calls you and I.

People leave church for people reasons, have you ever left stopped going to church, what were your reason's? Were they legit or were they just kind of petty? Here is a test – if you left for legit reasons then did you immediately seek another church to be a part of, if you left for principle or anything approaching that then you would also seek where you could find the Shepherd. I know one of you out there think I am talking about you but actually I am talking about myself. A time in the past we wanted to stop going to the church we were at but we only had petty reasons to stay, the world would have called the reasons legit but God wouldn't have, so we stayed and God worked it out.

Now you may see yourself as the one who wondered away, so what are you waiting for get back in the flock, or are you worried about the 99? That is what the crux of it is, and this is where most of you are at really. You see you are not the one who wondered away but you are one of the 99 who stayed. How will you treat the one who wondered away?

Slap them on the back or shake their hand and say nice to see you again, and then walk away again. How do we treat those who come back? I know we have new member courses but do we have a back again class, nope we just plug them back into the same class and maybe doing the same thing, isn't that where we were before and look what happened. We need to love them, not just shake their hand but look for them search where they are, not wonder why they are not where we are. Love and encourage and grow them not plug them into a slot hoping that will keep them close, it wont.

Whom do you know that you have not seen lately, what will you do about it?

Willing or weak

Matthew 26:41
Watch and pray, that ye enter not into temptation: the spirit indeed is willing, but the flesh is weak.

Are you living like you know you are supposed to be? Or what is "supposed to be," what is the right way anyway? Do you sleep well at night? What is right from wrong anyway?

Are those enough questions for you? There I go again asking another question will it ever end? All to often we are not watching nor are we praying and we succumb to the sins in the flesh. We fall asleep every once and a while don't we, spiritually I mean and not physically.

Now I am sure nudge-nudge wink-wink that all of you started your days off with a prayer of various lengths, some quick some longer some to the point some wordy. However did you stop and listen did you stop to look to see if your prayer was answered. After all you may have prayed for people at work, then when you got to work did you look to see if God had beat you there.

Sure the spirit is willing after all in your heart you know that God is God and that all blessings come from Him, but in your flesh you may seek gratification in the moment something tangible. Okay basically we want these answered prayers to fall into our laps. It doesn't work out that way though does it always. So sometimes we fall asleep instead of keeping watch maybe it is because we lack faith or anticipation of an answered prayer.

Stop – Selah – pause for just a moment and take a deep breath and focus solely on God

Selah – pause for just a moment to pray earnestly seeking God's blessing on your day and the day of others around you

Selah – pause and know that the LORD GOD — — — —- IS — — — — —-

We must keep watch that we may not enter into temptation of sin, all sin daily sin; gossip, hate, lust, greed, contentiousness, using the Lords name in vain, covetousness, and probably many others. In your walk with the LORD today you must be awake, keeping an eye open for the direction that He gives you. How awake are you?

If Today

Luke 18:8
I tell you that he will avenge them speedily. Nevertheless when the Son of man cometh, shall he find faith on the earth?

If today Christ were sent back would He find faith or works on the earth? Yes I know what James says about works and that if you have faith you will have works, show me faith without works is dead, that is a paraphrase. Yet are we showing our faith in our works? Hmmm mayhap yes and mayhap no –

Why are you doing what you do? You point to the fact that you teach Sunday school, or a deacon, or a pastor, or a youth guy, or a choir member, or a men's director, or a women's director that you were involved in the Thanksgiving Meal project, or taught at Vacation Bible School. Are these things checked off of your list to say look what I did or did you serve to serve the LORD GOD. Some say that they hope that God comes back while they are in the middle of doing Vacation Bible School or a church service, cause certainly then He will find them doing what is right, and yet these things matter not if in your heart you are doing them for yourself and your list of doing good. We can be busy doing and still miss the crux of the whole thing and that is God.

Do ya wantta know something, well I'll tell ya anyway. IF we who say we are doing this for God are really just doing it for ourselves then those whom we are trying to reach will miss it also. Why do you roof a house if you are ill with those whom you roof, why do you have a back yard bible group if you wonder where the volunteers are, why do you do anything and then wonder why it doesn't work, could it be that you are doing just for the sake of doing. BULLY FOR YOU!

I wonder when Christ will come back, I wonder if it will be today or tomorrow, I wonder if when He comes back He will find me being faithful to Him but ya know what all of those things matter not. Isn't that right? What matters is that Christ has already come, we don't need to wonder about when He will come back, He lives with you today by the power of the Holy Spirit. Our Helper is here today we must be living in faith today and tomorrow and the next day, but you say that is too hard. I say your right, but that is no reason to give up and not even try.

Will you fall yes, just as I have and probably will today and tomorrow and the next day? But now listen up, if we live in faith in Christ we will be okay, well better than just okay we will be caught up in the air and we will be with the LORD forevermore. Don't stop doing, but do for the right reason and maybe Christ will come back when you are teaching Sunday school, or delivering His word, or at a deacon meeting. It after all is not up to us when He comes back, but let us do everything we can to ensure that when He does come back He will find "faith on the earth."

Where to go

Psalm 43:3
Send forth your light and your truth, let them guide me; let them bring me to your holy mountain, to the place where you dwell.

When I was in Germany I had this car, no not the Hyundi, but an old Ford. It was a beater, just a car that was passed down from owner to owner as a person was transferred in or out they would buy one of these cars for a couple hundred dollars. Well I was in an accident with this car, it didn't do any damage to the German's car I hit but it put out one of the head lights glass front, not the bulb the light still shined it is just the glass was broken. So no Doug I didn't get it fixed, after all it still worked (sorta). The funny thing about this was that after that one light shined down on the road while the other shined well somewhere kind of front but yet off to the side. I guess it matters where the light shines so you can see where you are going.

You see during the day we don't run with the headlights on cause we don't have to, although some of you do turn your headlights on so you are more noticeable. Although at night everyone turns their lights on, yes Ricardo unless they are impaired, the thing is when do you turn the lights on? Do you turn them on quickly or do you wait to see if you can make it to your destination? The decision to turn a little switch (unless you drive a car like Tammy's) is a choice that we each make in a different way, and probably use different criteria to make that choice. So to it is in a person's relationship with God.

While things are going well we don't think about the light, we just plug along on our way doing our thing and well just living large if it were. Then as darkness approaches we try to figure out if we can make it to our destination without the Light, we figure for some reason that we can make it on our own and make it thru the gates or at the very least make it thru the darkness till the sun comes up again. Oh You Silly Man and Woman. Just turn the lights on.

Just as when you first get into your car and flick the lights on, even during the day, go ahead and ask God to shine His Light on your path so you can know where it is you are going. There is no shadow in God's light as there is from the sun or a light bulb so there is nothing that can be hidden when God's Light shines forth. His Light will guide you to His Holy Place and not into a brick wall that can be hidden in the darkness waiting for you to slam into it.

God is out there, and here and with you yes even now He is ready to shine His Light onto your path to lead you to where He is. Tell me isn't that where you desire to be?

Remission

Matthew 26:28
For this is My blood of the new covenant, which is shed for many for the remission of sins.

Ya know something I can never be good enough, I can never do enough good things, I can never act holy enough to gain remission of my sin. That no matter how hard I try without the blood of Christ I would be doomed for a pit of fire and you right along beside me. Yep that is right, we would suffer what we deserve if but for that Saving blood of Christ. So here we try to live up to Christ's sacrifice, ya know being worthy of what Christ did on the cross. It should be no wonder to us that we fail, but that is why there is a covenant, that the price has been paid the debt has been given and because of Christ we can stand back up.

This is His blood, no need to shed yours or mine or anyone else's after all our blood would gain nothing for the remission of your sin, my sin or anyone else's sin. Don't look at the wooden cross but at the blood that streamed out of Christ, nor should we blame the ones who drove the nails or turned Him over. It is really a matter of taking responsibility and you and I are responsible, because of His love for you and I He suffered and died.

You and I were purchased with each stripe, with each blow of the hammer and our debt was paid with every drop of blood. Not with how many meals we give away at Thanksgiving or how many missionaries we support or how much we tithe or anything that we do or say. That we forget about the cost is the same as we often forget about the penalty of our sin.

What does this new covenant mean to you? Really what does it mean to you, does this covenant mean enough to you to walk a different road today, to turn from your sin and confess it and accept the forgiveness that wipes the sin away? Don't beat yourself up, like I do too often, for not being good enough or smart enough but rather understand that forgiveness is available and the sin will be wiped clean. Maybe the world needs to see saints on their knees after messing up instead of pointing at others for their sin after all sin is sin.

Tell me something, when was the last time you truly sat back and thought about the blood of Christ and why it was shed for you, and not just for you but also for your enemy or rival? You see if we recognize that we are sinners and don't try to hide the fact then maybe others will see that we do not judge their sin but just seek to introduce them to the risen LORD. After all it is a covenant between you and Him not between man and man.

Seek First

Matthew 6:33
But seek first his kingdom and his righteousness, and all these things will be given to you as well.

What is the first thing on your list to do today?

Why God can't I seem to get this right, Lord I am doing what you want me to "do," come on LORD throw a dog a bone would ya? Maybe that is a bit of an over exaggeration but have you ever thought that God isn't paying attention to your life, to your needs and your desires? Well He is paying attention so that aint it, but are you paying attention to the rope He has already tossed you and you are just too busy checking numbers 2 thru 150 off of your list to see you haven't done number one first and that is to seek first His kingdom and His righteousness.

Sometimes we get so wrapped up in doing we don't stop to seek God first. Sure we say we are doing it for the LORD but really we are doing it to check off of our list the things that we feel comfortable doing. Let me ask you a dumb question, does God have average things waiting for you, does He only want to bless you in a bland sorta way, is that what you think of God? Hmmm Sad!

God's Hand, God Thing, Spirit Moving just to name a couple of things that we use to describe when God "shows up," funny God is already there it is just that we finally sought Him first. Are you Gail and Geri expecting to see God move today in your life, well how about you Danita are you anticipating His hand writing on the wall today, and you what about you in your chair right there are your eyes wide open seeking GOD?

Ya want Joy then seek God's Kingdom first and His Righteousness in all you do and where you go. Strive to keep always seeking, don't just sit back when you see God move and say wow that was a God Thing then go on about your business unchanged. No rather get back up and go meet God where God is working, be apart of His kingdom instead of being a part from it. There is always joy overflowing when God moves, when you see a God thing and feel the Spirit move and shouldn't we strive to seek it everyday almost like and addiction. That if we don't see God we have withdrawals, shouldn't we zealously seek after God. Do you want to experience joy, and then are you seeking His Kingdom?

How can you seek His kingdom if your head is down and defeated, how can you see His kingdom if your heart isn't seeking Him first? Look here Pate and Jesse and Joe as you continue on your day are you going to first endeavor to just make it to tomorrow or are you going to stop and seek God first. What about you?

All You Have

What is it that you have, as you look down into your hands what do you have is but vapor, here today and can be gone tomorrow. It sounds kind of sad at first thought but then again what you have in your hands isn't all you have, what is in your heart now this is what is lasting good or bad. I would appeal to you to check to see if it is good rather than bad for each have lasting consequences don't they? In the heart of all men lurks bad, our sinful nature is there but there is or also can be Christ who conquered sin and death who sits to the right of our Father. It occurs to me, something I knew but haven't thought of directly, now listen carefully and don't miss this. You have to accept Christ into your life where as sin is a byproduct of being human. This meaning to say you have to want Christ in your life and well sin is just there as it has always been.

As we launch into another day full of thoughts of doing right and living well we must launch ourselves into a life of righteousness and Christ-like living. As a premise to everything that we do God, Jesus and the Holy Spirit must be in our hearts and reflected thru our hands. Do that make a sense er what? We mustn't abandon the cause of Christ who came to reach and save the lost.

What with the great commission and the great commandment's if we would only apply these two things to our lives how much more could we be called sons and daughter's of God and brother's and sister's of Christ. Yet we know God's word but we are lax in using it and applying it to our everyday life situations. We look to see how empty are hands are and how full our schedules are, of what could happen instead of what will happen. In His word you find how to live today for the goal of tomorrow.

Oh my brothers and sisters in Christ we are still but babes and hope to mature but struggle against the growth that God brings. We fill our lives with idleness in a busy way if we don't use God's words for what they are to be used for. In everything we have an opportunity to grow closer to the LORD, do you believe that or do you just say it.

Each day we must be leaving the old self by the wayside and putting on a new self. I long for the day when Christ comes or calls me to the Big House, but until that day we must keep on keeping on, running the good race as Paul would say, till we also come to the end of the trail. In the end it won't be what you carry in your hands that will be judged but what is in your heart, who is in your heart.

Dear Lord God, I am but a sinner, I confess to you my sins of lust and greed of hate and disobedience and foul language and hurtful acts. Lord I accept that Christ came and died on a cross for these my sins and that on the third day You Oh God raised Him from the dead and now my Savior sits at your right hand. Lord I come to you as a child with a child's needs and ask you to teach me and grow me, and Lord be with me.

Don't just say the words but listen to the Lord and ask Him to come into your life, to change your life because you have been in open or hidden rebellion to Him.

Father's Protection

Psalm 17:8
Keep me as the apple of your eye; hide me in the shadow of your wings

The first tank action was in WW1, it got its name from a cistern something that holds water. As it rolled across the fields in France the soldiers (Brits) said it looked like a rolling cistern the name Tank stuck so here today we have tanks of varying degrees of weight, armament, protection, and yes lethality. The tanks armament both deflects incoming rounds and also absorbs strikes against it. In every war there is an enemy who figures ways around the shielding to knock the tank out of commission and those who are inside of the tank to their demise. That is why there is strategy in warfare, to defeat the enemy's tactics. In this battlefield of life we also have an enemy and that enemy knows how to knock you out, but if you are hid in the shadow of His wings there are no munitions to defeat His armament.

Now it may seem a bit depressing to put things this way but everywhere we go you are under assault or being scouted out to see what or where your weakness may lay. Lest you forget that Satan is like a hungry young lion roaming around to see whom he can devour. We may not often feel the assault but it is there, lurking if you will, waiting for you to do what? Step out from under the shadow of His wing.

We do not have to walk around hunched over, tense and worrying about where the dart will come, we don't have to pay the darts much attention. After all how mighty is your God, very Mighty indeed. As the apple of Your eye, some one who pleases Him, some one who is dear to Him.

My wife and kids are very dear to me, I'll give you a hint, if you speak ill even slightly of them I will protect them. If you try to harm them then you must first get thru me and you won't. Instilled in each father is the desire to protect those who are dear to them, to shield them from harm, and if you're a dad and you don't feel the need to protect your loved ones then you aint much of a dad. Do you think God is much different than this; after all He is the Ultimate Father. He will protect you and be there for you, for you Melissa, Gail, David, Charles, Clara, Martha, Beth, and you are very dear to Him.

We sometimes wonder out of His arms though don't we, this is not why bad things happen, we just forget what our Father taught us and we stray once and a while out from under the shadow of His wings. Ya know something Jenna, Walter and Tom we can go back, we can get back under the shadow of His wings, He doesn't throw you out because you made a mistake.

Today are you the apple of His eye or have you caused Him to shed a tear? Seek to be under His care and protection, He loves you, and even now looks down upon you ready and willing to love on ya.

You tell me

James 5:16
Confess your trespasses to one another, and pray for one another, that you may be healed. The effective, fervent prayer of a righteous man avails much.

Avail: aim, advantage, purpose, benefit, reward, gain – which one of these words mark your prayers? How about this, how fervent are your prayers or are they just the right words spoken in the right fashion, simple orations of requests made in a simple way with no great sense of urgency or desire to see God's will be done?

No I am sorry but we sometimes don't put all ourselves into the words that we say when we pray. Gotta make them sound good don'tcha know. Lodi-da – so what, if you can't muster even an once of emotion a sense of fervency then why in the world do you expect God to hear you? It isn't just in the words that we say when we pray that the prayer is conveyed to the Holy Hill, but it is with what is in your heart that the urgency comes. Do you have urgency in your prayer today, or are you just saying what you said yesterday as a script.

It is no small wonder that confession is in these verses; James knew that sin stands as a block between God and us, sin is not a hurdle but a wall that must come down first. There is no door that you can open when sin is in the way, you can't dig under it or climb over it, and the only way to deal with it is to confess it. We confess our sins to God, but when we have sinned against a brother do we confess it to them, when was the last time you confessed one to another, cleaned the slate with them so to speak. I tell you it is not easy looking some one in the eye and saying I have sinned against you, but it must be done and it is worth doing.

You know something, I would like to put something in here that would enlighten your day and turn your head and make you ponder the effectiveness of your prayers, but I can't think of anything. It is not that I lack the words but ya know something I can not determine in you how effective your prayer may be or how fervent you prayers are, nor if you are righteous, all of that said you have to look at yourself and ask yourself a couple of things.

Do I confess my sin: to God and one to another?
Do I pray or recite words?
Do I pour myself into my prayers, more than I pour myself into my job, hobby, or whatever else that I am passionate about?
Is my prayer time effective, fervent?
What do I need to do to change any or all of the above?

Stacks

Matthew 6:19
"Do not store up for yourselves treasures on earth, where moth and rust destroy, and where thieves break in and steal.

What do you got in the ole' storehouse of yours? Go ahead what do you spend your time earning, buying, storing, and packing away? Ya know what, a chipmunk stores up acorns in a stash to help it make it thru the winter, not because it has a conscious thought about hmm maybe I should store these things up it just does it out of the nature of things. SO we as humans with our weak nature sometimes store up what we naturally gravitate to. If we don't check every once and awhile to see what it is in the storehouse maybe we will be unpleasantly surprised when we go to make a withdrawal.

In Iowa you don't have to go a great distance to see a grain elevator or silo packed out with grain. In the fall the bins and silos and elevators can barley keep up with the influx of grain and they have to pile it up on the ground. You are pretty proud of Mt. Cheahaw, that it is a wondrous sight, well until you have seen a mountain a corn a couple of hundred feet high you aint seen anything. The harvest is plentiful and the storage is limited so it ends up sitting on the ground exposed to the elements and sometimes even rots right there. They have to get the grain moved as quickly as possible before it is rendered useless. They end up making room one way or the other, either by building bigger storehouses or by shipping it to other co-ops that have bigger storehouses.

What we do is build bigger houses or keep track of our bigger accounts to keep up with our treasures. Ye who dies with the most toys wins, right? Wrong, ye who dies without Christ well they die no matter what they got in the house or bank. No those who have nice homes and nice stuff are not evil folks but it is what is in ones heart as your storehouse. A person could live in a wooden shack and be just as lost as a person living in a 6.5 million dollar home. We each carry our storehouse with us, we wake up and go about our day seeing what we can put in it. Don't we, don't we live our lives to see what we can store up to make it thru till spring?

Sure I would like to retire with enough stuff to live comfortably until I die, not anytime soon for either of those things. What is the focus in our lives shouldn't be what we got that we can put our hands on but the thing we can't touch. Is your storehouse full of faith in Christ? Placing anything before God is placing the wrong treasure into the storehouse. If we live our lives in Christ for Christ rust and moth will not touch. You do need to check the balance of what is important to you, don't fudge. Honestly ask yourself is what I say I consider a treasure to me, what is in my storehouse worth the blood of Christ?

Luck

Luke 12:37

[37] Blessed *are* those servants whom the master, when he comes, will find watching. Assuredly, I say to you that he will gird himself and have them sit down *to eat,* and will come and serve them.

This one time I went to a Twins game, before the dome, we sat up in the club house row and I got to see Rod Carew play, he went two for three that day a single down the right field line and one over the shortstop. It was great! But somewhere in the later innings it wasn't so great for this one guy a section over from us, you see he stopped watching the game and found that he should have kept watching because a ball flew up into the stands and hit him in the side of the head. The guy got up but some one else got the ball, seemed kind of sad they could have given the ball to him to go along with the head ache (yes Tammy I probably would have kept it also). So tell me what inning are you in, are you watching the field or do you have your eyes in the stands?

We rely on some strange things don't we? I mean there are certain things that we do that we say work but really it is dumb luck. Sports are probably a good example of that, there are people who wear certain shorts, won't wash their uniform if they are in a streak, rabbits foot, don't walk under a ladder, don't step on a crack, salt over your shoulder, horse shoe open side up.... Some would call these superstitions and well that is all they are there isn't nothing to them that hasn't come out of our own super –stitions our quirks. Ya know what is amazing thou, how much attention people pay to them. It is kind of like looking into the stands instead of the field one day the ball will smack ya in the side of the head.

"If I just knew," or "but I could a," or "well I," could all be answered if we would just keep watch instead of relying on "if, but or well." Will that be our answer when the Master of the house comes, If I just knew when you would get here I would have cleaned up, or But I could a taken care of that had you let me know when to expect you, or Well I thought I still had time. How many people do you know because you have asked and not assumed are waiting to "get things right," till they are at the end of their life, that will be the time to get things right before you meet your maker. What they are relying on is just blind luck and not faith.

I wonder if part of our joy is that we are keeping watch, that we are at the edge of our seats, or on the top of our toes watching expectantly for the sky to split and the sound of trumpets and the Master to come home? Does it feel you with joy knowing that He is coming and that you are not relying on blind luck but in faith in Christ. Hey you are at the edge of your seat aren't you Doug, Walter, Tim, Rachel, Judy, Gail and you, you are on the tip of your toes looking into the game instead of in the stands? Please don't be blind-sided it isn't luck, Christ will be back or He may take you home today, place your faith in the Truth.

Selah

Does the ...

John 3:21
²¹ But he who does the truth comes to the light, that his deeds may be clearly seen, that they have been done in God."

Mark 1:35
Now in the morning, having risen a long while before daylight, He went out and departed to a solitary place; and there He prayed.

Here we are, all of us, each in our own place and situation. Some have hurt, some do not, some wonder why they do others with they could do something else, and some of have joy some wonder where the joy has gone. Yes you right there where you are may be and probably are dealing with your own set of "WHY," what do we do, where do we turn and how do we get there and will it ever end. You see two verses this morning, and no I didn't forget to delete one of them rather each verse ties into the other verse. Yes even though one is in Mark and one is from John and even thou each are not talking about the very same thing and yet they do speak of the same thing. Both talk of a relationship with God.

The King James in John says he who doeth the truth, we don't always doeth the truth do we. Sure we try we give it the old attempt but yet we don't. Let me give ya a for instance. Do we know that it is wrong to gossip and yet we do, what we do is we polish it up and call it anything but gossip but when you get down to the just of it you know it is gossip. Do we bring gossip into the light no, we try to hide it in the shadow, but we also know that in God's Light there is no shadow the light reveals all deeds for what they are.

When was the last time you went and prayed in a solitary place, to see that what you doeth is done in God. Sometimes the noise of life hides the truth, it is so loud that we have convinced ourselves that we are rightly motivated when in fact if we bring it into the light the flaws will be reveled.

I don't know, I am not a socailologist, I can't tell you stats or findings from one study or the other that would amount to a hill of beans. What I do know is that we don't we don't go to a solitary place and there pray near enough, that we don't doeth the truth in the light near as much as we should. After all the light will reveal the flaw and that is a bad thing right? No its not, if the flaw can be revealed then the flaw can be repaired.

You see ya'll it is easy to say we do the truth, it is easy to say I am right and you are wrong or I am better than you are. These things are easy to say that I try to do the best I can ya can't expect any better then my best. Your measure is not me or the guy next to you; your measure is the Truth, the Word, and the Light. Our excuses don't amount to didly when we bring them to where they are supposed to be brought, and that is to the altar of God.

Go to a quiet place and don't just read and pray but listen and apply – Learn from the Truth.

Slip

Psalm 17:5 Uphold my steps in Your paths, That my foot-steps may not slip.

Working in a kitchen the floors always seem to have something on them, from water to meal to oil, there just always seems to be something there. The staff has to wear slip resistant shoes and we also put mats down to help minimize the risk of slips and falls. These things along with cleaning as you go, one can say that we try to make it a safe work environment? Then again slips still happen, and people don't bounce like they used to, especially me, don't go there Douglas and Ricardo… and you don't need to ask what the deal is.

Uphold my steps - Support or sustain my steps. Is this what you have asked God to do today, to support your steps? I know that sometimes I don't ask I just assume that God knows that I want to walk in His path, then for some reason I notice that I have left the trail and have wondered off of the path and am on a different path. Have you ever done that, no sure you haven't you are much more focused than I am. Then again are you on the right path today and are you sure?

Here lately there have been some things that happened that I wish wouldn't have happened, and the situation really isn't that important but what is important is who is in control and who's path I choose, just as it is important for you to know what path you are on. You see we can be like water, yes H_2O. We can take the path of least resistance and avoid the situation but is that where God wants to take you, or does He want you to have enough faith that He will take care of you along the path that He has laid out for you.

You see He is the One who sets the path, gives you the slip resistant shoes and lays down mats to help you not slip and fall and bust your hurt (nudge-nudge). Upholding your steps isn't about blind followship but about a relationship of trust and faith. You see God will not let you down or push you down if you are on His path but He will lift you up when you slip and it will be Him who dusts you off. Now if you are not on your path and He wants to get your attention, as He has gotten mine from time to time, He may knock you down and as you look up ya wonder how this could happen and who will help you up. Then you realize you we trying to take the path of least resistance and weren't' relying on Him.

It doesn't matter who you are, you could be a CEO or RVP or RDO or DFNS or REV or Asst. REV or a Mr. or a Miss or a Mrs. or an Ms, your wealth or lack of wealth or brain power, you could be a hulked up Ex-Marine but all of this won't matter a hill of beans when you slip and we have slipped or do slip every once and a while. Who is upholding your steps, are you relying on you know how or God Authority? Well when ya put it that way, Father knows best. Let it go and just live for God in God's way upon His path you will not be alone.

Put aside

James 1:21 Therefore lay aside all filthiness and overflow of wickedness, and receive with meekness the implanted word, which is able to save your souls.

²² But be doers of the word, and not hearers only, deceiving yourselves.

What was the easiest thing for you to lay aside in your life before Christ? Was it easy to lay aside filthy language, adulterous relationships, being a drunk, greed, hate, or whatever? What is the hardest thing for you to lay aside is it filthy language, adulterous relationships, being a drunk, greed, hate, or whatever? How about this, how about are there some things that you don't want to lay aside such as pride, self, I wantta instead of He wants me ta. Just your basic humanistic stuff that keeps you from, well that really keeps you from Christ.

We are good about telling others to apply God's word to what they are doing but how good are we about applying God's word to our lives. Shouldn't we first remove the plank from our eye, hmm that is probably in the Word somewhere isn't it? If we use God's word to be our example then when we disagree with things we can shake hands and walk away without harsh or hurt feelings.

It is my contention that until we put aside ourselves that we wont truly experience God in His fullness. The filthiness of pride can overflow just as quickly as the filthiness of adultery, theft, or any other sin. It is just that we don't keep a watchful eye out on the green monster of pride, or is jealousy the green monster. What ever it doesn't matter much what color it is the only thing that matter is we keep an eye out for it. In so doing what is the challenge to your day, what is the challenge to your ministry today?

Are you focused on what you can do or focused on what God wants you to do? Are you treating the men and women, boys and girls in your ministry as numbers instead of as individuals? That may sound like it is only going out to pastors or associate pastors but it isn't just them. But you right there have a ministry that is just as important as speaking behind a pulpit or music stand, your ministry lies with those whom you see everyday.

Each of us need from time to time look at ourselves and ask ourselves are we doing for the sake of doing, do our actions reflect what we say. Do we need to but aside self and our wants to serve God better? In the past months I have learned something that I consider important, I can preach to the congregation but if I don't speak to that person in the pew I am not doing the ministry that God has called me to do.

It is hard to put aside self and what we think should be done because we all have our opinions. But you know what Hugh, Stanley, Jerome and Tim our ministry isn't about the mass congregation but about that person in the pew whom we miss. Ya know what Doug, James, Debbie and you, your ministry isn't about what you want to do but it is about doing what God has equipped you to do. When will we get it thru our hearts and heads that God is our role model and His word reveals what He wants us to do not a program book or seminar. Be doers of the Word and put aside self today and let God use you in His plan

Him,

2 Timothy 2: [11] *This is* a faithful saying: For if we died with *Him,* We shall also live with *Him.* [12] If we endure, We shall also reign with *Him.* If we deny *Him,* He also will deny us. [13] If we are faithless, He remains faithful; He cannot deny Himself.

2 Timothy 1:2 To Timothy, a beloved son:
Grace, mercy, *and* peace from God the Father and Christ Jesus our Lord.

To Jesse, James, Tom, Helen, Tim(s), Joe(s), Trish, Doug(s), Tammy, Hugh, Stanley, Russell(s) and you, my beloved brothers and sisters:

Grace, mercy, and peace from God the Father and Christ Jesus our Lord

Tell me brothers and sisters have we forgotten that all things are for Christ and Glory to the LORD? Tell me have you died with Him, are you enduring, do we deny Him in our petty arguments, do we seek humility in reconciliation with others or is it still about us. No wonder we weep, no wonder we get frustrated because all of this to your left and right is about you and for you and is totally dependant upon you. My-my what big shoulders you must have to carry the weight of the world upon them. Have you forgotten Grace, mercy and peace are from God the Father and Christ Jesus our Lord and not thru your groaning.

Paul used these words as a greeting to Timothy, but the Holy Spirit means them as a greeting of encouragement to you also. Greetings are often a reminder in a way of how we feel about a person or people, we express how we feel about some one with a nod a hug or a Howdy. We get so wrapped up with our to-do list that we sometimes have to get our head straight about who we are supposed to be serving.

Paul said this is a faithful saying so now also do I ask you how are you doing with these things. Sure we get caught up with the our lives and the stuff that we have filled them with, what we need to do is remember the cross upon which our Lord died and leave our desires there, our desires are our selves. We must more than just exist but we must endure, not balled up waiting for the end but continuing on thru the blasting storm. We must not deny Him, not just in words but also in our actions most assuredly not in our actions. Don't do the things that others expect you to do rather do the things, which God commands you to do. Have faith, He cannot deny Himself nor will He deny His own.

Endure, encourage, strive, greet, faith, serve, humility, mercy, peace and Grace let these things be the cornerstone of you relationship with Christ, let these be the things shine forth in your walk with Him, be the light in the storm.

Church Folks

2 Timothy 3:[1] But know this, that in the last days perilous times will come: [2] For men will be lovers of themselves, lovers of money, boasters, proud, blasphemers, disobedient to parents, unthankful, unholy, [3] unloving, unforgiving, slanderers, without self-control, brutal, despisers of good, [4] traitors, headstrong, haughty, lovers of pleasure rather than lovers of God, [5] having a form of godliness but denying its power. And from such people turn away

Turn away from instead of turn towards!
Seems to be quite the list that Paul was giving ole Timothy and us doesn't it? Okay stop right here and don't check mark off the list of things you may not be. Look at the things that you may be, not that you are bad because after all certainly there is some one else that you know who is more of a boaster than you, or more headstrong, or more haughty or more of a lover of pleasure. Right you and yes I are not so bad when we compare ourselves to then guy next to us. What about Christ? Was He any of these things?

Who were the people that Paul was talking about, church people or people outside of the church? Look at verse 5 again, having the "form of godliness," they know the churchy words they know the churchy ways they may even know the good book but they don't live by the gospel they live for themselves. So I guess it is boggling why we still to this day are talking about ill acting church folk. Let me see if I can say this as delicately as I possibly can muster in a non-haughty way and with self-control, achem-achem. It is because not all of the people in the church have a relationship with God thru Christ Jesus and we don't turn away from such people but wallow in their same blah blah blah.

Tell me something when was the last time you called a member to account? When was the last time you pulled a member to the side and asked them about their relationship with God? Is everyone that you know "Saved," or do you just figure they are? A lot of people learn the form of godliness the way to do church but until they learn to live by His Power they are just learning law. Yes Tim we should be about evangelizing the lost outside of the church but we also must evangelize the lost within its walls also. This is what I have heard it said and I agree to a point, "well if they are in church at least they are <u>hearing</u> the word," that is just it thou ya'll they are not hearing at all. Unless we go to each person and challenge him or her about his or her relationship with God we have failed.

This is a radical thought, but what if we just did away with church rolls and the like, what if we just stopped keeping record of who belonged to what church. What if they only thing that people would have would be their relationship with God as their indicator of salvation? It is sad but there are more people worried about having their name on a card in the church office instead of having their name written in the book of life. What is the fruit you are bearing, or going to bear today? Check out Paul's list again, where do you see yourself.

Listen Online

Psalm 81:13
"Oh, that My people would listen to Me, That Israel would walk in My ways!

How many of you listen to your favorite radio station online? I listen to two stations, not at the same time duh. To listen you have to click on the stations tab that they have set up for you, one station's says "Listen Online," while the other says "Listen Live." If you don't click on the tab you won't be able to listen at all, then again how are we about listening online or live, it don't matter if your ears aren't in tune all you get is static, tune it in instead of just cranking up the volume.

"Oh, that My people would listen to Me," When was the last time you stopped to listen, no really just to stop and listen, well not just listening but listening with intent to hear. I know that may sound like double talk but let me give you an example. When some one comes into your office with a complaint or just comes in to ramble you may listen but it is more like listening to help them get it out of their system. Then there is imagine you are the hunter, oh I don't know say a turkey hunter. When you are sitting in the blind or concealed in brush you try to be as motionless as possible even to the point of your can falls asleep. Then there is a faint sound of a hen clucking your ears prick up for where there is a female there is also a male. The adrenaline surges thru your body, all other things have passed away it is only the sound of the hen that is your attention, not the snake at your feet, not the troubles of the day, not anything but that hen. Now if you are not a turkey hunter you may not get that but if you substitute shopping for hunting and a debit card for the gun and a sale for the turkey it is roughly the same.

My point is this sometimes we need to concentrate a bit more on our listening then maybe we wouldn't get off on the wrong way. When God has your focus your attention it is the same thing, the adrenaline shoots thru you as you can barely wait for the next word. We say God what are you trying to say thru your word, well first ya gotta read it with the intent of learning from it, God's word is pretty plain. "Love your neighbor as yourself," how are you doing just with that one, oh I listen I just don't do, then you are not listening at all and you have gone the wrong way.

Oh that you would walk in My ways, do you need to listen live, listen online, have you forgotten to click on the tab. Each day we can walk in His ways if we will but listen with intent to what God has to say.

Pick it up

Matthew 10:38 And he who does not take his cross and follow after Me is not worthy of Me.

Matthew 7:1 "Judge not, that you be not judged."

First off I would like to say that I know that judgment is God's not mine, and I as you thank Him for this each and every day! It is something that we must get in our heads and live out in our hearts without self and without reservation, judging must start with you and I looking at ourselves and taking responsibility for our own actions with out the "buts" or the "well" and most certainly not the what ever.

Are you picking up your cross today or is it left down along the bed or in the closet or well you have know idea where it is? Can you tell me what it is to pick up your own cross? Is it simply saying you are a Christian and that you are following Him who died upon the cross? Could your cross be your self, those things of yourself that you give over to serve the Lord, what have you sacrificed really to follow Christ? If you pick up your cross you cannot use the but I excuse because what is brought to the cross is left there.

There is this thing that bugs me, it is in-sincere apologies, it is one of those things to me that is like when we sin and then repent and then go out and without measure or care sin the same knowing that we can repent again and all will be well. It wont thou, the sin will harden your heart. Is it sincere to go and apologize about something then go down to your office and laugh about what you said and deliberately slander the person you "apologized" to. When we confess to the Lord that which we have done wrong we must turn without reservation by admitting we are at fault for what we have done, for what I have done without the buts or wells. Don't excuse your sin or excuse anyone else's sin with an excuse.

Political correctness dictates that there are excuses for why people sin or fall into sin. But Christ calls all those who would follow Him to be as He is not as society is. Christ was sinless and blameless, He is righteous and Holy and you and I are to be the same as He. Place the buts and the wells on the cross. Who is it that you are following anyway, if you pick up your cross the weight of it will dictate whom you have given your life over to. The only out to sin is death, we will not be able to excuse our sins away when we face the Judge. Can you look up and see Christ on the cross and say "Well I know I have sinned but ya know what they really ticked me off," I am sure that will work.

We are not the judge of people's sincerity, least of all me, nor are we anyone's judge about anything. It is all we can do to keep each day picking up the cross to follow Christ and understand that we must be set apart from those who don't pick up the cross. Because thru it all you maybe some ones but I or well I excuse. Shirt, pants, socks, shoes and cross are you really fully dressed yet.

Gift to giving

1 Corinthians 13:2 And though I have the gift of prophecy, and understand all mysteries, and all knowledge; and though I have all faith, so that I could remove mountains, and have not charity, I am nothing.

In the NKJV it says "and have not love, I am nothing" so do you have charity and do you have love is this what you show to others, oops it doesn't say show it says have not. You can't fake love nor can you fake charity, especially with kids cause they see right thru it especially when there was an absence of it before. We can have all these bells and whistles in the world that sparkle and shine but if we don't live God's word then we are nothing, if you don't have love. I feel sorry for those who don't love cause they are missing out on quite a bit.

I know at times we get wrapped up in the doing instead of the hugging. There is this guy who tells a story of when he was a lot younger and he and other guys would go to a hospital and they would hug and touch the patients there, but this one guy who was nice enough wouldn't touch the patients. He suffered from what a lot of people suffer from, the contagious if I touch I will get sick syndrome. Alas it wasn't that he was a bad guy or anything like that it is just that he missed out on love. The patients needed the loving touch not a fearful "oh God don't let me get sick".

Don't confuse charity with throwing money at a problem, it isn't the green that will show God's love but it is you and I getting off our keister's and swinging a hammer and hugging a neck. God don't need our stinking smelling rotting money, He desires to see love, our genuine love in action. After all God loved you so much He sent Christ. Was Christ thrown into the fray just to solve the problem cause there was no other answer, no He was sent because of the LOVE Factor.

Oh I don't know I don't have all the answers, sure I have an opinion on just about everything, but opinions are not answers. What would happen today Mike if we loved those around us, what if we stopped faking love and stopped trying to solve everything with the talent in our heads and started solving things with a loving touch. Instead of looking down our noses and giving charity started looking into eyes and extended charity.

The same charity that we were shown on a cross.

Selah

I wish I could convey to you Russell and Joe and ya'll about what my heart says is right, what my spirit urges me on to do. If we don't do out of love we need to stop doing cause we are faking it then, we are just doing. When will we stop relying on what we can do and start relying on God's love to abound in us and to follow His pulling His leading. I guess we will stop when we look first at the "I" and that is for each of us to look at first.

Lathered Up

John 2: [16] And He said to those who sold doves, "Take these things away! Do not make My Father's house a house of merchandise!" [17] Then His disciples remembered that it was written, *"Zeal for Your house has eaten[a] Me up."*

When was the last time you walked away from a worship service worked up in a lather? I know we do church aerobic way to much, stand up, sit down, stand up shake hands sit down, take a nap stand up and walk out. I would be willing to say that there wasn't anyone nodding off to sleep when Christ started driving the oxen out of the temple. Maybe a few people thought to themselves, am I next. Well maybe you are next, what have you made the house of the Lord.

Hold on there boy-oh we don't sell oxen or have money changers or any of that stuff, no doves allowed in here. BLAH-BLAH spare me, what have you allowed to enter in thou – gossip, envy, dis-unity, clubs, social committees and what ever that detracts from God.

Can you picture Christ standing in front of those who sold doves, whip in hand sweat dripping from His brow (driving cattle is work) breathing heavy and well worked up into a lather. I'd get out of dodge also rather then face this guy who drove these others out.

I tell ya what if you want to buy something go to Lifeway.com or a local store, if you want to join a club or mix in a clique join the red hat society or whatever, but don't bring the world into the church. That is what we have done and that is why the churches have become ineffective because we have started treating church as a social club instead of a house of prayer. We don't want to fight that battle we don't want to make a whip and drive out the gossipers, the busy bodies, we don't want to look at ourselves and see if we are part of the problem. We are weak fleshly and human —- oh that is not that good of a reason but it is the one that people use.

We are not Jesus Christ, that is true enough. We are however supposed to follow His example and not Mary Jane Joe Jefferies' example. How can you make a cord a whip and drive out the gossips and the busy bodies, make worship about God and not about the pastor or deacon or deacon's wife or about the youth or about the adults or about the middle aged or about the social committee. MAKE WORSHIP ABOUT GOD, look at your activities if they are glorifying Christ.

When was the last time you let your zeal for the LORD – consume you – been your everything, your total focus and your total desire. I am not talking about jumping or shouting or raising your hands or any of that but when was the last time you encountered the LORD in His house? Ya know what is sad, some people don't go to church anticipating an encounter with the LORD but they expect to see their buddies

As you walk thru this day are you anticipating an encounter with GOD. Be zealous for the LORD, get rid of those things in your life that detract from God and get back to the basics by making God's house a house of prayer again where everyone who enters expects to see the LORD.

Remembrance

Psalm 97: Rejoice in the LORD, you righteous, And give thanks at the remembrance of His holy name.

Focus – focus – focus

How do you rejoice in the LORD, gee thanks God way to go ho hum wahoo gee wilikers whooped de do. No I am not asking about how you corporately worship but there where you are right now how do you worship, how do you rejoice. Now pictures of Dougs and Jo Annes jumping and shouting just shot thru my head, and Jans and Tams saying "praise God," right there along side the jumping and shouting. Which ya'll is a good, a very good thought that you do rejoice in the LORD right there where you are. That was the sugar, some of you don't have the sugar but are the plain salt that has lost its flavor.

Have you forgotten His holy name? Have you forgotten the why of what you do, are doing, have done, used to do or are you just focused on how stuff happens? Some have lost their flavor because they have forgotten what it is that God has saved them from, done for them, blessed them, guided them, and held them. We don't rejoice because we seem to always say thanks but then we say what's next, what are you going to do now God.

Mark 9:50 Salt is good, but if the salt loses its flavor, how will you season it? Have salt in yourselves, and have peace with one another."

Do you know what is sad, there are entire churches that have lost their flavor because of splits, arguments, bull pucky and stupid stuff. That the church is the body of believers is true, but my question is what do we believe in if it HAS got to be my way or the highway, or one groups way the taste is bitter without the sweet. To regain the flavor we must remember whom we are to serve. GOD who sits upon HIS throne on His Holy Hill.

When was the last time you bowed down, when was the last time you called upon the name of the LORD to say thanks to rejoice in who HE IS. The Great I Am! Does the flavor need to come back into your life, into your relationship with God, Are you seeking and speaking with HIM? MY oh my but aren't we a selfish lot, quick to forget and closed off in remembering.

Maybe you want your taste buds to explode with the flavor of the LORD, maybe right now you are worshiping and are just seeking more and more, then dive deeper and deeper into relationship with Him who is and was and will always be. Then today right now even remember who He is and recall what mighty works God has already accomplished in your life and REJOICE.

Win

1 John 5:4 For whatever is born of God overcomes the world. And this is the victory that has overcome the world—our faith. ⁵ Who is he who overcomes the world, but he who believes that Jesus is the Son of God?

The bottom of the 9ᵗʰ with one out a guy on second and third base my senior year in high school arch rival we were down one and a hit would bring in two runs a sac would tie the game so what do you do. Well if you are me ya just go up try to win the game with a homer. Now not to pat myself on the back but I had the highest batting average and led the team in singles, doubles and triples but I had no home runs as of yet. Instead of playing my game what happened was well a backwards K and we ended up loosing the game, I didn't rely on what I knew but wanted to swing for the fence. How often do we want to do this each day, swing for the fence instead of just living in faith, for it is in our faith in Christ where we truly have the victory.

Ya know what today lets not rely on the grey matter between our ears but lets rely on the Spirit that fills us. How would that be, just saying GOD ya know what here are the reins you are the Man lets go. I know sometimes we feel like we gotta do this and that and control this and rein in that, pretty soon we look like one of those ole 20 mule team drivers, and we have fists full of reins. Well after all the wagon wouldn't get anywhere if you were not in the drivers seat. BLAH-BLAH

Today keep His commandments, concern yourself with: Exodus 20:1-17, I am the LORD your God, You shall have no other gods before me, You shall not take the name of the LORD your God in vain, Remember to keep the Sabbath HOLY (set apart), Honor your Father and Mother, You shall not murder, You shall not steal, You shall not commit adultery, You shall not covet your neighbor's stuff, You shall not bear false witness, You shall not make for yourself a carved image of any likeness ... Love your neighbor as yourself, Love God with your whole heart, mind and spirit...

You don't have victory in yourself but only in the things that God delivers to you. Is your faith strong enough to let go of the reins and live in the victory of Christ, of having faith in He who is and was and will always be, in Jesus who was born in a manger, lived as a man, died as a criminal, buried in a loaner tomb, rose in victory from the grave and now sits in Glory at the right hand of the FATHER. Tell me something who knows about winning you or God? Then who do you really want with the reins in their hand.

I know that you and I can have victory today because of CHRIST, our faith has to be stronger then our doubts, can you do this today will you do this today, will you try, start with a prayer on your knees and look up and see that the victory is already there.

Closer Still

James 4:8
Draw near to God and He will draw near to you. Cleanse your hands, you sinners; and purify your hearts, you double-minded. — [10] Humble yourselves in the sight of the Lord, and He will lift you up.

How close are you to God this morning? Do ya need to get closer, do you even want to get closer, or are you just happy with keeping God at arm distance?

There is so much to say about these verses so I ask you to look them up dwell on them for a time and just listen and ask yourself when was the last time you looked to see how close you are to God.

Can you cleanse your hands, can you wash them so clean that they will be surgical sterile so you won't even have to wear gloves? Probably not huh, no matter how much you scrub you will have some sort of bacteria growing living on your skin. Now there is a nice picture bacteria growing on ya. So it is with sin, without confessing your sin to God your hands will never be clean, as long as you have the sin un-confessed, un-repented, it will be un-forgiven. Try drawing close to God with that sin in-between you, good luck it won't happen, God is not going to draw near to you if you will not draw near to Him.

When was the last time you mourned when you sinned against God, your laughter to tears for the affront to God that is our sin.

I sin but hey God I still love ya, even though I gossip, even thou I use your name in vain Hey God I love ya can't-cha tell? If you love Him obey His commandments, don't obey your excuses. If we use excuses to why we sin, then are we really repentant of that sin, certainly we are not mournful of sinning.

Doug can you tell me why we don't walk a holy life, with each step we take Jesse are we serving the LORD or serving ourselves. I know Joe it is easy to lash back at others when they upset us? But what about each of us, are you going to walk a holy life today, with each step you take will be a step claiming no declaring God as Holy and instead of sinning because some one sinned remember that they are not a good enough reason for your sin.

"He will lift you up." Thru it all, thru all the bull and blabber we must remember that to be humble is to be lifted up by He who spoke the world into existence. That when we mourn for sin that when we weep because we have sinned that we can come before a Holy God and turn from our sin and be washed clean and be lifted up. And that we can draw close to God and not keep at arms length but rather to dwell with you thru the power of the Holy Spirit.

We must each day turn to God and draw closer to Him and now don't miss this "He will draw Closer to YOU!!!!!!!!!!"

Worship Time or Time to Worship

Psalm 34:1 I will bless the LORD at all times; His praise *shall* continually *be* in my mouth.

David praised God with his whole heart, He trusted God and believed in his holy word. Because of that, his prayers were answered. He did not limit his praise when it came to magnifying our Lord and Savior.

It's different with many of us. We limit our worship and praise to God. Many churches have a time limit in their worship. When the Holy Ghost is strongly in the house of the Lord or anywhere else, don't limit the Spirit. Now, let me ask you this, when God was pouring out all of the blessings you have received did He limit your blessing? When your pay check was less than the bills you had to pay did He ignore the prayers you sent up to Him? We don't look at what God does for us, we only look at what God can give us. When the praises go up the blessing come down. Don't limit praising God, don't set a time limit on the word of God, because you might miss something.

May God Continue to Bless Each of You – Helen Fears

Watch watchers don't always get it, but neither do those who act out seeking to draw the attention of the members to them. How can we who have limited time in this life put God on a time limit, God

179

who owns time is not limited. The important thing in worship is not the time or dress or the glass pulpit but whom you came to worship. David worshiped in good times and bad, when stuff was going well for him and when he was fleeing for his life.

It doesn't matter if you worship for 5 minutes or 5 hours if God isn't in it you just as well have stayed home and watched the game. I know people love to look at their watches to make sure everything is going according to schedule and that they can get the good seat at the Cracker Barrel, but to boast about spending 5 hrs in church is as bad. Ya want to know what is the important thing about time and church? Nothing! Not one thing if you are there for the wrong reasons and pre-occupied with either time or doing church.

Ya know what time it is, it is time to worship God and that is the most important thing about coming together as the assembly, to worship and praise God. All the glitz and glamour of technology and who wears what and how long or short you stay wont amount to a hill of beans if God isn't the focus of your time there instead of the program of church.

Having praises to God continually on your lips is not just a Sunday thing but it is a today thing, an everyday of the week thing. Yet how we limit Him during the week by not taking the time to praise Him, to draw closer to Him. Is this your focus to draw closer to Him, to praise Him as much on a Tuesday as I do on a Sunday.

God!

Psalm 3:8
Salvation belongs to the LORD. Your blessing is upon Your
people. Selah

Where do you find God, where do you look, is your eyes open
to see. When I look at the world I don't wonder that people
are seeking a god, because they are, I wonder what god they have
found. All to often they find the wrong god, it isn't the true GOD.
People find god in their bank account, in their position and possessions and in them-selves. No man is God now will ever be a god but
to themselves for who among us can save our self? Salvation is only
from GOD.

Ya know I understand the aspect when people say they are good
enough because of what they do, that they have a tally sheet about
getting things done as if they could earn their way to heaven. We in
the US can really buy into that sort of mind set because we believe
that if we work hard we can move up and up till we get to the top.
So we apply what we learn in society to the hope of a here after. Sad
thought aint it, but am I really off of the mark on that one. If I am jut
good enough ya'll won't get me in any book of life but may get me
in the Who's Who of the Valley.

I was reading this one book and it talked about "natural revelation," the revelation that there is God that thru nature He reveals
Himself. This is true God does reveal Himself thru nature, each and
everyday even before the sun comes up God reveals Himself. If you
were to get up at 0400 and go out side or to a lake and just stop and

listen you will see God has nature perfectly balanced and working in dare I say harmony. That everything is working itself out to the way God has it designed. It isn't until those two legged human creatures wake up do we get things zapped and messed up.

You are also a part of God's creation, as a matter of fact your were created in His likeness. It is just that we go against God and rely on our human nature, it used to be survival of the fittest now it is survival of the meanest. To be perfectly honest with you I detest my human nature do you? I say that because when I am rely on my human nature it causes me to sin and to be separate from God, if you were to look at the sins that you commit you also will se it is out of your human nature.

Salvation comes only from God and His nature in His Love. We can never be good enough to earn our way to heaven, there is no tally sheet with a bottom line that you have to reach before you earn your salvation. If there was a tally sheet there would be debts and credits, so you would find that they at best at best balance.

His blessing is upon His people, those whom He has revealed Himself to and who have accepted the sacrifice of the cross and who have come to believe that there the Son has died for their sin and not Jesus Christ sits at the right hand of the Father. Isn't it a blessing just knowing that God loves you, and that He holds your salvation in the palm of His hand that no man may wrench it from His fingers.

No matter how beautiful the sunrise is salvation doesn't come from the sun but thru the Son who's Father, your Father, created that sunrise.

Start to Finish

2 Timothy 4:7 I have fought the good fight, I have finished the race, I have kept the faith.

1 John 2:25 And this is the promise that He has promised us—eternal life.

Have you fought the good fight, are you on the ropes, is it round one or round 101 that you are now in. Don't throw in the towel just yet but keep faith endure till the final bell rings and rest in the arms of GOD.

Ya'll know something, we often, well maybe it's just me, wonder about finishing the race and how it will end. This past weekend this one guy lets just call him Tim so as not to embarrass him (how was that Tim) said something at a men's conference/retreat about making an impact for Christ where you are at. If you were no longer in Nashville would you have left a crater, an impact for Christ in others lives or in the community. How about you in Mobile, have you impacted your family-neighborhood-community for Christ? Feel free to put your city in either of those lines.

If you haven't impacted then have you been fighting to good fight? Or are ya just kind of coasting to the end? Paul saw that the end was near, he knew that the race was about to end and the bell was now beginning to ring. For many today the race is also coming to a close, that we may be in the final rounds is a possibility but not a certainty. We are not promised tomorrow but we do have a promise that we can hang onto and that is eternal life. Sometimes we get tired of the shots and jabs that we take, but that doesn't mean we can get out of the ring, it may mean at times to sit down and take a rest.

I don't know this Christian walk seemed so easy when I didn't know Christ, all those guys going to church on Sunday but living like they were the same as me every other day of the week. It seemed like it didn't really matter where they spent their time on Sunday because it didn't make a difference in their life. Sure I used the hypocrite excuse to not believe in Christ, but then who was the biggest hypocrite I was. People in church are no better or worse than anyone else, I judged them for their stumbling not for their repentance.

You see this race that we are on isn't a matter of who comes in first or who has the most awards or medals this race is about finishing, and to me that is also finishing well. This race is about how you can help others who are along the route get into and also stay in the race.

Look I don't have all or even many of the answers, but what I do know is who is at the finish line and I want to get there to the end. That each of us has an opportunity to impact our families-neighbors-community-county-state-nation-world for Christ is a reality, but if we are hanging onto the ropes instead of getting into the fight our impact will be limited. IS your faith strong enough to take a shot here and there, even if the world knocks you down will you have the strength to get up, shoot boy-oh look who you got in your corner, Jesus Christ cheering you on, encouraging you to finish that which you have started.

Sit Down – Slow Down

Mark 4:39
Then He arose and rebuked the wind, and said to the sea, "Peace, be still!" And the wind ceased and there was a great calm.

Yeah I know, how many times can we talk about wind and waves and how Christ has power of that which was called into existence. Well we could talk about it till I am blue in the face but that would defeat the purpose, because some times we need to get the message all by ourselves and not try to get people to understand it our way or to do things our way but to let their faith grow in God's way. I know some where in the Bible it talks about being patient with others in their maturity, and I also know that sometimes I just want people to see God as I see Him. But ya know what maybe we just need to sit down and slow down not stop mind you even thou that is what you may think what I mean by sit down, sit down and slow down to wait to be still and to enjoy the great calm.

I have been accused, rightly so, of umm how to say this of being overly demanding, pushy and aggressive about some things. The more I think about it the more I know that I just need to sit down and not think that people need to keep up with me or do the things I do. Are there people whom you know that you just wish they would get as involved as you are, why maybe they really are not ready so you sit down and wait on them. God is the one doing the calling, follow what He calls you to do.

So what does this have to do with wind and the sea, well maybe you are the wind and waves at times. Today maybe Christ needs you and calls out to you "Peace, be still!" let Him deal with the faith of those in the boat. We can not force understanding on anyone else we just blow and blow and nothing is accomplished but a storm. Those in the boat may have a deer in the headlights look and don't know what to do, give them time they will have understanding. Sit down and encourage instead of discourage them, don't chastise them for where they are but encourage them for where they are.

Hey Ya'll would it be too much just to sit down and let God have control, let go before He rebukes you but if you are rebuked then obey and do what He says. Isn't it funny kinda that Christ called out "Peace" what does wind and water know about peace? Well what do you know about peace, be calm and maybe you will learn. Oh if only we would obey God as well as nature does, if we listened, if I listened half as well as the sea did.

Each of us today need to maybe just sit down, be still Doug, Walter, Doris, Jeff, Charles (1-2-3), Burton, Rachel, Deanna, Shelly, Jesse, Jo Ann, Joe, you and I.

Straight-Up

Genesis 15:1

[God's Covenant with Abram] After these things the word of the LORD came to Abram in a vision, saying, "Do not be afraid, Abram. I am your shield, your exceedingly great reward."

You know what do you trust in, no really what is it that you are relying on today as you go about your business what is it that you are trusting in? Self reliant and ready to take on any problem any foe or just trying to keep your head down low and not be a target for anyone or anything. Possibly could we trust in the Lord who has said over and over time and time again "I am with you".

All to often we rely on what we know instead of Who we know, that some how the grey- matter is more important than God. We try to hide instead of relying on the shield to go forward into the fray. I guess we at times lack trust in God other wise wouldn't we take a stand shielded by Him. Aren't we a foolish lot, by not trusting God to carry out that which He has promised in His Word. Oh maybe that is it, maybe we don't trust the Word.

Tell me this ya'll do you trust the Word? Abraham was worried about not having an heir, the only heir he had was his servant not a son from Sarah. God showed him that he would have an heir and gave Him a look at what this nation would go thru. God not only said that Abraham would have an heir but multiplied the descendants to be a nation. Wouldn't that be a thing to scare ya, a nation of Irmiter's. Holy Cow, what fun we would have but I digress.

We read God's word we look into it for answers hoping that something will click in our lives something that we can hang onto. We miss the application and promise of it sometimes because lets face it we all at times like to do things Fran's way, oops I mean our way. The problem with that is God's way is the Way the Truth and the Light not my way or your way or the by-law way or what-ever churchy way you or I come up with. I can't remember who it was, but it was at a revival and the speaker said something like, if what I say is contrary to what your pastor says listen to your pastor if what you pastor says is contrary to what God says listen to God.

I guess the jest of it is one must trust in God straight-up, no excuses no blustering, no blah blahs, but solely to take God's Word and apply it to your life and live it instead of living contrary to it. If all you are standing on is what you have build from gray matter then you have built on sand and I just say beware the storm. Do you think you are any different then Abraham in God's eye, certainly the example of how God kept His word to Abraham should lend itself to you that He will be faithful to you also.

A shield is for battle not for cowards, don't quiver behind the shield but stand up, firmly grasp it and go forward. Take back the land that God has led you into and rely on HIM, He shall be faithful.

Love part 153

1 John 3:11
For this is the message that you heard from the beginning,
that we should love one another,

What, don't-cha got anything else to talk about than this love thing again we get it, alright already man give me a break. Some times I worry about repeating the devotionals both in message and verses used, but then again I don't worry much about that at all. I know don't try to figure me out it will add to your grey hair right Doug and Jesse?

How many times did Jesus talk about love over and over again, and God did He ever talk about love, yep over and over again. Yet with all of these messages of love, about love and in love when was the last time you applied love to your life and showed it to some one else. I know we sometimes get callused over with bunk and junk so we feel like we aint got time or opportunity to show love, extend love, reach out our hands, and give love. When in fact our excuses are just bunk and junk.

This message you have heard from the beginning that we should love one another, but do we, have we or even can we? Do you, have you, and can you?

If we have really heard this message time and time again then are we applying it to our lives, and to those whom we come in contact with in our lives. You see it isn't a matter of just hearing but also in applying this in our lives. Daily!! Sure I know that when things go to pot and there is a disaster or something people send money, cloths, food, and even go to help out. Not these are good things and should be done but what about today in the average person's life will you have opportunity to just love some one.

To hold a hand, to encourage with a word, to correct some one in love, will we stop just saying this warm fuzzy things but actually living them out. Why aren't these hands holding, because they are clenched into a fist ready to defend that which is ours instead of reaching out to those whom we can give to. You see today, right where you are at there will be some one whom just needs to hear a loving word from you, or will need you just to put down your pen or turn away from your computer so you can listen. Love them, you may not love the thing that they are doing but love them.

You ask who we are putting our trust in today? The Sweet Holy Spirit... Jesus said in John chapter 16:7 ... Tells us He must go so that the Comforter would come... Praise Him! Praise Him! God is so good... He knows our every need and his supply of grace and mercy are sufficient to meet those needs... I can't even imagine how anyone can get through their daily struggles without Him... The Father, The Son, and the Holy Spirit! they are my daily guide and inspiration.... Without them I would be nothing! My life would be in vain... Thanks for giving me the opportunity to share my Faith! – Jo Anne Shows

Suprise

Matthew 6:21
For where your treasure is, there your heart will be also.

Matthew 9:4
But Jesus, knowing their thoughts, said, "Why do you think evil in your hearts?

S pace was limited when I was a kid, wasn't it Deanna. There were very few places one could stash their treasure, I kept my stuff in an old brown (not rust) tin suitcase. I kept everything in there that was important to me. Pictures and cards of and from different people mementoes from this event or that event. Just chocked full of stuff that I wanted to keep, to you thou it would have been trash – junk – a joke – nothing. Each one of us has a tin suitcase that we store our treasure in, metaphorically Douglas, is God the thing in your treasure that you hold dearest to?

Some where along the way of traveling to and fro around the country and world and back to the new world I have lost that tin suitcase. Then again my memories no matter how dear to me are not my treasure, you see Tammy, Amanda and Daniel are my treasure it is only because God is first that we can see the real treasure.

To many times people think their treasure is what name brand they got, how many rooms in the house, what is parked in the garage and how much they can spend – this is not a rich verses poor. It is a matter of your heart, what is it that you desire what is it that you lusts after and why don't we see that God is the real treasure and His Word is where real life begins.

Christ knowing their thoughts – now that would be a perplexing thing – right there in the middle of your conversation, which in your heart is an attack of evil, Christ calls you on it. Is it because we hold onto the evil in our hearts rather than dumping out the suitcase of stuff, dump out the evil and repent of it and turn from it and let it go as far as the east is from the west.

If you treasure something it will come first in your life and you wont have to make time for it, rather time for the Treasure in your life will come first. We at times abandon our true treasure for human treasure and we let our hearts grow heavy with the weight of sin and of lusting after that which will be but ash. Each and everyday we must search our heart with God's help, with His Light shining into each nook and cranny revealing that which if left un-checked, un-repented can become our treasure.

What is it that you have placed into your heart, is it treasure that can withstand the heat of a fire, or will it be burnt up? Don't be surprised if Christ asks you one day, "why do you think evil in your heart", if that is what you have treasured.

Look Up

Psalm 5:3
My voice You shall hear in the morning, O LORD; In the morning I will direct it to You, And I will look up.

One just has to look up, I need to look up, sometimes everything just seems to bubble up and over and we fall down and pray asking God to lift us up but we don't look up to see His hand there waiting to help us up. I know it is proper form to pray with head bowed and an angelic expression upon your face and to say the correct words in the correct sequential way and to hold the pose just long enough to seem holy enough, but sometimes don't ya just want to shout to God WHY - WHAT - HELP – HOW.

When was the last time when you prayed you wept over your sin, when was the last time you screamed and shouted in your sorrow, how "deep" do you go? Now I know it is the good Christian way to fold your hands and bow your head and to speak in a calm voice when you pray, I know that but is that the way you talk normally? NO, it isn't could you imagine if we all spoke in the same way that we pray in? Should you be humble when you pray Tim, should you must you bow you neck and pray yes we should but we shouldn't put on airs and an act like this is what prayer is about, an act.

If My people would humble themselves and turn from their wicked ways then will I hear their prayers and heal their land. It doesn't matter how much you bend your neck and act like you are humble if you don't turn from your ways, your words will be as wind with no voice to be heard.

Has God heard your voice this morning, or the whisper of your thoughts?

Cry out to the LORD in your prayers talk to Him, come before Him with humility and boldness, let Him get to know your voice and don't but on airs.

But also look up! In the morning we can look up and see that dawning of the day, the golden tendrils of light cascading thru the trees and clouds, the golden rapture of a new day. (how was that) All of that aside there are no words or pictures that can express the Glory of the Day that the LORD has made!! Don't miss it ya'll, rather look up and keep your eyes upon it and know in your heart that God hears you. Let Him hear you and not the scripted message of an empty prayer.

Be Glad

Psalm 4:7
You have put gladness in my heart, More than in the season
that their grain and wine increased.

Where does your gladness come from, is it because you have toys or is it because you know the LORD, Abba, and Yahweh? Where does your joy come from, what can you and I do to create our own joy that is lasting but look at what God -Eloheem (sp) mighty and strong has created for you.

You know some of the happiest moments in my life are no-cost moments, now does that make sense? A smile on a Christmas morning, a twinkle in the eye of one of the kids, handing some one a meal at Thanksgiving, having good friends whom I can count on, and on and on are just some of the things that have brought me glad-ness. Each of you have moments of gladness that came not from what you could put on your credit card but what God has given you thru the blessings He has given you.

I don't know, Russell but do you think people have gladness in their heart as much as they did why you were much younger? Could it be Jo Ann that we are looking to create our own gladness? Tell me Rusty when was the last time you genuinely felt glad for the things God has given you? Each day the great "I AM," blesses us with things to make us glad but so much of the time we are only glad when our cup is overflowing instead of half full, think of this if there was just one swallow left in the cup that is still more than you or I deserve.

I don't really care how much you have or think you don't have if you are trying to fill up your cup on your own then the cup is still dry. Look here ya'll it isn't about he who dies with the most toys wins after all your toys are just that toys no different then that model airplane you built then blew up with fire-crackers bringing you a chuckle or two but then you had to clean up the mess (please don't tell me I am the only one who blew up a toy airplane). Sure it was fun for the moment but it took you longer to clean it up then to blow it up.

Gladness that comes from God is lasting and filling, there isn't anyone out there who can tell me that they can't remember the sheer gladness/joy of when their children were born and you brought them home.

Who has put gladness in your heart? Is it yourself or is it GOD?

Is your glass dry? Is your glass half full? Is your glass filled to the rim? Is your glass overflowing? Ya know something share a cup of cool water with some one who thinks that their cup is half full or dry, I betcha that God fills your cup right back up.

Walk with

Psalm 23:2 He makes me to lie down in green pastures; He leads me beside the still waters.

As you walk around today are you going to be lead beside the still waters or is the torrent of the world going to sweep you by? It is easy to get swept up with all that is going on these days with tragedies and stuff that is going on, so even more we need to let God guide us to and along side of the still waters this is where we will find true rest not in bed.

Have you ever felt like the guy floating, not really floating, but getting swept away down the river after falling out of the boat. Getting battered and beaten by the rocks that lie just under the waves and being pounded by the crashing waves that seemingly try to push you down. Arm flailing reaching up to hold on to some thing or some one, hoping praying that some one would be there to save you. There is the thing right there, praying, crying out to God with arms outstretched, and ready to hold on.

It would be an easy thing to let the waves keep you down wouldn't it? This is not where God leads you though, this is where you fall into. We get ourselves into some pretty hairy predicaments at times and we wonder why GOD the LORD has let us fall into the on rush of the river. Is this what you think GOD has in store for you, it isn't He doesn't wish you to drown but to live. We shouldn't cry out WHY GOD WHY, rather we should ask GOD for a hand and we should reach out for His hand.

Every day it seems God reminds me of a green field where I can go, if but in my heart, and remember His whisper and feel His hand I can see the wind bend the grass and hear the stream move by. This is something that no one can take away from me, do you have a place that you can go, if but in your heart, that you can feel the very presence of GOD.

[1] The LORD *is* my shepherd;
        I shall not want.
[2] He makes me to lie down in green pastures;
    He leads me beside the still waters.
[3] He restores my soul;
    He leads me in the paths of righteousness
    For His name's sake.

[4] Yea, though I walk through the valley of the shadow of death,
    I will fear no evil;
    For You *are* with me;
    Your rod and Your staff, they comfort me.

[5] You prepare a table before me in the presence of my enemies;
    You anoint my head with oil;
    My cup runs over.
[6] Surely goodness and mercy shall follow me
    All the days of my life;
    And I will dwell[a] in the house of the LORD
    Forever.

Learn What?

Matthew 9:13
But go and learn what this means: 'I desire mercy and not sacrifice.' For I did not come to call the righteous, but sinners, to repentance."

I still haven't had time to fully compartmentalize the trip to Mobile / Pascagoula yesterday. Why this hurricane hit and who is to blame seem all but irrelevant at this time. Much more irrelevant today as I felt they did yesterday before I went down. You see those things are not the important things and I really could care less what any media outlet has to say about that. Do you know what matters, mercy, hope and love.

Christ said that He desires mercy not sacrifice. And ya know what I believe Him. So many times we have heard in the past week why, why, why maybe we don't feel like we have been shown mercy but judgment. We drove around the destruction and there was a sign at one house that was totaled, well actually it was gone, the sign read "Don't let Katrina steal your joy", then of course there were already some road side vendor selling tee-shirts "I survived Katrina" tell me who feels as if they have been shown mercy?

Some lives were taken, and this is sad and devastating to everyone, to the families and friends and it breaks the heart of a nation (it should). There is the life that we lead and the choices we make that places where we are. If some one is killed in a hurricane or in a tornado or earthquake it is no less tragic and the grief is no less sorrowful. Mourn the dead, it is right. But don't forget to celebrate with the living.

Do you want to know where I saw God's mercy, it was on the faces of those who helped unload the truck(s) it was on the faces of those organizing the shelters, it was on the face of a lady holding some one clsc's nephew, it was on the face of superman who was a kid maybe 5 who carried what he could and others may have thought was to much. It was mercy that their lives were spared.

It is mercy that our lives each day are spared. Who among us has not sinned, will not sin none are righteous when we apply God's commandments to our own choices. We have not earned mercy but been given mercy to live today to make the right choice to admit that we are sinners and that it is only thru Christ Jesus that we can come to the Father's house. He has come to call a sinner, that is you and I, to repentance. Not well those bunch of hypocrites but me and you.

Will we stumble and mess up, yes and each and every time we do we need to turn and repent. He has called us to repentance, when was the last time you truly turned? Are you struggling with sin, if so why do you go back to where you know you will sin again, could the possibility exists that you have only said your sorry and not repented. Tell me how much mercy do you think you deserve anyway?

Your Fruit

Matthew 14:[18]"Bring them here to me," he said. [19]And he directed the people to sit down on the grass. Taking the five loaves and the two fish and looking up to heaven, he gave thanks and broke the loaves. Then he gave them to the disciples, and the disciples gave them to the people. [20]They all ate and were satisfied, and the disciples picked up twelve basketfuls of broken pieces that were left over. [21]The number of those who ate was about five thousand men, besides women and children

Here is a poser, what would it take to feed 5 thousand today? Take a moment to figure that one out?

Done, good.

Lets see if your answer matches mine. The same thing that it took back then, God + our obedience = miracle

Why are we satisfied with just doing what we can, and using the talents of just a few to accomplish that which we think is a mighty thing? Ya know what God has more for us than what we can do just within ourselves, look around you and see all of the people whom He has placed in your life. All we have to do is be obedient when He leads us to His miracle.

What would Christ do if He was in Alabama, Georgia, Florida, Nebraska, Iowa, or Tennessee and there were people who were hungry in Biloxi? He would tell them to bring your fish and your loaves and direct the people to sit on the grass and they would eat their fill and there would be left over. But we can't do something like that, that would be way to complicated way to over my head and for those very reasons it would be a God thing.

If any of ya'll are familiar with the "Prayer of Jabez," it talks about expanding your territory, it is time to expand your territory.

When was the last time you let go and let God do a God sized event thru you, by just using the talent that you have and all of those around you?

Would you be willing to feed 5 thousand?

Basics

Genesis 1:1 In the beginning God created the heavens and the earth. (NKJV)

Genesis 1:[1]In the beginning God created the heaven and the earth.(KJV)

Genesis 1:[1]In the beginning God created the heavens and the earth.(NASB)

Genesis 1:[1] In the beginning God created the heavens and the earth. (HCSB)

Genesis 1:[1]First this: God created the Heavens and Earth--all you see, all you don't see. (MSG)

Ya know what, there is a lot of debate about creationism or Darwinism or intelligent design. That we evolved from apes or what ever that we crawled out of the cesspool of a swamp or something. *Genesis 2:7 And the LORD God formed man of the dust of the ground, and breathed into his nostrils the breath of life; and man became a living being.* To me that ends the debate, people try to explain things from their own view point, but none of them can explain everything. The first five words in the bible say it all.

Sometimes it is good to get back to basics especially when we think everything is getting to much and that it seems as if no one is in control. God is of that there is no doubt, you don't have to make up God you just have to look. In the beginning GOD created, it doesn't say in the beginning God consulted a polling group, or got a board of scientific angels together to discuss the possibilities of the best way to go about this. GOD –Mighty-Awesome-Powerful and Omnipotent created the heavens and the earth, the birds and the fish, the four legged animals and those with more or less legs and the LORD God, personnel Yahweh – Abba – Father – Daddy- Mighty-Awesome-Powerful and Omnipotent breathed into a lifeless form created from the dust of the earth, and the form breathed its first breath there as God looked on.

SO what can God accomplish, anything He wills. For His will is but a thought, He doesn't need hooky pocus or a magic incantation to create. He but has to call it into existence and there it is. Is this the GOD you serve, is this even the GOD you know, is this the GOD you love? Ya know we need to not rely on what is at our fingertips but rather rely on the very Word of God who is Jesus Christ.

Getting back to basics is just that it is starting with the things that we should have learned and should apply first in our lives. I know we should always be maturing and all of that but if we forget the basics we sometimes loose focus on what kind of an Awesome God it is that we say we serve. We do serve an awesome wonderful powerful GOD, tell me if He can speak the world into existence, if His very breath can bring life then what are you worried about or what can come against you and defeat you. Maybe we find ourselves outside of His arms, maybe we have wondered off a bit. Return to basics and turn from our reliance on what the world says is right and follow what God says is right.

Return to Holiness, be separate from the world and rely on God let Him use you for His purposes instead of you trying to use Him for your purpose.

Joy Comes

Psalm 30:5
For His anger is but for a moment, His favor is for life;
Weeping may endure for a night, But joy comes in the
morning.

How can we endure in the Lord if we don't surrender to Him?
Man I know there have been times when I probably have
royally ticked God off. He knows I am not perfect but still can I do
no better than that. You see we all know what is the right thing to
do, but sometimes maybe not all of the time we do things that well
just make God angry. Isn't it a good thing that His anger is but for a
moment, how about yours or mine?

Every once and a while I get a big head like I am some one,
leave it to God to use people to knock me down to size. Kind of
helps one focus when one isn't self reliant and actually depends on
others. Even if every once and a while others may let you down and
not do the things that they know you have taught them, they just
kind of hypocsyia (brain burp). Ya want to just lash out and ya get
all upset but when you think about it, you have done the same thing
to God and He still never leaves you.

Weeping may endure for the night but when the night fades and
the dawn breaks joy comes. I know sometimes the night seems like
it is a long time, kind a like up in Alaska when they have months of
night but even up there the dawn does come. His favor is for life.

Joy comes in the dawn because His favor is for life, our life. His joy is also in us when we obey His commands, to know Him, to love Him and to serve Him.

Let your anger be also but for a moment, extend that which was granted to you mercy and love. IF you have received freely then shouldn't you also give freely? Tell ya what why don't you turn someone's night into a dawn by letting God guide you instead of lashing out because you can.

Maybe the dawn will break thru the night and joy will sweep over our nation today, but first it must start with those who Know the Lord and that is you and I.

Drink the right water

¹³ Jesus answered and said to her, "Whoever drinks of this water will thirst again, ¹⁴ "but whoever drinks of the water that I shall give him will never thirst. But the water that I shall give him will become in him a fountain of water springing up into everlasting life."
John 4:13-14 (NKJV)

Have ya'll seen these flavored water things that have been coming out in droves. You can get raspberry, lemon, strawberry, fruit punch, peach and on and on. We all have our favorite, mine happens to be raspberry and I think there are only two or three people in the entire county that like that one, most prefer lemon. With all of these flavor and all of these choices how can one make up their mind, well I guess it is just a matter of what works for you huh. Lets hope that we don't have this same attitude about salvation, there is but one flavor, and that is Jesus Christ.

We sometimes go to a well to get our daily fill of water and then away with even less of a sense of refreshment all because we sipped it instead of drank it. Do ya get that, sipping instead of drinking it in. We sip hot beverages so we don't scold ourselves, nobody like that scolded feeling in their mouth when is numbs your mouth and then you can't taste very well for a couple of days and stuff like that. No rather we sip it in, trying not to take too much in but then how refreshing is that. Depends on what your sipping doesn't it?

Now ya'll may think this is to literal and all that but Christ said "whoever drinks of the water," drinks of the water, taking it in. Have you ever been so thirsty that when you drank something that it would overflow your mouth and run down the sides of your cheeks and down your chin and running off onto you shirt. If you were thirsty enough it didn't matter that your shirt got soaked you were drinking it in. When was the last time you drank in the word of God like that or are you still trying to sip at it worrying about getting convicted by it?

The water that He gives is the fountain of water <u>springing</u> up into everlasting life, springing up in you. Ya remember the *Beverly Hill Billie's* when Jed shot the ground a oil sprung up, is that the kind of spring that God provides in you or is He the spring that came from the rock when Moses place the staff on it and water flowed that refreshed the people. My point is one was a story and one was a miracle of God, which would you rather have inside you?

We can come to the well everyday and if we only try to get enough just to fill a jug or jar we are trying to fill the wrong vessel. You and I should be filled with the living water of Christ and in His word drinking it in. Drink the right water, let the spring of everlasting life overflow you cup.

The Harvest

John 4: [34] Jesus said to them, "My food is to do the will of Him who sent Me, and to finish His work. [35] Do you not say, 'There are still four months and *then* comes the harvest'? Behold, I say to you, lift up your eyes and look at the fields, for they are already white for harvest!

What are you going to do today, are you going to talk with people concerning what their plans are for the weekend, for the evening, if they are going to the game tonight or tomorrow? Hey Doug do ya mind if I pick on you? No, thanks man. When you are talking with people about activities that are being planned for the month or the year do you also wonder about where their eternal weekend, month or years will be spent. Do we, that is each of us discuss what is really relevant and that is where we will spend eternity.

In Iowa now the fields are probably still a little green, the bottom leaves of the corn stalks may be showing signs of brown. Soon the harvest will take place and that which was planted in fertile soil will be swept up into the bins and bens. Each farmer is already preparing their combine getting the teeth sharp and greasing the augers so that everything will go smoothly, they hope. Today the fields are ripe for the harvest, but who among us is really that concerned with reaping the harvest, or are we just hoping some one else does it?

Whose job is it to talk about Jesus Christ? Is it your job Gail, Linda, Bob, Stewart, Kevin, and you right there? I know sometimes we think it is only the pastor's job to talk about Jesus, so tell me then how effective is that? In a day and age where church attendance is going down in many places whose job is it to seek out those who just know who Jesus is but don't bear the fruit of a relationship with Christ. Is it the job of one combine or the task of all those who are called by His Name.

When was the last time you talked, I mean really talked about who Christ is. Not just inviting some one to church but talking with them about the Savior who saved you Elaine, this Jesus who died on a cross for your sin Brenda, the Messiah who was raised on the third day. Maybe you have forgotten what it was to be lost before you met Christ ask Savior and not as a baby in a manger. Can you Jane think of all those things that God has brought you thru, saved you from. IS your testimony not worth sharing, I betcha it is but when was the last time you actually shared it.

These are not question as much as they are statements, each of us can do better can't we the question really is Will We? Get into the field that God has placed you in and reap from the harvest that which you have not sowed.

First Things

Matthew 6:33
But seek first the kingdom of God and His righteousness,
and all these things shall be added to you.

A re you searching harder for your keys in the morning than you
seek the kingdom of God each day? Keep the main thing the
main thing, is God the first thing and the main thing in your life?

Most things that we do we do in steps, policies have procedures,
ways to do and get things done. Follow step one to get to step thirty
four and don't skip steps twelve or twenty and don't try to put step
forty two in front of step thirty six. You will end up with pie in
your face and you will just end up having to redo it. This life you
are leading thou have no redo button. Once it is over it is over, end
game. As much as I would like to go back in time to redo some of
the things that I have done and do them over again I can't. Maybe
that is a good thing, I guess that is where we learn to avoid things in
the present or future.

Today we must seek out His kingdom first, not oh I forgot or I'll
get to it or if I can squeeze it in but first we must seek His kingdom.
There is little that can be added to this, matter of fact Christ's words
are in themselves good enough it is our application of His words
that I ask you about. SO if Christ said it we should do it right? Then
what keeps us from doing the things of God, ourselves, picking and
choosing what we want to live by, learn and apply? Go ahead I am

sure that will be a good answer, "Yeah God I know that we were supposed to seek your kingdom I remember reading something about that. But ya know something I had to get a better job, work on a promotion, I had to take the kids to ball and dance and God ya know I needed my time so I wouldn't burn out I just ran out of time."

Ya know I used to figure that God's kingdom would just fall in my lap, that when I came to know Christ in a personnel relationship that everything would just be hunky dory. To seek out His Kingdom man alls ya got to do is open your eyes. Some where along the way I had closed my eyes and just looked at what I could do. Let me see if I can say this better, I just looked at what I knew I could do even sometimes without God, but for God. When do we start looking for God's size results, when we start looking for His kingdom.

Keep the main thing the main thing, sure we know it but do we do it? Seek FIRST the kingdom of GOD! The first thought of this day is how can we be set apart for God if we allow sin and self to prevail in our lives, when we walk in darkness we just bump our head. Step back into the light out of the grey or pitch and plant both feet in His Light, seek His kingdom with passion with a sense of urgency and emergency let the seeking be your passion your hunger. Place your all and all in the seeking to look for the finding, you will find that His kingdom isn't in a far off distant land but maybe just at the tip of your nose.

Is He

Luke 1:79
To give light to those who sit in darkness and the shadow of death, To guide our feet into the way of peace."

Ya know something, today I don't feel like planning a thing, I know that probably shocks a bunch of you. Today I would much rather go along with the day and the people in it and just let things happen that will happen and not take the hurdles personnel. Does that sound good to you?

You see sometimes I try to knock down the hurdles instead of letting God guide me over the hurdles, the problem with what I do is I can't knock the hurdles down and just bludgeon my knuckles on them. Also when you try to knock hurdles down they inevitably just get knocked down on some one else and this doesn't do anything but cause friction. Now I am not saying we shouldn't work a plan El Timo but we should be working the plan that God has laid before us.

Light doesn't just reveal the problem that is in the path but it also illuminates the way to deal with the hurdle. For where God is there is also a solution, let the light reveal it and then you and I should follow it. I know we think it is much quicker to just bull thru the situation but it isn't because you will find more hurdles beyond that hurdle. I am not saying this to anyone but myself.

We should not be sitting in darkness but we must be following the Light that is there to guide our feet in the way of peace. You see sometimes we sit in darkness because we have clicked the light off or because we just well sit down and stop following the Light. Well I guess I am just saying maybe it is time to stand up and start following the Light like we are supposed to do.

The way we overcome the world in not by a 12 step program or a flow chart organizational piece of paper but by the Word of God. To guide our feet, is not taking over your steps, maybe He should but maybe we need to surrender everyday those steps that we would go and ask God to lead us then we should follow. We each have so much to give that if we only want to give in our way then we will not end up giving at all. This may sound a bit like rambling today but the jest of it is that we must let God be our guide and the Guide is Christ, He is the Light He is the Word and He is the Savior. Let His words guide you today.

Hmm maybe I'll even be late for things today and not worry about it?????

Pray

Matthew 6:9
In this manner, therefore, pray: Our Father in heaven, Hallowed be Your name.

The manner in which we pray matters!

It is called the model for prayer but when was the last time we considered its words, did we start off our day this morning with considering who and where He is and how sacred His name is? I know I was rushed this morning also, I had to get going and didn't even have time to iron my pants, just a shower and a shave then off so I wouldn't be late picking some one up and getting to work on time. So when will I take the time to actually consider these things that I am asking you to consider, how about now.

Who: Our Father – we are created in the very image of God, "Let us make man in Our image." So we have character traits of God in our image, well it the image of God what you saw when you looked into the mirror this morning? Yeah me neither. Just as people know you as your fathers son so to should we also know our Father. We did not evolve from an ape, otherwise we would look like an ape and have chip like qualities. No matter how strange some of us may be, some of you more than others, we have been created in the image of God, not a god but THE GOD. He is our Father, yours and mine and when we pray we should pray with the intimacy of a Father and a son. We do not pray to a stranger who doesn't know us, maybe we don't know the Father very well but the Father knows us.

Where: in Heaven – Our Father is not in some mystical Shangri-La but in a place of His own creation, the same place where you will dwell with Him one day. When you pray do you consider that God is where you wish to be one day. Certainly you desire to be with the Father on that Holy Hill, certainly you desire to walk into the throne room and lay prostrate on the floor and worship the Most High in the most Holy of places. Christ said that in His Fathers House there are many mansions, are you praying considering that you have a place to go to? Just as God created the heavens so did He create where you now sit. Our Father who is sitting upon His throne can hear your prayer. He does not lie in state somewhere but His ears are attentive to your words. God hears you Jesse, Rod, Joe, Doug, Tim, and All of us.

Sacred: Hallowed be thy Name – What is in a name, well if you consider that this is the name that causes demons to flee and it is the name of the one who's very words spoke the world into being then we must consider this name sacred don't cha think? If you go to Ringsted Iowa and tell some one there that you know me, most will say who is that, some may say is that one of Jerry's kids, some may say so and some may say cool so what is he up to. None will say lets roll out the red carpet and invite you in to our house. How sacred to we consider the name of God or is it just an expression we use when we excited or upset? How holy do we treat the name of GOD, with what umm uh reverence to we place upon those three letters, GOD. When we pray we must consider the manner in which we pray along with the state of our heart.

Side Effects

Mark 7:13 making the word of God of no effect through your tradition which you have handed down. And many such things you do."

Have you ever watched some of these drug commercials, the legal ones Joe don't give me that boy! You know these drug commercials that say if you take this it will help with hair growth but some of the side effects would be in some cases diarrhea, bloating, rash, pealing skin, soreness in the joints and in rare cases death. Makes me want to run out there and get some of that stuff, wahoo!! But I guess you can take some medicine for those things so we can really be a pill popping society. Take this med for this problem and take these meds for the side effects of the one med, now what sense does this in general make?

Well now so is the same thing when we try to be cultural Christians, by softening up why the church is supposed to be here by saying we should be doing this or that to be more inclusive. Nor should we be making rules that are contrary to the Word of God. The word is divisive, it calls what is right-right and what is wrong-wrong it is not a matter for interpretation it is a matter of fact. Christ came to call us to repentance, it was the first message that He taught after being baptized in the Jordan. Tell me how can we be called into repentance if we are not convicted?

We say that the Holy Spirit convicts us of a sin when we commit it, but do we listen to the Spirit or do we listen to the committee on social ed-I-kit (thru spell check into overdrive) but you know what I kind of like the way that is spelt, the I is capitalized because we want the me and our clique personified instead of doing what is right. When we put the I into things than we have just taken medicine that nullifies the effect of the word of God. I tell you the truth I would much rather lash back at some one then listen to God when He says "Love those who persecute you," but if we do what we know is wrong what do you call that, I call it sin. To do what we know is wrong is not just wrong, a convenient word that we use since we don't want to call it what it really is and that is SIN.

Cultural Christians have made the Word of no affect because it doesn't change us/them/me/you. This is something that God's Word came to do, to change you from the worm with sin to the holy and righteous men and women of God!!! The word is what we should be living by and applying in our lives, we must practice what we preach first so the Word will have the effect that it was intended to have. Christ said, "I have come to divide," tell me ya'll biblical scholars out there, if there is division are there two sides and are those sides sinful and righteous?

When we go forward in this day and consider the things that we do and say are we encouraging a brother and sister in a growing faith in Christ or in this is how we do Church. Go there fore and make disciples in where you are at, teaching them the commands of Christ not the-this is how we do church. One thing is true, the side effect of death is real and eternal.

No Title

Luke 22:44
And being in agony, He prayed more earnestly. Then His sweat became like great drops of blood falling down to the ground.

Mark 1:35
Now in the morning, having risen a long while before daylight, He went out and departed to a solitary place; and there He prayed.

Mark 16:2
Very early in the morning, on the first day of the week, they came to the tomb when the sun had risen.

If every day we rose early and walked out to be in a solitary place to pray, what would be your reaction?

I wish I had the words this morning to encourage you to do mighty things for the Lord, to rise up and take the world by storm, even in Decatur. But alas the words escape me, then again how about this how about you take your world by storm, where ever it is you plant your feet that is your world, you go and claim that for God.

Christ prayed "more earnestly," not that He wasn't praying earnestly or praying at all but rather He poured even more of Himself into His prayers. How exhausted He must have been after this prayer.

If you think sure He prayed and still look what happened, they still turned Him over to be crucified, also remember that He prayed for God's will to be done. How much of yourself do you pour into your prayers, I have to admit that sometimes mine are quick fast and in a hurry, I need at times to remind myself to slow down and pray in the Spirit for God's will to be done. Ya know what prayer works, God hears.

Christ rose early in the morning to go pray off by Himself, it doesn't say what He prayed for or if He had His prayer list in hand. Ya'll if we don't make the time to spend with God why should He make the time to be with us? We do the things we want to do, we make the time to do the things we really want to do. The best of intentions get you what, nothing but the best of intentions. Are you willing to place God in a special place in your life or are you still trying to fit Him into your free time? Isn't that a shame?

Christ had risen, the tomb is empty, and now to this day it remains empty. You see Christ Jesus, Messiah, Prince of Peace, and many other titles sits at the right hand of God. By praying with intent and making the time to commit yourself to lift up your prayers via the Holy Spirit, Christ brings them to the Father. Christ hands your prayer to the Father with scars in His hands, feet, side, and head. God can't hear you if you don't pray to Him, so go off and pray and ya'll pray more earnestly.

Narrow Gate

Luke 13:24 "Strive to enter through the narrow gate, for many, I say to you, will seek to enter and will not be able.

Have you ever been in a parking lot and there is a parked car on one side and some other guy waiting to pick some one up on the other side and you looked in-between them going, "hmm I wonder if I can make that gap?" Well we don't need to worry about parked cars or even how we are going to squeeze in, when you know Christ as your Lord and Savior the gate will be open to you, right.

Are we striving today to enter the narrow gate? There is this lady that has just passed away and from knowing her and yes her family I can be sure that she is already thru the narrow gate. You see this gate isn't based upon if you are thin enough to enter but who you know, think of it this way (you bible scholars cringe when I say that). Christ is the bouncer at the gate and He will deny access to those whom don't know Him. Christ knew this lady not because of who she was but because she had a relationship with Him for more than 70 years, that is a lot of getting to know.

If you think about it, for even one year, how well do we strive to enter the narrow gate. Please notice that I didn't say want to or even to desire to enter the gate but actually striving to enter the narrow gate. Each day that we know Christ we should strive to enter that gate, but do we earnestly seek His path every day.

Have you ever seen those country roads that have grass growing in-between the tire ruts? These are roads that are less travel, for one you gotta know who owns the land that the road is on, but you also need to know where those roads lead. This gate is at the end of the road for all of us, yes that is right for all of us will meet up with the bouncer one day, the old adage is "live each day as it were your last," well it could be I guess. If you had to ask yourself are you just seeking to enter the narrow gate or are you assured of an entry.

Each day we walk and talk about Christ and what He means to us. You have goals for your life here on earth and that is a good thing, have a goal for your eternal life and strive with vigor towards that end, each and every day from today till you reach the end strive for the narrow gate. Get to know God more and more each and everyday instead of just knowing who He is in name. We can be on the right road everyday and we don't have to worry about trying to squeeze in, there are no technicalities in gaining entrance.

Here is a thought, tell me what ya think! If when you pray today has your prayer been passed thru the gate? If you are praying in the Spirit and Christ receives that prayer and God hears that prayer isn't He getting to know you and your voice.

Things of God

Matthew 6:26 Look at the birds of the air, for they neither sow nor reap nor gather into barns; yet your heavenly Father feeds them. Are you not of more value than they?

The things of God have more value than all the plunder on the earth, do you agree with that? How about this does your life reflect your agreement of that?

AHHHHHHHHHHHHHHHHHHHHHHHHHHHHHHHHHHHHHHH HHHHHHHHHHH!!!!!!

My God how wonderful are Your works that You LORD have made all these things that we see and have created them in perfect harmony and all we have to do is take it in and know that YOU ABBA Father are Alive. We can be alive more each day when we stop taking for granted the work of His hands and know that this is but a taste of what is in store for us beyond the narrow gate.

It doesn't matter if you look across the fields of Iowa seeing the green fields in the spring or the golden fields of the harvest in the fall. God is the one who has given you that view. Maybe you look across the Lake of Eufaula, a "man made lake," doink who filled it gave one the ability to create it, man did not create the water or the fish or the trees or the ground that it was created on, basically man just backed up the water. Yet one can look across that Lake and see the birds swooping in to catch the fish and one can be awe struck by the life in the air around the lake. Possibly one can look across the hills of Clay and Randolph Counties in Alabama and you may need to stop and just take it all in. This is one view that I can not begin to describe.

With all of these things, yes many more things, that God has done you Tammy and Danita have more value, that you Jesse and Rod and Joe and David and you Walter and Hugh and Stanley and you over there Randy and Deanna and Lisa and Gail and you Doug and hey even me are more valued then all of these things. We were created in the very image of God Kat and Trisha each of us, not a one of us was created contrary to His image. Black or White, Yellow or Brown we each are more valued then everything else that He created.

Ya know, it is really very simple if you meditate on it, God will provide because God knows you for He created you. Sure sometimes the choices that we have made have caused us to question our value and sometimes we may struggle to fill our store room. Because what must come first in each choice is God's will and we gotta ask Him and then follow His lead. Maybe we don't do so good following huh?

There are three words that need to be on your breath today, something to constantly remind you of your value, God Loves You. Go a head and say it Bob "God Loves me!!!"

Lift Up

Psalm 3:4
I cried to the LORD with my voice, And He heard me from His holy hill. Selah

Psalm 4:7
You have put gladness in my heart, More than in the season that their grain and wine increased.

Are you glad because of what you have or who you know? If you are sad because you don't have a new bass boat then a ski-boat will do it gets ya to where the fish are doesn't it. If you are sad because you don't have a new big screen plasma T.V. (hint-hint Doug and Jesse)((Just kidding)) to play X-Men II on then to bad your 40" screen will have to do. Are you glad because of how God has blessed you or because you know Him well enough to cry out to Him and HE HEARS YOU.

Ya know there are a lot of folks out there, some of them Christians, who are not glad about anything. Woe is me woe is me, when will I get my fair share when will I get stuff cause that is how I know God blesses me. Give me a break, spare me and holy cow what a pity we only look to our stuff to see if God blesses you.

Look I don't want to sound holy or anything like that because that would be well right, but there is one thing that you and I should feel different about and that is, are ya ready for it.

God has put gladness in our hearts, more than the stuff in our house or the increase in our accounts. It isn't the stuff but the Giver the HOLY ONE who hears us and listens to us. Who in moments of sorrow can give us peace and in moments of joy can fill us to overflowing.

Selah

Man there is no reason for me to ever be down because He should be my gladness all of the time and I should share that gladness with others. Gladness doesn't cost a pretty penny it is free; it doesn't cost you anything to smile at some one and tell them hello does it. I know sometimes we get down, I get down, but at those times then the rest of us should lift each other up. This gladness we shouldn't cup in our hands trying to keep it locked up no but rather we should share it with some one, you know the person you are supposed to share it with so go do it. If for some reason you need more gladness then CRY OUT to God He will hear you.

Not a Challenge

Matthew 22:39
And the second is like it: 'You shall love your neighbor as yourself.'

This is more of a challenge for each day than I can stand, oh but the title is not a challenge, jinkers. Oh that is write Christ didn't say and I challenge you to love you neighbor as yourself, good luck. It is not a challenge it is a command that we shall love our neighbors as ourselves. So tell me Pat how are we doing with that one, and Doug how's it going are we able to love those people who get under our skin or just do stupid things that make no sense to us why they do them?

Christ didn't give us a suggestion but He told us what we must do, not should do or if we got time or well if you could see fit to help out, no we must love them. I know what we do we substitute the word love and place in that spot umm like them, or feed them or cloth them or visit them or be nice to them or whatever kind of ___ ___ them that you have been doing to avoid loving them. Now for you who said what's wrong with liking them, feeding them, clothing them, or visiting them isn't that what we are supposed to do, and yes that is what you and I are supposed to do but first we must love them and that is why we love them and feed them and cloth them and visit them. Do we really love them if we see that they are cold and then walk away instead of going to our closet and getting that extra coat out and giving it to them.

Hey can I ask you something Nancy? Aren't each one of us each others neighbor? I mean you may be in Nebraska or Alabama or Mobile or Valley or Lanett or Lafayette but we are still each others neighbor. SO where is the limit that we say okay out to here these guys are our neighbors, every one else out there your some one else's neighbor good luck.

Like I said this is not a challenge, it is a command not given by Fran but given to us by God. How are you doing? Loving your neighbor is one of those fruits that people see, what are they seeing in you?

Guest Writer (my better half)

Ephesians 1:7 In Him we have redemption through His blood, the forgiveness of sins, according to the riches of His grace

Ephesians 2:13 But now in Christ Jesus you who once were far off have been brought near by the blood of Christ.

Thanks to all of you who supported me and prayed for me during my recent trip to Thailand. It was a trip of answered prayers, and many lessons. One lesson was that we may make plans, but God has bigger (and better!) ones. I planned to build a house…God planned for me to do no actual construction, but to build on what He has already taught me.

When my team got to the first house we worked on, we were informed that the house was used as a brothel. Surprise! My first thought was "why in the world should we be helping put a brothel back in business?" Well, I went there to be flexible, and to do whatever it took to get the job done, so I picked up my paint roller and started painting. As I painted, I prayed. "Lord, why here? Why this house? Couldn't we make a difference in someone else's house, someone who deserved it more?" God spoke to me as I painted. Jesus didn't choose to minister to only those who were deemed "worthy"; he sought out the harlots, and sinners, and tax collectors. His blood was shed to cover the sins of ALL, and His blood is sufficient. His blood covers our sins, just as that paint covered those walls. It was my job to serve Him WHEREVER he called me to serve, and so as I painted, I prayed for each soul that walked through the doors. I prayed for the owner and his wife, for the girls who may work there, and for the men who may frequent the house. I prayed that somehow, our service would make a difference, and that somehow, God would work in the lives of the people there, to show them that they, too, could be forgiven, through Jesus, according to the riches of His grace.

I was responsible for leading the group devotional one night. I thought about giving my testimony, but while lying in my bed in my room the day my team wouldn't let me go to work (my feet were too swollen to walk), I changed my mind. Or God changed it. My testimony would be that I am forgiven. That is all we really have to say. I am a sinner, but I am forgiven. *In Him we have redemption through His blood, the forgiveness of sins, according to the riches of His grace.* Just like those who are a part of that "sunshine house". We share the Gospel to others so that they may know that they, too, are forgiven, if they will accept Jesus as their Savior. That is what we are all called to do – to go, to do whatever it takes to get the job done.

Were my prayers in that house answered? Yes. God always answers prayer. I may never know the answers this side of heaven, but the seeds were planted, and God answered. That's all that matters.

By the way, my feet got better, and I was able to work the rest of the trip. Another answered prayer!

In His Service,

Tammy Irmiter

Pound it In

There are times when I am working on something at home and I don't have the right tools for the job. You know like you can't find the hammer but those vice grips are pretty heavy they will do the job, or if that screw doesn't seem to want to go any further so you flip it around and use the handle for a hammer. Hmm I guess the theme with that is anything can be used to pound something in. If the vice grips or screw driver get a little worse for wear then oh well I guess I should have stopped to find the hammer. Tammy loves it when I do those things by the way, right honey? Now ya'll may not believe this but sometimes duct tap and bailing wire are not the right tools for the job either, granted most time but not all of the time ya bunch of rednecks.

Now what in the world does this have to do with any kind of a devotional? Not much I am just rambling. No really it has a lot to do with our relationship is with God. Come here let me show you.

1) Christ said that He was the way the truth and the light that no one comes to the Father but thru Him. Do you believe that? Or are we still trying to be good enough not using the right tool but rather pounding thinking there must be another way. That maybe if we just do good things for others that God will have mercy on us and that will be good enough. But you see God has shown us mercy by sending His one and only son to us, to teach us, to lead us and to die for our sins. We may

think that the price was too high but it was a price that had to be paid. You see there is only one way to get into the heaven and the ticket has been purchased by the blood of Christ.

2) Even though God has given us His word we try to just pick and choose the verses that we will live by. We want to look down on those who live sinful lives but we don't want to be judged by our own sins, judge not lest you be judged by the same measure. At times people are quick to point out that they are not as bad as say me but yet they are, for isn't all sin a vile stench to God, isn't it because of sin that Christ had to pay the ultimate price.

Using the right tool for the job is essential, it helps to maintain order cause even if you pound that nail in with the vise grips it will be askew and won't hold like it should. When we talk to people about God, Christ and Heaven we mustn't forget to listen to the Holy Spirit. Only God is judge over our enemy and neighbor, no matter how frustrating they can be. You see the Romans used the right hammer to pound in the nails.

Happy

It seems like such a corny simple word doesn't it but yet at times this simple thing eludes us, me and you that is. We try all sorts of things to make us happy but really these are things that kill time in-between work days. Like to stay busy doing something anything don't we, when really it seems the happiest that I have been is when I have been quiet and just sat back and listened and watched. If you are a parent you sit back and watch your kids and the quirky thing that kids do and these things make you happy they bring a joy to your heart. It isn't that they are trying to do quirky things its just that kids don't care nearly as much as adults care about making the "right" impression they are well kids they aren't trying to impress anyone. So if we are children of God then who are we trying to impress, ya want to be happy just be a kid.

Happiness is not something you can buy, you can't go to the local Wally-World and on isle six mid way down third shelf from the top and get you some happiness. Sure you can go buy you a John Wayne video and that will entertain you but once it is over well its over. You can go buy you a radio controlled plane and once you crash it and destroy the wings (speaking from experience) it is over. There are far too many people out there trying to buy their happiness with stuff and it is up to you and I to show them that stuff is just stuff but happiness comes from a vibrant maturing relationship with God.

You see it is thru your relationship with the LORD that you can really experience joy, happiness, love, comfort, abundance, and all sorts of warm fuzzies. DO you have this kind of happiness or are you still trying to get your joy out of a bottle, something canned prepackaged. Most things that I deal with in the kitchen that are packaged have expiration dates on them so if you're looking for joy in a package it won't last. Only God lasts. How you/I meet with Him each day can bring more joy and happiness then I/you ever-ever thought imaginable.

When God reveals Himself to you, when His word and Spirit touches you at the core you can know that God is looking at you and that He sees the quirky thing that you do and gets a chuckle out of it. "Why are they still trying to purchase their happiness don't they know that lasting happiness starts with Me," not that I am putting words into God's mouth but lets face it sometimes you do the darndest things.

Today sit back and don't stress so much but just listen to God, hear the still small voice calling you back to Him.

Live Worthy

John 19:30 -So when Jesus had received the sour wine, He said, "It is finished!" And bowing His head, He gave up His spirit.

I was going to call this one, live worthy – good luck but it isn't luck that will cause you to live worthy and you can live worthy today and everyday.

There is this movie that one of the final scenes was people around a tombstone and the older actor conveyed the story of the man who's stone they were in front of and how since so many died to protect him that he should live a life worthy of their sacrifice. This is what the man tried to do for the rest of his life was to live up to the sacrifice paid. In a country screaming out for true hero's this is a good message that everyone should hold dear and not debase the sacrifice that we have been given, its called freedom. So when I see people at a high school sporting event not even taking their hat off during the national anthem it drives me nuts. How cheap we hold this freedom that we have. Then again people treat the sacrifice of Christ even worse.

Tell me are you living a life worthy of the stripes that Christ endured for you? Are the things that you do worthy of the nail pierced wrists and feet? Are the words that flow from your mouth worthy of the death of Jesus Christ on the cross? Oh but if only we would think of who and why it was that Christ died on the cross before we spoke or acted in a manner contrary to being worthy of Christ. I know there are plenty of times that had I thought about Christ before I spoke that maybe some words wouldn't have tumbled out or instead of getting angry considering that it was Christ who died for them also. Not always a pleasant picture is our sin is it, if that wasn't bad enough thou we didn't even pay the cost for those sins but Christ did, He bore the welt for my and your sin(s).

How will this help you to live a worthy life of Christ? As He cried out "it is finished," scripture was fulfilled and the penalty was paid so we no longer have to be burdened with sin but have available repentance and forgiveness thru no other means than Christ. That you and I can live a life worthy of His sacrifice is something that should be our goal each and every day. We mustn't quit even before we start and say we can't do it but rather we should realize that we can't do it of our selves and can only live a life worthy of Christ with Christ, not apart from Him. To be honest with you, there are some of you who know that you are living apart from Christ and not as a part of Christ, I ask you to come back to His family.

Wouldn't it be an awesome thing to be able to say you are living a life worthy of Christ? That the next time you partake of the Lord's Supper that when you examine yourself with the Holy Spirit that you know that you are all confessed up and are living a life worthy of God because you take to heart and action why Christ died on the cross.

Ask, seek and knock

Matthew 7:7-12 -7 "Ask, and it will be given to you; seek, and you will find; knock, and it will be opened to you. 8 For everyone who asks receives, and he who seeks finds, and to him who knocks it will be opened. 9 Or what man is there among you who, if his son asks for bread, will give him a stone? 10 Or if he asks for a fish, will he give him a serpent? 11 If you then, being evil, know how to give good gifts to your children, how much more will your Father who is in heaven give good things to those who ask Him! 12 Therefore, whatever you want men to do to you, do also to them, for this is the Law and the Prophets.

What are you asking for, what are you really seeking, what door are you knocking at? It may seem that we don't receive because we are not asking or we are not really seeking because we really don't want to find and we are not knocking because we don't want that door to be opened. FEAR, I know this may seem a bit preposterous but for me sometimes I know that I don't ask because God will give, I don't seek because I will find and I don't knock because the next door will be open. I can't I can't I don't know how I am tired (lazy) I have done enough can't I just stop here for a while.

Ya know what that is not what we should do, look at this a sec. Christ said ask not asked, He said seek not sought, and He said knock not sit there all of these things are doing something, they are actions not past-tenses. There are many times after we ask that God answers and we have received that we like to sit back and go, "that's cool" or "what a God thing" and we should thank God for answering but then we should go forward seeking and knocking and asking.

The Father who is in heaven gives good things to those who ask HIM!

Maybe we don't ask because we don't think we are good enough to receive, that maybe we don't want to seem bratish or that we have been given so much that it wouldn't be fare to ask for more. What a bunch of well there maybe a little truth in there. Let me ask you something though. If you have given your children more than they have even asked for does that make them brats, spoiled maybe but not brats, I know I have spoiled my kids but they are not brats. Do you think God doesn't want to spoil you, He doesn't want you to be a brat and look down on others, but as for spoiling you He does have much good to give to you?

Ask, seek and knock without fear for if God is in it God will work thru you to achieve His goal. Today if you are hurting or joyful if you are discouraged or strong turn to God who gives as only the One who has authority to give completely.

GO to His House

Psalm 26:[8] LORD, I have loved the habitation of Your house,
And the place where Your glory dwells.

Do you miss going to church, I know its Wednesday and that some of you will go to church tonight and all that but do you miss going when you are out of your normal routine? Or how about going on a Thursday Night also, man if attendance was like it was on Wednesday night then how much less it would be on Thursday Night you would need some outstanding program to get people there on a Thursday night huh. Hey Doug(s) and David(s) can you do me a favor go to church about a ½ hour early before most everyone gets there and go to a different place in the pews and tell me God didn't beat you there. It is after all HIS entire house not ours, we aught to be going to meet with HIM and His son's and daughter's not to go thru a program. CHURCH IS NOT A PROGRAM it is each of us coming together in HIS houses.

Church has got to be about what the pastor says or what the choir sings or who is at Sunday School or blah-blah-blah .. blah-blah. It isn't about any of those individual things it is about GOD. All of the reasons that we go should be about meeting with God. It is the place where His glory dwells. Man just thinking about that is awesome, the place where God is. There have been times where I have gone in early before an event and just sat in the darkness of the room and have not been alone, its one of those moments where you can be still and take a deep breath and just, well just be not in the moment but in His presence.

Let me see if I can explain this so you don't go wow what a transcendental moment. You see if you are thinking this is just a point and time just some sort of thing you can point to and say wow that was cool then the moment will flee, but you see God doesn't flee He doesn't evaporate and leave He is well He IS. No you don't have to be in His house to reach out to God, but isn't in nice to be able to go into His house to meet with Him there?

David was not from the South other wise he would have said something like, "Hey Lord, I love going to your house cause listen up here son that's where You are," or something like that (maybe not). There is no reason why we should program attendance to be the important thing about our fellowships, rather if we can get people to come to Church to see God then they may feel His presence also and wouldn't that be awesome.

It is His house no matter how big or small the building is, it is still the place where He dwells. Ya'll go ahead and go to church tonight be involved in what is going on but don't loose site of who's house you have been invited to and meet with Him there.

Rememberer

James 1:²¹ Therefore lay aside all filthiness and overflow of wickedness, and receive with meekness the implanted word, which is able to save your souls.
²² But be doers of the word, and not hearers only, deceiving yourselves. ²³ For if anyone is a hearer of the word and not a doer, he is like a man observing his natural face in a mirror;

I know rememberer isn't a word but for the sake of today let me ask you is your rememberer broken? Do we at times walk away and quickly forget what we just read? Okay maybe its just me so I'll quit right there, then again maybe its you also hmm could be.

If today we could just lay aside all filthiness and overflow of wickedness and receive with meekness the implanted word. If we could lay aside the junk that we learned from the world and rely on that which we have been taught from the Word. When we start to apply the Word to our individual lives in every facet of our lives and remember what it is we learn and apply it in our lives then everything will be hunky dory right? All is well with my soul doesn't mean you are not under attack from the enemy.

We struggle at times because at times we are not in the word as much as we should be so we don't really rely on God but on our own abilities to cope or deal with issues as they arise. SO how is that working for you, …. Me neither. It is actually kind of stupid of us to think that we can do it on our own, we can't even see what is going to happen five minutes ahead of us so how can we know what will happen tomorrow, but the one who inspired the word had those who wrote It down to put down in ink that which will help you today and tomorrow.

What does it mean anyway that you need to get into the word, and we are supposed to receive it with meekness? Well some one who religiously reads their bible according to their read the bible in a year plan is this getting into the word? Look first of all lets get something straight meekness is not weakness okay being meek doesn't mean you are weak, a matter of fact if you are meek then you are strong and have given up trying to do it on your own and realize you can't.

Receive the word with meekness because it is how you can live a life of victory in Christ thru the Holy Spirit. It is only after you realize that you don't know diddely that you need to learn anew and put aside all that you thought you knew for what God would have you learn. That when you open up the paper or leather or inagahide cover to your bible, to God's word that and read it to learn for the application to your life that one can truly be in the word.

Don't walk away from the word and forget what it is you have read, but go out and live it. Don't say my rememberer is broken, if you live what you read then you can talk of what you know.

Reminder

Matthew 6:33 -But seek first the kingdom of God and His righteousness, and all these things shall be added to you.

I know we got bills that we got to pay, we have homes we have to upkeep, the kids need money for the band trip or the new game system and the wife needs a cedar chest and you need a new set of irons because you keep breaking them. Woo there boy-oh are these really things you need or are these your wants? What is it that you need a place to live, something to eat, clothes to wear, and some one to love? So sift the needs from the wants and start there.

You need a place to live well try this one on for size: <u>John 14:2 -In My Father's house are many mansions; if it were not so, I would have told you. I go to prepare a place for you</u>. Hey David and Beth where would you rather live Shawmut Circle or in a mansion in Heaven? No contest huh, so what are we doing spending all of our time seeking that home that the world says we should have? As far as I can tell you can have a mansion here on earth as a triple wide when your place is written in the Lambs book of life.

— You need something to eat, okay here ya go chew on this one: <u>Matthew 4:4 -But He answered and said, "It is written, 'Man shall not live by bread alone, but by every word that proceeds from the mouth of God.'"</u> Does your heart think you are going on a diet from the Word of God? That being said we sure do like our steak don't we, meat and potatoes (rice for some of us) is the meal we love but soon enough you are hungry again. When was the last time that you fed your soul, dished up some of God's words and gobbled them up? We should be spending more of our time enriching our lives with Gods word.

— You need something to wear, well then put this on: Revelation 3:5 He who overcomes shall be clothed in white garments, and I will not blot out his name from the Book of Life; but I will confess his name before My Father and before His angels. An Armani Suit would be nice but those fibers will rot. Will you overcome and be clothed in a white garment? We like to look nice with ironed shirts and pants but no matter how much starch you use the wrinkles will come and when you eat spaghetti stains will come. Oh but to be clothed in a garment of white, what are you worrying about today how your dressed on the outside or on the inside. Heaven is not a fashion show.

— You need some one to love, then love some one who loved you first: John 3:16 For God so loved the world that He gave His only begotten Son, that whoever believes in Him should not perish but have everlasting life. In our day to day live to find what joy or what we call happiness we forget that God is the one who loved us first, that we were created to Love God. Love may sound corny to you but it isn't corny or heartsy flopsy it is something in the deepness of your heart that we all need. God sent Jesus to live and then die on a cross because of His great love for you. If He would sacrifice His Son then what have you to worry about.

Maybe you worry because you need to turn fully to Him or maybe you just need a reminder that God will cloth you, feed you, give you a place to live and that He loves you..

Appraise

Matthew 6:22 "The lamp of the body is the eye. If therefore your eye is good, your whole body will be full of light. [23] But if your eye is bad, your whole body will be full of darkness. If therefore the light that is in you is darkness, how great *is* that darkness!

When you go into a new home that you are looking at to buy from oh lets say Wood Real Estate who have been helping families find quality homes in the Greater Valley area for years (shameless plug) do you look at the view from the windows? Oh we have to have a good view, a good view in Alabama includes oh about 1 kazillion trees, a good view from Iowa includes about 1 kazillion and one cornstalks (for a season). This view that we have from our home we appraise each day. We take it in on a morning before everyone wakes up, we may stand just on the back porch and view all that is around us and just take it in.

Oh if we could just have those moments every moment of the day, there would be no worries. In this day and age of pop-ups and spam email you just never know what you are going to see. Maybe even watching a show at night and then all of the sudden you see on a commercial something that well flashes across the screen that you wouldn't have seen 10 years ago. You and I are inundated with images each and every day, do you protect what you see, and do you keep your view good?

We like to say what choice do we have, we don't produce the commercials or the adds or the spam's or the pop-ups but we do have a choice we could turn the channel or skip the add and make a choice not to involve ourselves in those things. Oh I know some one is going to say, it is okay to appraise a picture if you don't take it home but is your appraisal how you want some one to look at your daughter?

We don't protect our eyes as well as we should, we pause because we are after all human right. I am sure that will be a good answer. Now look here God you're the one who created man and woman you created that we would have desire for each other. Sure you go ahead and try that, no please don't really don't blame anyone else for you leaving the channel on the station it is on. We figure after all that we can handle it, until we fall that is. Oh but if we would pause and appraise the things of God like we should,

If therefore your eye is good, your whole body will be full of light. Is your whole body full of light, the light that is good? There are also things that are all around us that we should appraise the view from the window that we choose. It seems to me that looking at the kids and the wife and seeing how the kids have grown and are becoming more like their mom, seeing the wife how she has ever put up with me for these years. There is that view from your favorite window or on your back porch where you can go and just sit down and watch the sun come up over the trees or corn and just see the rays of light chase the darkness away. I guess our eyes need to be more like a sunrise, only lighting on those things that are good, chasing the darkness away giving it no quarter or excuse.

Let your eyes be on the things of God so that your body can be full of the things of God so that others see God in you.

We are

John 9:16 -Therefore some of the Pharisees said, "This Man is not from God, because He does not keep the Sabbath." Others said, "How can a man who is a sinner do such signs?" And there was a division among them.

This is one of those verses that ya just gotta go, don't you see why, come on its so plain you even answered it for yourself and you still don't get it. Do you see it? "How can a man who is a sinner do such signs?" Jesus was not a sinner nor was He just a man; Billy Graham called Him a God-man. He is of God we are in the likeness of God. We worry about the churchy things Jesus did His Fathers work when it needed to be done. We are sinners Paul said he was the chief among sinners, I guess I am giving him a run for his money on that one. Man can not be used by God when we have the blackness of sin in our hearts.

This Man, this Jesus Christ who is God's only Son what an awesome Savior. I have wondered from time to time if I just typed the name of Jesus Christ over and over and that to be the devotional for the day. No not chanting it but saying it and listening to His name. It is a name that speaks of authority and a name that has power we need to realize that and not use His name in vain.

There are times when we act as though we were the Pharisees, when we don't rely on His name by not calling on His name when we aught to. Instead we try to see what we can do what we can take care of and let's face it sometimes we couldn't work our way out of a wet paper-bag with a hammer and chisel. (How was that R.N.) ((Not talking registered nurse)) We act sometimes that we have power when we really at the best of times are just a vessel that God has filled up to use for His Glory, and that is good for me too.

We are to keep the Sabbath Holy, Christ when He followed His Father's plan kept it Holy set apart from a work day because on the Sabbath when He healed it was showing God presence and power among the people. We are the sinner and it was Christ who died for that sin, chief sinner or well I don't sin all that bad sin is still sin.

This Man can do so such signs because He is sinless and blameless. We sin and we must repent and turn from our sin, unless you just want to keep that sin or we don't want to be used by God which maybe there is a problem there. Ya think?

Selah – pause and take a moment to think about if there is something in your life that keeps you from being used by God.

How we deal with the sin in our life tells a story about what kind of relationship with have with God.

Commitment

John 19:30 -So when Jesus had received the sour wine, He said, "It is finished!" And bowing His head, He gave up His spirit.

How committed are you to the cause of Christ? How committed are you to the plan of God? Even to death, even to hardship or is there only a certain limit that we will go thru for Christ because hey after all we are just weak anyway.

Will God ask for your death to show your commitment for Him? If I said yes would that shock you, it shouldn't we are supposed to die to self right, but we don't always do a good job of dying to self we call it human nature. We sometimes just do things out of our sin nature than out of His nature. There are a lot of reasons why I don't want to bedraggle that point, just work on it okay.

The thing is we talk a lot of commissions and commands, of God's plan, of being led by the Spirit, of programs and opportunities all of these things are well and good but do we get it that we must continue on till God calls us to the Big House. That we must strive with a kind of passion to end the race that we have started, this race is our life. Sometimes we get side tracked and may get a bit off kilter with the race and take a pit stop or just get completely off of the path.

When I think of Christ saying it is finished, I don't just think of His life on the cross but I also think of His life as an example to us of how we should touch others lives while living out our own. I know for me sometimes I get self absorbed with the things that I have going on that an opportunity may be missed because I am only concerned with what is in front of me at the time. I like to go from item to item one thing at a time so to speak, but our commitment need not be on the item but on the Will of God.

When we die this carbon unit is finished, sorry but it is, but the life that we led is the example that we leave behind for others to follow. Last nigh we talked about WWJD, and how we are supposed to be examples of what Jesus did. That others see you and hear you and that our actions support what we say or our actions discount what we say. It isn't what is good for the goose is good for the gander, but that both goose and gander should reflect what the Creator directed.

No I am not saying that we should all go out and die on a cross, but we should die to self and pick up our cross and bear with one another. This may be morbid but when you breathe your last, will you say with assurance that, it is finished. Ya'll don't leave things undone but do. Live your life as an example of Christ Jesus.

I want to ask you something and I don't want you to go on till you can answer it.

Does you faith in Christ make sense at all?

With no other parameters to that question, just simply does your faith in Christ make any sense at all. Some will say yes and some will say no some will just say I am off my rocker and well maybe all of those answers are correct except one, no DA and Bob I am not off my rocker that is the one that is wrong.

> *Matthew 6: 24 "No one can serve two masters; for either he will hate the one and love the other, or else he will be loyal to the one and despise the other. You cannot serve God and mammon.*

Your faith makes sense when you live it because well you recognize that it is God who is in control and it is you who is not. That even thou things may be dim now doesn't mean they will stay that way or when things are going good that it is a blessing from God. You see faith is un-tangible, is that right? You can't place your finger on it and say here it is, see what God has done. Yet does this make sense in our self contained thought and reasoning? To me this is what makes it faith, because I can't explain to the letter of why I have placed my faith in some one I have not seen. Sure we see the results of God everyday but we have yet to look upon His face.

Yet the world says that we should only believe in what is proven and what is before us, things we can touch or scientifically prove. What does the world know, after all the reasoning of the world is flawed because it discounts God because you can't touch Him? That things come and go in random order is its self flawed because even in a boiling pot there is order there is a flow of how things go.

We serve what we have faith in, we serve what we know don't we? We serve God because we know that His Son died on a cross for our sins, we serve God because on the third day He raised Jesus from the grave. That even thou the world says our thinking is weak it can not deny that our faith is strong. The world can say that our faith makes no sense but we are not the ones trying to reason the tangible. That faith in our Master is what we cling to and time and time again He has pulled us thru and out of situations that we have gotten ourselves into.

Whom will you serve today? Is it God or is it the world?

Turn

Matthew 7:14 -Because narrow is the gate and difficult is the way which leads to life, and there are few who find it.

This morning on the way to work I am just not sure I was paying that much attention to the road. No, I didn't hit anything or anyone but I got up to this stop sign that I have come up to for lets see 8 years x 248 days (or so) = 1984 times and have turned left at that sign but today for some reason I turned right then I turned right at the next sign which led me away from the hospital. Why did I do that, I have know idea but then I had to make a big circle just to get back on the right road. Maybe I should have just gone home and went back to sleep. Life is about a series of turns isn't it, by turns I mean choices are you turning down the right path today or have you turned off the right path and heading into a circle?

I am sure that the reason why I turned will remain a mystery that will ponder the ages but when I guess you get down to it some times we just get distracted and do stupid stuff. No I am sure you never do stupid stuff like taking the wrong road but then again maybe you run into a door in the pitch dark while trying to be stealthy so as not to wake up the folks. Come to think of it some times we do stupid stuff and that maybe called sin, if we are not paying attention or minding the road we can take a right when we know that we should have taken a left. I guess then before we know it we may take another right and not notice till the Holy Spirit brings it to our attention that we are heading in the wrong direction.

Now Doug and Walter let me ask you this, how do we get back onto the right path? If the quickest way between two points is a straight line then why do we circle around sometimes and try to come back around? We figure we gotta get it right so we kind of meander around taking a wide loop and then we get back on the right path after a while. What would happen Rod and Joe if instead of taking a wide loop around if we cut the wheel back the other way and just turned around? Ya may not wanta try that on the road with your car/truck but if you are talking about your relationship with God Deborah go ahead and get back on the right path the quickest way possible.

Christ said that "difficult is the way," and ya know what, He is right isn't He? Obstacles come up along the way, stones on which to stumble litter your path and we must remain vigilant along the path. I say difficult with no measure of frivolousness, they say pride comes before the fall and Randy you are right it often does, that is why we need some one to hold us accountable. Proverbs 27:17 As iron sharpens iron, So a man sharpens the countenance of his friend. Do you have some one sharpening you?

If today you find that you have taken your own wrong turn don't despair or think ill of yourself, there isn't one person who reads this (including me) who hasn't found themselves off the right path. We must however get back on the path and to do that we must go on our knees with a humble heart and repent and turn from our way and cling to His. In saying that it would be difficult Christ also said that we would have a Helper, well

Ya'll listen to the Holy Spirit and follow His lead.

High Beams

Psalm 18:28 For You will light my lamp; The LORD my God will enlighten my darkness.

What happens when you drive without lights at night, full moon or not, that's right you take the chance of more than just a fender bender. When I go up to Pleasant Hill on Wednesday nights there are all sorts of little creatures (I didn't put cats there) darting across the road and some make it while others don't make it. One has to stay alert for deer because even thou they are not as big as say Iowa deer you can still do some serious damage to your car. When I can I flip the high-beams on so I can see better what is in the ditches and what is further in front of me. You look for the tale tell sign of the light hitting their eyes then look for other eyes cause where there is one there is two and you don't want the other to get you.

God enlightens the darkness revealing to us the obstacles that lay on the road. We can avoid that what we see or we can run smack into them, because hey we don't always slow up. Sure we may be looking out for that big sin that may just be off of the road so we can avoid it but as we crash into the one from the other side or that little (we call it little) sin that scurries in front of us we still damage our vehicles on the little sin because SIN IS SIN. Maybe we didn't turn the High Beams on so we could see what was in front of us better.

There is something that gives us reassurance knowing that God is our Light, that He is our Way. It isn't just that He is "The Man," but that because He lives we know He is always there. That the Light that is our light is holding back the darkness is something we can have joy in.

Light is a funny thing what from flashlights to sunsets it is all about revealing what is around you. After all no matter how good you are you can not play golf in the dark, you can't drive in the dark; you can't hunt and shoot at something in the dark without taking a chance on your health. If you walk in the darkness you can't help but to stub your toe, if you drive in the darkness you will run into a tree. It is only when we walk in the light that we walk in the Glory of God, hmm Glory of God now that to me is an awesome thing. Just think about that His Glory is your high beams.

It may be the ramblings of a strange man but to walk with the high beams on everyday is what my desire is and sometimes I just don't sometimes I don't even have the regular lights on or just the fog lights and sometimes not even the fog lights. I know I should turn the light on be I don't, I convince myself I don't have time, that I am running late or what not no wonder I twisted my ankle again. When we sin the pain is just as real, why don't we learn to turn the light on everyday and hey while you're at it flip on the high beams.

Bread

Matthew 4:4 -But He answered and said, "It is written, 'Man shall not live by bread alone, but by every word that proceeds from the mouth of God.'"

Today what word are you going to live by, what is the verse in your life that you will amplify in your walk today? Hmm, I am just not sure there is just so many that I it is hard just to pick one, then again will I even be able to live up to that one? I guess that can be frustrating can't it, then again maybe not if you just start applying it all in your life and working at it by living it out.

This is the third time today that I have tried to write a devotional, I know kind of but not really writers block again. Then again maybe not, let's see the other two were going to be about mercy and hearing. Both probably good subjects but they can't be separated today along with love, hope, light, obedience, and salvation. We must live all these things today, not just picking the one that we would either like to live by or the one today that we are going to work on.

There is nothing that we can do that would show better what Christ means in our life then to actually apply His words in our life. We like to get a cup of coffee or two in the morning and say this is what we like and this is the way we start out our day instead of getting a biscuit to go along with the coffee. We like to put ourselves on a diet of the word but do we realize that a diet is really what you eat? That we all have a diet just some have bad diets, so to is it with the word when we just pick and choose what we want.

Wouldn't it be an awesome thing if we all started acting like we know we should, ya know what acting is a bad word there. It implies to me just a façade, how about we live like we know Christ wants us to live. That we look at His word as nourishment for our souls and we all want healthy souls don't we.

In your daily walk, in your daily prayer have you asked God lately to give me today my daily bread? Not the soft white bread that is almost like a cake but maybe the coarse bread that you get at a Russian Bakery that you gotta chew about 100 times just to soften it up so it doesn't tare up your digestive tract, ya know get enough fiber. Sometimes we need the coarse bread to clean us out and get everything back on track.

Live by the Word and be in the word.

First Place

Matthew 22:37 -Jesus said to him, "'You shall love the LORD your God with all your heart, with all your soul, and with all your mind.'

When was the last time you put as much energy into your relationship with the LORD as you would your relationship with your job? I tell you this to ask you to also beware of the first commandment, *Exodus 20:³ "You shall have no other gods before me.* Let's put it this way shall we, if you are treating your relationship with God as a weekend activity/hobby something you do on Sunday then who do you love with your heart with all your soul and with your entire mind? But of course none of us do this, and we don't know anyone else who does this, ya know what though I do know church folks like that.

No I am not saying that we hobbies are a bad thing, maybe I should get a hobby I can do more than once a month maybe that would ebb the flow of grey hair sprouting up. Hobbies are a good thing they can help keep distract us from the stress of the grind. There is nothing wrong with hunting, fishing, golf, needle point, or what-ever but these are hobbies. A hobby did not save you. I am afraid that in today's culture that we are saying that these things are more important than God is. Why is that, if a sports team has a practice on a Sunday morning the kids go to the practice but it is the parents who take them, thusly condoning it.

There is also nothing wrong with coming in first, winning is not a bad word just like profit is not a bad word and doing what you can to win or make a profit is okay as long as it doesn't bring disgrace upon the one you call LORD. So this is how we justify working on Sunday or practicing on Sunday, well we gotta win. Now I don't know about you but having a growing maturing relationship with God makes me a winner right there, that there is more profit for me to know God than there is dollars in an account.

So knowing who should come first, do we strive each day to keep Him first in our lives? I tell you this if we really want Him to be first in our lives then we must love Him first each day that we should put Him first in our heart, first in our mind. That we must have the audacity to stand up and yell and shout and pour everything that we are into Loving God. Not just saying we do but to step out of our "comfort-zone" and let everyone know who it is that we love. Not just putting a fish on the back of you highlander or putting a cross on your neck but to actually reflect Christ in all that you do.

That we should each passionately serve the LORD and making sure each day we place Him first.

Glory

Luke 2:14 -"Glory to God in the highest, And on earth peace, goodwill toward men!"

I got some of the best advice yesterday that I have ever gotten, this person said that they liked it better when I just told them from the heart instead of reading it off my notes. So just tell'em from the heart, okay.

This message that was sent to the Shepherds was also sent to Regional V.P.s, CFOs, CEOs, DFNSs, Secretaries, Cooks, Janitors, Teachers, Retirees, Moms, Dads, RDOs, to everyone no matter what position you have or job you fill. That to me is so cool, this message of GLORY TO GOD IN THE HIGHEST, peace and good will toward men. Doesn't' that just make your heart soar?

I hear these words again, glory to God, peace on earth and good will toward men and I wonder if we get it sometimes. Do we act like we understand that GOD IS IN HIS HIGHEST? That right now at this very moment God is there in His Glory watching and listening to what we are doing and saying that we can either at this moment bring a smile to His face because we get it or we can bring a frown to His face because we miss it. What is the "it" now that is a good question Joe so let's see? The "it" is a lot of things but lets just look at this verse again shall we. Do we get peace; do we show goodwill toward men?

We try so hard to satisfy ourselves each day, we work hard at trying to bring home a good check so we can take care of our spouse, our kids and the dog, yet there are some who have no peace in their lives. Are you looking for peace in the right direction, peace doesn't come thru your paycheck no matter how large or small you think it is. Dollar signs can not bring you peace; dollars can get you a hotel room in Jamaica or Des Moines, get you a break from it but this is not peace. Peace like wisdom only can come thru the Father. Christ came to give you peace, that if you look to Him you will find peace for your soul, your heart. That because He came once He will come again to bring you to Himself, think about that that where He is there you will be also if you trust in Him.

How much good will do we show towards our fellow man? Ya think some one has an angle to get something out of you, that you have worked hard for what you have and you think some one wants what you got, man if we only treated our relationship with God like that. Not the hording part of that but that we had such a relationship with God those others wanted what we had. Ya want goodwill toward man, fine then do it and stop talking about it. That Christ came as the ultimate sign of goodwill toward man that HE didn't come because it was well convenient for Him to come or that it would be a good time on the beach. He came ya'll for you.

Glory to God in His Highest, peace and goodwill towards all man kind, as this holiday season gets cranked up think about where you are in your relationship with the LORD. Do you have peace or are you still seeking it out, look in the right direction. Look to the highest place where God dwells.

Awesome Compassion

I am letting God permeate my life more and more. HE is "sanding" off my rough edges little by little. One day I hope to be "smooth." I am thinking and concentrating much less on "things and stuff" and more on heaven. I am much more aware of the needs of others and acting on them in HIS name, not mine. It is my desire to keep Christ in Christmas!

Lynn

Matthew 14:14 -And when Jesus went out He saw a great multitude; and He was moved with compassion for them, and healed their sick.

I like to flip thru the channels at a high rate of speed, trying to get to each channel in under thirty seconds is a test of immortal skill, okay maybe not. I don't stop until something catches my eye that I may actually want to watch, this is getting harder and harder each year as the new series roll out. I certainly don't stop for any commercials, a matter of fact when I do actually find something I like to watch I don't like to watch the commercials during that show, so I will flip the channel and then make it back to the show in just about the time the commercials are off. Okay sometimes a little after the commercials are over and its into the show again. My point is, hum let me think, what was my point? Oh yeah, sometimes we miss the brief moments in our lives that we should be showing compassion because we are more interested in the show.

There isn't a bunch of moments lumped up into one event that we should be showing compassion but there are brief moments each day that if we just put down the remote and watch we will see them. Maybe you don't want to see them, maybe you just feel it is all you can handle just making it thru your day? But maybe just maybe you see them and don't know what to do, don't know how you can help, that it is more than you can deal with. Then you know it is a God thing. God things are more than you can do on your own, that only God can do them and that at those moments He has invited you to be with Him to show His LOVE and GLORY. Now that is awesome.

You know what Walter we should have a hunger for those God moments shouldn't we, I mean Jeff if everyone in your church had the desire to serve God first and to show His compassion to others wouldn't services be more of a celebration? Hey Doug do you want to be shown compassion, sure we do then shouldn't we show compassion, sure we should. So what stops us, now I guess that is the big question that needs to be answered by you only. What is stopping you from showing compassion?

Is it that we look out on the multitudes and see people who are different for us, so we deduce that they are just out to get something or they may in someway take advantage of your "generosity?" Be careful, haven't you taken advantage of God's generosity? Didn't you do what you had to do to receive it, something that was freely given you freely received, and yet we are not perfect but we are but working out our sanctification. We mess up and God does not pull His mercy from you, He does not take away His love from you. Look at the brief moments each day and show compassion.

Flexible

Luke 2:7 -And she brought forth her firstborn Son, and wrapped Him in swaddling cloths, and laid Him in a manger, because there was no room for them in the inn.

In all the best laid plans that we make God still has His own plan so guess which one will actually end up happening? No matter what we do to anticipate things there are still things that happen and we should roll with them instead of rolling against them. Where would Christ had been born had there not been a census being done, or what would have happened if upon hearing there was no room at the inn and that the only place available was a barn and Mary would have said no way we will go on. These are not what if questions today because we see that Joseph and Mary were on mission for God and that they were flexible enough to be thankful for shelter.

We some times get caught up in our own plans, the way we want it to be that we fail to see that God just wants you and I to be obedient to His way. That if it causes you a bit of discomfort or having to change what you have planned then be flexible enough to go along with it. Ya know what I don't know how God does it, putting up with us sometimes. Like when we want things just so and if it doesn't go just so then we fuss at some one or fume cause this isn't how it was supposed to work out. If we are on mission for God shouldn't we then look for His plan in the thing we have been asked to be flexible about without ripping into someone?

It is amazing that Mary and Joseph didn't ask God what He was doing after all this was His Son, the Messiah that was going to be born. One would think that God could have kept a room at the inn open for them at least, but a manger a manger are you kidding me. The Son of God being born in a straw filled animal occupied stable. Something tells me that they hadn't expected that one. Now we can see that this was an awesome example to us, an example of humility and promise.

That the Prince of Peace came as the lowliest of lowly, the King of kings came to earth wrapped in swaddling clothes not silk or gold laced cloth. He wasn't placed in a crib with jewels and gold inlaid around the sides His first bed was a bed of straw. We that is you and I should really consider each day who we are on mission for today, that we should be flexible to God's plan and not relying on a man program.

Look here there really isn't anything that we can do to reach even one person for God when we try to do it on our own. We can't save anyone anyway only God can and He is also the one who prepares their heart to hear His message. Stop trying to plan every detail of how you are going to reach out, just be available and if you are relying on your plan you are not being available.

It is easy to go out and serve God if you only want to do it your way anyway, the thing we should be doing is just follow God's plan and remember that His plan is well better then your or my plan.

Exalted

Psalm 46:10 -Be still, and know that I am God; I will be exalted among the nations, I will be exalted in the earth!

Before you start your day will you exalt the Father, no not just Father but God. If I have learned anything in the past couple of years it is that how the Bible is written conveys so much meaning by what word is used in whatever verse. You see this verse is God, Mighty and Powerful the Great I am, where as LORD is personnel Abba Father some one you look up to. Both LORD and God are the same being they are both God.

Tell me Patrick and Ron before you go into a patients room do you be still and know that He is God and has equipped you? Before you enter an account Doug do you pause and ponder that it is God who has placed you over these accounts? How about you Jesse, when your at a hospital do you ponder that God is the one who really makes all of this happen? I don't know Rod but if we don't every once and a while stop – selah- pause and take a deep breath and know that we are not here to say how good we are but how awesome is our God then have we missed it? How about you Bob and Douglas and you Walter and Tammy, yes you Joe and Pat, include yourself Obie and Jerome and you right there, are we exalting God in everything that we do? Maybe we should take more than a moment, more than just a deep breath and just stop and be still and listen to God.

"And know that I am God," when was the last time you really thought about this, knowing that He is God? Now I know that you are sitting there saying, every morning when I have my quiet time I know He is God, and this is true but through out your day He is also God! Sometimes we need to stop during the day and just be still and understand that He is God, by understanding I mean looking at God who is above all things and that all things are under His authority, that you are under His authority.

If we take a moment before a meeting or before an encounter and look to God who hovered over the waters and then spoke the world into existence, the God who parted an entire sea so that His people could walk upon Dry land, this God who has been with you when your wife passed after the birth of your child, this God who has been with you when your mother and father passed away, this God who was with you during a hurricane or with you during a storm of mans making. God is God, it is a fact that you can cling to and maybe during the business of the day you may want to cling to even more.

The world tells us to keep quiet about God, to keep it at home or at church. That we shouldn't talk about Him at work or at play or out in public and many have taken to that cover. But God deserves to be exalted in every facet of our lives, when people see us should they not see the Father, is the Holy Spirit not in you?

"Be ____, and know that _ __ ___; _ will be _____ among the nations, _ will be _____ in the earth!" Don't take God out of your life.

God Is

Psalm 145:5
I will meditate on the glorious splendor of Your majesty, And
on Your wondrous works.

God is??
We like to look for what adjectives to describe God but all of
them seem to pale from moment to moment. If you were to describe
who God is to you one would have to see where you are at in the
moment of time, in other words what you are going thru today and
how God is carrying your thru that moment will help you describe
Him. Woe to those who don't know Him, for they only see a sunset
or sunrise as mineral reflection of light as the sunlight strikes the
partials of dust. Also how sad it is to those who say they know Him
but don't ask for His help, or even think to call on His name.

I was reminded several times this past week about who it is that I
call God, see if you can remember His works in your life along with
me. If one accepts Christ there is a change in their life, not just in
where they spend their time on Sunday but how they live Monday
thru Saturday. I recall the day that I accepted Christ as Savior and
Lord that night going home and dumping the rum and beer down the
sink and looking thru the video tapes and tossing the less than favor-
able movies into the trash. These are just two examples of things I
did but looking back what God did was, gave me a hunger for His
word, cleaned up the way I talked, and any number of things. To me

an adjective for God then would have been incredible because to me the change wasn't noticeable but to others it was.

Today God is still incredible but He is also awesome and majestic and powerful and wonderful and He is also Friend-Father-Discipliner-Creator. If you have ever been to Lake Okeechobee down in Florida all the way down in Florida and headed out to go fishing and the sun is just coming over east and the light is sparkling off of the water one can only wonder how great He is and how planned life is, not a random smashing together of atoms, God is the BIG BANG.

We don't often spend much time meditating on the glorious splendor of His majesty and the wonders of His works do we? Yet there it is today just outside your window waiting for you to notice God today. You see even thou we have accepted Christ and God we sometimes don't open up our eyes wide enough to notice His majesty each and everyday, I know we are busy too busy to notice God so we go off to work to get the day started and hopefully sometime throughout the day we have a God encounter. You see we already have had a God encounter, you woke up, and we didn't notice Him there we just went into our routine, hmm I wonder if we made it a point to look for God everyday that we would notice Him more and be thankful for that God encounter.

I am sure that God knows who you are but do you know who God is? Tell me what adjectives would you use to describe Him in your life?

Doubt

Matthew 14:31 -And immediately Jesus stretched out His hand and caught him, and said to him, "O you of little faith, why did you doubt?"

Fear keeps you humble before God, on your knees so to speak and this is a good fear. It also keeps you in the boat or if you get out of the boat you notice that you are doing what God wants you to do then you NOTICE THAT THERE ARE NO ROPES TO HANG ONTO AND THERE IS NO NET and instead of keeping focused fear causes you to drown. These are just two examples of fear one good one not so good. Do you know Bill that if we step out of the boat that God is with us from the first step, your right Debbie from the first twitch of a muscle that we leap out of the boat. When we surrender fear is the last thing in our mind, we just are so excited that God wants to use us we leap.

There is just no doubt about doubt of the unknown makes our knees grow weak and are palms go sweaty, because if you really surrender you just don't know where you will end up. Imagine this would you trust me to lead you around a room if you were blind-folded, oh add a twist to that, how about if there were nails and glass around that room would you worry that I may lead you into a pitfall. I don't think I would trust any of you enough to do that one. But this is what we must do when we surrender our lives to God; we have to rely on His plan and His control.

I think it is easy for us to say we surrender but in all actuality we have a tough time with it because we have to give up control. Even though we know God is in control we sometimes worry more about the waves lapping at our feet and the peril of what could happen that we turn around and try to get back into the boat. Oh we of little faith, Oh me of little faith. Why we worry over the detail when it is God who is the detail and control of every hair on your head.

When you walk around today and see that God is in control don't have little faith, a faith that lacks being surrendered to Him but relax and keep your eyes on Him who is more than a rope but a hand that will lift you out of the water. Oh Peter, he was such a typical guy, willing to leap out of the boat with out the first thought of what he was doing, but soon he noticed that he wasn't on dry land. That is my prayer for you today that you notice that what you do that you notice the water and still keep your eyes on God.

Let me share with you something that I most definitely know. God has something in store for you today, an encounter if you will but more of an opportunity to get out of the boat. That when you surrender your day and your life to Him that He will always be with you and guide you about the room, that if you relinquish the control that you have worked so hard to maintain then He will keep you out of the glass and nails, that He will guide you along the path He has chosen for you. Do you believe that? Do you really most sincerely believe Johnny and Bill and Jeanne and Catherine and Doug and Jesse and Pat and Joe and You do you believe with all that is in you Danita and Gerri that God is with you? Then don't doubt but surrender and keep your eyes on Him and not your plan.

Joy

Matthew 28:8 -So they went out quickly from the tomb with fear and great joy, and ran to bring His disciples word.

Luke 1:14 -And you will have joy and gladness, and many will rejoice at his birth.

Okay this is a test, just a test what do you have more joy about Christ's resurrection or Christ's birth? Go ahead and answer that one, I'll wait. .... Hmmmm....

Is it all that hard to decide which or are you like Douglas Clyde and have already figured out that you can have great joy because of both of these two events. They are both a part of God's plan for you, take joy in each of them. You want a blessing then understand something that an old pastor once told me, "the manger and the tomb are both empty."

I was just going to tell you this morning that we can be joyful even when things bite, is that deeply theological? I went to bible-gateway to look up a couple of verses and these two were right next to each other, then it dawned on me, no I wouldn't say I had an epiphany or anything deep like that right Charles. There are two Sundays that churches have high attendance and those two Sundays are Christmas Special Sunday, and Easter Sunday. There are some basic reasons why these are high attendance days, one is that this is when families gather and then the go to church together and two these are two Sundays that people make an appearance coming back after a hiatus.

Shelly is it a strange thing that people can't find joy, so they look to other avenues to find it? My contention is ya'll that if you are only looking in the manger and in the tomb then you will find them both empty, some will get that some wont. You see some come back to church looking into the manger wanting to find Christ as a baby there and some will come to church on Easter to see if the tomb really is empty but walk away and forgetting that they are empty.

The joy comes in knowing that these two places are empty because Jesus Christ lives. Because He lives He hears you, because He is not a baby He will understand you, because He is God's Son He is the way. JOY oh JOY not because we get to decorate a tree or an egg but because our Savior lives. Really do you have joy because He lives, is your life different today because He lives?

If your life is different because you know He lives then praise God, but if you don't really know or are just kind of lethargic about your response then can I ask you something, how far away from Him are you? Let your joy draw Him closer to you; let your joy be focused not on things of this world but on things of God. Maybe that is where real and lasting joy comes from anyway from God? Now there's a deep thought. Joy doesn't come from being able to hit a golf ball 325 yards, or to catch a 10lb bass but it comes from the one who blessed you, who looks out for you and places different things in your life that will bring you joy.

Joy is yours for the receiving hang onto it with both hands. Jesus lives and knowing that fact alone should brighten your day.

Bring them in

Matthew 14:35 And when the men of that place recognized Him, they sent out into all that surrounding region, brought to Him all who were sick,

For crying out loud is this the only reason why people came to see Christ, so that they could get their sick healed and their lame to walk, why did these people take advantage of Christ? They should have taken the opportunity to learn from Him, they should have sat at His feet and listened to Him. Right No not right but exceedingly WRONG. They came because they had a need and Christ being well Christ had compassion on them and healed their sick and healed their lame oh and by the way while they were their they got the Gospel first hand.

Christians who clutch their money purse tighter then they open the Word bewilder me? One can bring you a Porsche but the other brings you Eternity of Joy, fifty years from now the Porsche will be either gone or in some one's collection where will you be in fifty years. When have your recognized Christ and brought others to Him, by others I mean those whom don't know Him. It took the men of the place to send out to the surrounding region to get the sick to come and be healed. Christ didn't have an apostle designated for Outreach to go up ahead of them and get people getting together.

For some reason it seems that folks worry more about the finances of the church rather than the business of the church, to two are not the same. The business of the church is to reach the lost and dying world not to make sure the carpet matches the curtains. But I'll tell you this I can't remember the last business meeting that I heard a report of who has been reached and who isn't coming or a Sunday school report. Nope we have our breakdown of how much we have. Ya'll we aint got diddely if we aint talking about Christ.

Tell ya what drive around the neighborhood where your church is at, are you reaching those right-outside your doors; do you want to reach those outside your doors? Now this may seem harsh, if you don't want to reach those in your neighborhood then close your doors and move now. Because lets face it you are not going to go out and send for them to come in to meet Christ. Where is your compassion at?

Each of us today have an opportunity to reach some one who is hurting, who is destitute, who is sick and we will shy from our responsibility to bring them to Christ because we are uncomfortable or skittish but our comfort is not Christ's problem our skittishness is not Christ's fault it is ours. What better way to see God glorified than for you and I to step out and bring some one to meet with Christ.

I ask you, is the Christ you know worth sharing about? Is what God has done in your life worth telling some one about? Then go tell some one your story, tell them that God will help them, that Only thru Christ can one come to the Father. Love them enough to share with them the truth.

Restore me

Psalm 51:12 -Restore to me the joy of Your salvation, And uphold me by Your generous Spirit.

Y a ever watch those car shows? You know the ones that they take an ole beater and restore it to mint some would even say cherry condition, why are both those analogies food, sorry Obie it just popped into my head. ANYWAY the cars have rust holes and rotted interiors so they gut them down to the frame and start with that and even there they put new pieces on it and putty it to fill in the gaps. I guess you can tell I am not a car guy, because you see my first thought is to just scrap it and go get a new one, boy am I glad God doesn't do that with us, with me.

God, well He just wants to take you down to the bare bones, and gut you out and the change you. Not your basic frame but gutting out all the rotted parts in your life. You know the paint that you put on everyday trying to hide the rust that lies just beneath. Getting rid of your interior that has rotted and no matter how much you try to patch it up with duct tape the filling is still a bunch of junk and pokes out. Then there is the rust spots in our lives, those places we don't talk about because well they are just ugly, not your physical looks but those places in your heart that seem beyond hope and you just want to avoid them.

One thing I have noticed is that God doesn't just trim around the edge of a rust spot but He whacks the whole section out, Kah-

Chunk, then He tosses it out of the picture. I saw this one show that they didn't get rid of all the rust spot but kind of filled it in with putty after using some sort of bonding agent. The rust was still there thou, no matter how much you try to seal it up or putty it up Sin is still there. Only when you come to God and ask Him to remove it will it truly be gone.

Some are at different levels of the re-build, some are letting God do the work that He needs to do to finish it, to put them back in mint condition while some are well lets say not so far along. The thing is ya'll most of us are in the latter of those two groups. In our weakness we expose ourselves to the elements and then we let the rust creep back in. Oh no not you, I am sure you've not sinned at all today or yesterday? Then again I wouldn't exactly bet on it either.

Have you repented, have you turned, have you asked God to cut it out like a rust spot? Or are you just going to gloss it over and say but I was justified or it really wasn't that bad, or what ever lame excuse you want to use. Oops there I go, I am sorry you don't use lame excuses, just really bad ones. Please, for crying out loud be honest with yourself and with your sin and to your Lord. "for all have sinned and fallen short of the Glory of God," we are all in the repair shop, we have all come to Him because, well because we know that only He can complete the work of Salvation. Let Him do His work in your life, stay out of the rain.

The Name

Matthew 10:32 -"Therefore whoever confesses Me before men, him I will also confess before My Father who is in heaven.

A las it is well documented that a goober is a peanut, but goober grease is both peanut butter and also peanut oil. It is also well documented that not everyone has heard that a peanut is a goober, depending largely upon the region where you grew up. What to me is funny about this is that there were some people when asked what a goober is actually looked it up in dictionaries and web searches and actually research its word history both to prove their point and cause they know that I will ask why, so they were trying to get one step ahead of me I guess. Hey Tammy guess what Renee came back with the goober-pea song, but I have to give it to my sister Deanna she went and asked some one from the South to get the answer. We are a funny lot aren't we, I mean hey some knew the answer and some looked it up and some well some just had no clue.

Even thou it is funny about a goober there is nothing funny about not knowing the name of Christ and who Christ is, yet there are people we each know who have heard of Christ and still don't know who He is. Tell me if you think of Christ do you think of Him in the manger, or on the cross, or floating on some cloud some where? Jesus Christ is with His Father, He is up there with God right now in the real Holiest of Holies next to the throne of God. Tell me does He know you?

You see as with the kind of silly exercise of finding out what a peanut is called we come to find out that people knew and some had to look it up. That they were inquisitive enough to research it to just find the answer tells me that people just want to know and have evidence to support their argument. Now listen up, there are people that you know who are looking to you to see if you really have faith in this name of Christ, they may not ask you directly but will look to see how you deal with them or with stuff.

"Confesses Me before men," how do you confess Him before men, before your co-worker, your employee, the sales lady at the store, the driver who has the thump turned up in the car next to you, how do you confess Jesus Christ before men. Would it worry you a bit if I said your actions are part of your confessions? NO-NO to confess you have to say it, nah uh sorry. You and I can talk a good game a lot of the time but sometimes our actions trip us up, how we treat each other how we look down our noses at others. Is it too hard to confess Him before men all of the time, well you are supposed to be Holy right, and Christ never said it would be easy.

Look ya'll we are supposed to be Holy and no it isn't easy but when we rely on the name of Christ we rely on some one a lot stronger than we are. What people need to see is that you and I who call upon the name of Christ actually have faith in what we say and believe that God will hear and carry us thru. Not taking just one verse out of the bible and putting it on a card but living each commandment and obeying God's word and well and just giving to God what is His. We are His; You are or can be His when and if you call upon the name of Christ. Get to know Him and He will get to know you and you just be ready for a change okay.

Your Heart

Matthew 15:8 -'These people draw near to Me with their mouth, And honor Me with their lips, But their heart is far from Me.

There is all this hoopla today about where and when you can say Christ or talk about God or taking Christ out of Christmas and all of this is very good. That being said where is Christ in your life, how close is your heart to Him? Are ya talking a good game or are you really living the life you say you are, I don't say that without any small measure of hesitancy. Let me tell you something if we are the Christians that we say we are then where are we on Sunday? Most of the churches are in decline not because a store has stopped saying Merry Christmas but rather because we have stopped living Christ year round.

Now I am not talking to you, because after all you make it a point each and everyday to read God's word not so you can say you read the bible in a year but because you want to learn from God's word. Really I am talking to that deacon who shows up every once and awhile when there is a money vote or that person who huffs about what music is being played or well that person we all know whom just doesn't seem to get it. This is what I know, we as brothers and sisters in Christ must help encourage each other to stand firm in faith, in Christ not in a church, in God not in a shopping season.

We must check where we are first so that we can see if there is any hypocrisy in us before we cast a stone.

What worries me is not that a store doesn't have a Christmas banner what worries me is that we don't have the banner on our foreheads. Now that would be cool, walking around everyday with a tattoo that says Christ has come and He will come again. Yes we must stand the gap we must stand up for Christ and we also must start taking back the ground that we have let go of, and that starts where you are standing and then working out.

These Pharisees and Sadducees were more concerned about the traditions of the church rather then who established the church, it is a sad kind of funny how they kept missing it because they were steeped in how they felt people should act. They missed Christ who was right in-front of their eyes, I mean can you imagine that? There Jesus was right in-front of them and all they could see was an upstart carpenter's kid instead of seeing the Son of God. The only Jesus some people will ever see is Jesus in you?

This morning the moon was like at three quarters and there was just a little cloud cover over it. Just another cool moment in the morning, ya'll non-morning folks sure miss out. The sun's light reflecting off of the moon was obscured by the clouds and yet the trim around the clouds shown in silhouette of the moon. I know that may not be the best description. Sometimes we let clouds block the Light we are supposed to be reflecting, endeavor each day to make sure the cloud cover is removed and let the full force of Christ in you radiate around. Let Jesus shine thru.

Pray

Romans 12:12-rejoicing in hope, patient in tribulation, continuing steadfastly in prayer;

Ya know something some times I am so full of it that it even surprises me? Sure I do a good job at times of faking you out with a warm fuzzy devotional or the like but I never fake out God. So He never leaves me off the hook, THANK GOD. I would worry if I didn't get smacked in the head when I messed up. Ya know what I am guilty of what great and grave thing have I done. Well I have forgotten these words to rejoice in hope, to be patient in tribulation, and worst of all to continue steadfastly in prayer. I would venture to say that maybe sometimes you have also, whatcha think?

Look I could probably excuse it away, I know Dr. Wynn I know an excuse is just a lie wrapped up in respectability. I have been busy lately, we got a lot of stuff on the plate right now, things will get better next month when all of this is over. Take it from me something else always comes up next month to keep you off balance. This is why a relationship that is growing each day is so important huh James? It is only when you have that constant contact with God thru prayer can one really be at peace.

Rejoice in hope that one day you will be Home that one day you will see Christ face to face. That one day you will walk with Him on the streets paved with gold, walk next to the crystal sea, maybe even do a little fishing there on the shore. It is more than just holding onto that hope but it is rejoicing in it, celebrating the Hope you have in Him. Man that is what is exciting isn't it, rejoice in HOPE, your hope is not placed on stuff of this world but on the Creator of this world.

Being patient in tribulation, that is my strong suit – NOT- I would just as soon it was over then to let it work out. I know I am flirting with disaster but I really don't know a lot of folks who are patient in tribulation. There is not many people who enjoy going thru junk in their lives, yes even those of you who are more mature in your faith then some of us. We would all just as soon not even go thru a trial. It is thru trials thou that we can get a good measure of our faith, and in the end we have hopefully grown stronger in faith.

Let me ask you this last thing, are you continuing steadfastly in prayer or is your steadfastly more like a well I got time right now? Look ya need to make the time for God? Mano-e-God, just some time for Him to hear your voice, a time also for Him to touch your soul. That is where it all comes together ya know, when God touches your heart, that is when you know that He smiles. Our lives should be marked by our prayer life, our communication with God. Look you either communicate with Him or He will get your attention, would it worry you if He didn't smack you in the head?

Hmmm

Psalm 24:10 -Who is this King of glory? The LORD of hosts, He is the King of glory. Selah

Acts 16:25 -But at midnight Paul and Silas were praying and singing hymns to God, and the prisoners were listening to them.

Do ya think Paul and Silas got it?
Do ya think they understood who the King of glory is, the LORD of hosts?
For crying out loud it isn't hard to see that, yes they got it but also they were willing to share it.

Selah

When is the right time to sing praise, to sing hymns to God? Is it just when things are going right or is it when things are going bad, I know don't sing hymns at the table that is just rude. When is the right time to sing praise to GOD, hmm maybe it would be better to ask when is the wrong time to sing praises to God. Ya ever wonder who is listening to your song when you sing and that is why you don't, try this try thinking who you are singing praises to. Not for the person on the back row but God who sits on His throne.

Selah

Do you think that Paul and Silas sang praises and sung hymns because they were bored? They were just trying to kill time so they will sing some songs, don't really think so. What did they have to be thankful for, beaten and bruised and thrown in jail, now that's not my idea of a mission trip? They didn't stand there at the window bewailing their predicament, they sang and worshiped God.

Selah

Who is this King of glory indeed, who is He that makes the sun rise and set, who is He that lines the evening clouds with silver and the sunset with gold, who is He that makes the breeze stir and the rain fall, who is He that breathes the breath of life into all of us? He is the King, He is LORD, He is Abba, He is the Great I am.

Selah

We have all been given but a few moments of time here on this earth. In a thousand years we will all be but a wisp, at best a foot-note in a family tree, we only have so much time to touch people's lives for God. We all have opportunity to sing praises and hymns not just in the churches or cathedrals but on the streets, in the shopping centers, at work and at play. Just as the other prisoners overheard and the jailer over heard, let some one ask you why you sing when all seems less than perfect, then you tell them why you sing.

Joy etc..

Psalm 16:11 -You will show me the path of life; In Your presence is fullness of joy; At Your right hand are pleasures forevermore.

Where is your joy, what is it in, is your joy based upon who you know instead of what you know?

Have you ever tried to make your self happy? How did that work for you not very well, didn't last long, didn't work at all something like one of those? Yeah me neither, when ever I try to do some thing that is supposed to make me happy it may work for a moment or two but then it is gone and then I start looking for the next thing to do. Ya know what that aint bad it just is the wrong way for lasting joy. God provides lasting joy if only we would listen to Him.

Oh I don't know it seems odd to me that we really don't have to do anything but be still and listen for God to know His joy for us. There is not meditation chant or steps to it, that all we need to do is stop and listen. At times we think we need to get away from every-thing so we can find rest, yet we don't even rest on the day we are supposed to rest. Your Sundays are as busy at your Mondays, way to follow the commandment about keeping the Sabbath.

If only we would shut up and just listen better, if only we would stop and read and then obey what God has set down for us to do and we will find this fullness in our life that we all desire. Many may say but I can't stop doing what I am doing, if I don't do it-it won't get done, I know I am the worst. We have put more on our plate than God has placed there, so much so God's stuff gets covered up and we wonder why we are not satisfied. DUH, you're not listening to God your listening to your head and what it tells you that you need to be happy.

Ya wonder why some people walk around with a sour look; well it is from sucking on their own bitterness, that if they can't be made happy their mission is to make you less happy. They haven't experienced what I hope you have and that is the presence of God. Man oh man just feeling God's very presence around ya now that is awesome that is joyful that is so well cool. I guess some people don't want to feel God that close to them huh, like if God's there then they will be shown where they have messed up and maybe they like that feeling, eeh gads that is an awful thought.

What about you, are you walking in the presence of God right now, at this moment at this time during this hour in this second? Can you feel the fullness of God as He holds you close Johnny, Glen and Hugh? Doesn't it warm your heart Rusty, Doug and Rachel to know that GOD ALMIGHTY AND MAGNIFICENT is right there next to you right now? Ya'll there is nothing in your life that God can't help you with, there is nothing in your life that God doesn't want to be a part of, if you say He doesn't want to be a part of your sin that is right but He also wants to forgive you of that sin so that you can come closer to HIM. If we would just listen more closely, walk and talk with the intent of Love.

Search

John 5:39 -You search the Scriptures, for in them you think you have eternal life; and these are they which testify of Me.

When I was a kid, or just younger than I am now I would look at these Tele-Evangelists and say what is the act all about, why are they shouting at me? They would be up on stage arms flailing about spit flying out of their mouth and their faces would be read. While one night B.C. when I was stationed down at Eglin AFB my friends and I went off to Pensacola to some bars there and outside one of the bars was this guy. He was wearing one of those placards you know one of those signs that you see that read "REPENT THE END IS NEAR," his didn't say that, it said something like, "Do you know God or of God?" While we were waiting to go in the bar I watched this guy as people came up to him and insulted him and taunted him but he just stood there reading God's word. The thing is ya know I think he was praying for all of us who were going into the bar with less then honorable intentions, some there were searching and knew what they were doing was wrong but just weren't brave enough to say no.

Look here ya'll there are people in our churches who have read the bible front to back, that can quote the verses that they like and can live by back to you night and day. Still I wonder if Christ were before them if they would see Him. The old problem of culture and color remain today as they did back then. Most of ya have probably heard if Christ came the first time today would we be so accepting of the manger, if Joseph was a cook or a steel worker or a garbage collector would we say but this guys dad was just a cook who does he think he is, he didn't even go to Alabama or Harvard he didn't even go to Southern Union or Iowa Lakes who does he think he is, he isn't Euro-white.

Can you show me where it is that any of the old prophets said that the Savior would come in gold or born in the finest of homes? No it just said that He would be the King of kings, that his name would be Emmanuel, that the government would be upon His shoulders, that he would be of the line of David was no guarantee that he would come into a family of wealth. Every one had their preconceived idea of what kind of Christ they would find acceptable and scripture had little to do with it. We want a savior we can connect with right? If that is so then we need to know the scripture so we can know who He is and not our idea of who he should be.

You see that guy waiting to go into the bar, well he wasn't looking for Christ outside of a bar, but God knew that there were people He was preparing who were going to be at that bar so he sent a humble guy in a placard with a simple question. Do you know something, there are people in your life, as we have said before, that are searching for Christ. This thought to them may be the most remote thought in the world, but in their heart they are searching. Will you just hold up a card and show them Christ, ask them a simple question and give them a simple answer? I know we don't want to get insulted or spit on or ridiculed or hurt but isn't that friend of yours worth it, isn't your family worth it. They just need to see the Christ of scripture in you.

Kneel

Matthew 17:14 -And when they had come to the multitude, a man came to Him, kneeling down to Him and saying,

When was the last time you brought your petition before God on bended knee? Gotta think to hard about when it was, yeah me too.

You know what excuse I use, when I was in high school I ripped my knee and it still gives me problems, so I can't kneel on it. Yepper that is the one I use what is yours. Tell ya what sometimes the truth of the matter is that we don't ask kneeling is because we are just lazy. I know your not lazy physically after all you put in your 8 hours a day or your 12 hours a day, I know you brag about what all you gotta do and how long it takes you. Hey can you tell me how many hours a day God puts in, and yet He is never too busy to hear you. Look I don't really give a rip what you do, oh oops that don't sound very theological sorry Hugh you tried, or how you or I justify our laziness the simple matter is how humbly do you come before the throne?

Is that it Tim are we just not thinking about being humble before God are we just so concerned about ourselves that we don't see God on His throne and who He is? Maybe I am just ranting again or maybe there is some truth to the matter of this praying thing that we should be more considerate of whom we are asking for healing, or health or strength, or well what-ever it is that you are going to pray about today. Hey Johnny do we have an earnestness an urgency in our prayers or are they like the priest who stands up and prays before man to hear himself use big words and so people say that was a good prayer.

Ya know this guy who came before Christ wasn't asking for riches or a better position at work or for things to go right but he was asking Christ to help a family member whom he had already brought to the disciples. He tried different things and they just didn't work, it wasn't until he went before Christ on His knees that he was heard. Maybe before he couldn't get to Christ, maybe all he could do or settle for was to see a disciple or maybe it wasn't until he was broken enough to go do what he had to do to get to Christ Himself. What do we have to do before we have this sense of urgency in our prayers that brings us to our knees, must you be broken before your knees bend?

Look I am just well me, I don't like to be broken but sometimes that is what God does so that we reach for Him with urgency instead of with lethargic hands. Does that make any sense to you? Who will reach for a life saver circle more some one who is drowning or some one who can tread water, but even the person who treads water will reach desperately for the life saver when the seas about them boil and are tossing them around. Maybe the rough seas are there to get you to reach out and cling to the Savior.

I would suggest that we humble ourselves before God humbles us. See if you are not humbly going before God then really do you want God to help you, to show you mercy, to have compassion upon you or even to hear you.

Gifts

Romans 12: 3 For by the grace given me I say to every one of you: Do not think of yourself more highly than you ought, but rather think of yourself with sober judgment, in accordance with the measure of faith God has given you. 4Just as each of us has one body with many members, and these members do not all have the same function, 5so in Christ we who are many form one body, and each member belongs to all the others.

When I was getting out of the Air Force they did this out brief thing kind of a personality test. It was to see what kind of job you would be better suited for, don't ask me why they didn't give that test prior to going into the Air Force that would make sense. Anyway I love it when some one give you a test and says "there are no wrong answers," bull-own-knee. The results were given and I tested out with number one being clergy number two being some sort of service organization like oh I don't know food service. Man was that test really off. Not saying any test will give you all the results that you want but I guess it was fairly close, some times it takes a test for us to figure out what gifts we have.

There are a lot of people who go around wanting to be the head or an eye but never want to be the toe or a finger and if they are put as a finger it is going to be the index finger and certainly not the pinky finger or the big toe and not the pinky toe. What are you, are you where you aught to be or are you where you want to be?

Forgive

Matthew 18:35 -"So My heavenly Father also will do to you if each of you, from his heart, does not forgive his brother his trespasses."

What you expect to be given do you give?
Have you ever wanted to be forgiven and yet you yourself are unwilling to forgive?

Well if you put it like that it kind of sounds bad doesn't it, yet it is bad. Whom have you forgiven, who has forgiven you. Are the infractions we commit less than those infractions that have been committed against us? Some yes and some no, it is a matter of what society says is acceptable and at times not what God says is right. Society says its okay to talk about people behind their back and to undermine if it helps you get ahead, God says it is wrong to gossip, and may even be murder and yet we still have a time taming our tongue. We certainly don't like it when some one talks about us behind our back but what does it take for you to talk about some one else?

There are times when we well just mess up, that we stumble and slip and slide, almost like the two steps forward and three steps back thing. Yet it is a step forward if we can forgive from the heart and not just with words. We are good at saying forgive me but not so good at really being sorry for what we have done. When was the last time that sin has broken your heart and you cried out to God to forgive you from your heart, has it been awhile? How about this when some one has messed up and asked you to forgive them? Did you forgive them from your heart or did you put it away in the memory banks, storing it away for future use.

Mark 11:26 -But if you do not forgive, neither will your Father in heaven forgive your trespasses."

Have you ever noticed in this Christian life that there is just as much responsibility on the forgiver as there is on the sinner? Now if I got this right, feel free to correct me Jerome or Hugh, but is some one who has sinned against us and they come and ask us to forgive them, and they are sincere in their request they can be free of that sin. Yet if the person who is being asked to forgive doesn't forgive but continues to harbor then they are the ones guilty of sin? Is that right Tracey?

Tell me Doug and Doug is it easy for you to forgive some one who has harmed you, by harmed I do mean sinned against you? Tell me Rusty, Jesse and Joe is it easy for you to wipe the slate clean after some one has messed up then come to you with a repentant heart? Is it easy to forgive the rapist, the slanderer, the murderer, the back stabbing piece of dirt that tried to undercut you, is it easy to forgive the liar, the gossip, tell me please did God say it would be easy?

You see if we are the sinner or the forgiver we need the strength that can only come from God, we can't forgive or confess but unless GOD helps us. Do you need to forgive some one or do you need to ask some one to forgive you?

Faith

Mark 11:22 -So Jesus answered and said to them, "Have faith in God.

1 a : allegiance to duty or a person : LOYALTY b (1) : fidelity to one's promises (2) : sincerity of intentions
2 a (1) : belief and trust in and loyalty to God (2) : belief in the traditional doctrines of a religion b (1) : firm belief in something for which there is no proof (2) : complete trust
3 : something that is believed especially with strong conviction; *especially* : a system of religious beliefs

Ya know at times it seems such a simple answer, "Have faith in God." Hmm after all it is the best answer there is because it is the only answer period. Yet these four little words are so complex because we add definitions to them that are more then they need to be. "Have faith in God." Do your actions reflect that you have faith in God, do the words that come out of your mouth reveal that God is in your heart. Holy cow we are so stupid at times, we say we have faith in God but then we try to do everything our way.

The disciples still marveled because a fig tree withered after Christ had spoken against it, they were still trying to put things into tangible terms and not living in faith. Ya know what I don't think I would not want to be surprised at a God thing either, but to recognize things as a God thing. Tell me please is it a surprise to you that

God hears your prayers and petitions, is it a surprise to you that He answers your prayers and petitions, if it surprises you then why do you pray? We pray because we "Have faith in God." Don't we?

I recall the first time I read this verse, thinking wow that's cool you mean if I have faith in God and ask Him to move this mountain then He will cast it into the sea. Now that's just cool, so me being who well I am, asked (sarcastically) for a tree to be moved. Like you didn't think of that when you read this verse. No the tree didn't move because I lacked faith in God. We don't move mountains because sometimes we lack faith in God.

For some reason people pray acting like God won't hear them, or the answer will be no so why even bother. Maybe we are trying to move the wrong mountain. Having faith in God doesn't mean that you can move mountains, no rather it is because God can move mountains. Ya know Nathan God has moved mountains in your life, ya know Julie and David God is with you moving debris out of your way to make your path flat. Most of the mountains we need to move are mountains of our own making, or bull that people have placed before us, "Have faith in God," He will move those mountains that lay in your path.

I know sometimes it is just easier to say "Have faith in God," then it is to actually live by it, not like it but to actually believing in HIM. Your faith in God will be reflected in the foot-prints of where you go and who you touch in this life. Ya know what, pray earnestly with anticipation of the mountain being cast into the sea.

Example

John 13:15 -For I have given you an example, that you should do as I have done to you.

A re you the example of Christ that you aught to be, or is your willingness to help others out just limited to a season on a calendar or thru a charitable gift that you then put on your taxes to get it written off? No nothing wrong with any of those gifts or opportunities to give, but then again isn't it a bit sad that the gifts come in the last week of the year, I wonder if the interest earned is applied to the gift. Just a thought, is this just an example of washing some ones feet or just meeting an obligation, you decide.

There are times when we ponder the greatness of God, the majesty of His creation, the awesomeness of His Son and then we think that there is no way we can ever be the example that Christ was. We forget that the Holy Spirit is with us, or over look Him, we say we can't we are too weak too human too selfish, oh maybe we don't call ourselves selfish though huh. We go on mission trips building fellowship hall, or delivering Thanksgiving meals, or lending a hand at an orphanage with the power or plumbing but if we don't share the gospel then we have failed to be the example of Christ that we should have been.

I was listening to this article well more like a book of our blindness; this was a mission group who had a 59 page book of how to conduct a mission trip. It was very retentive, covered everything from healthcare and first aid to what materials to take to complete the mission. Some where along page 40 something is when they talked about having a missionary covenant and that is where it talked about sharing the gospel. Can you tell me how or why this would be buried in the 40 pages of get this and make sure you have that?

Christ went out to preach and share the gospel, along the way He asked His Father to heal, to feed and restore those who were brought to Him. His mission was the great commission some of the fruit of that mission was that people were healed. Now we flip it around at times, we go out on a mission trip to roof and feed and if given the opportunity we then will share the gospel, maybe if we are bold enough or recognize the opportunity.

You are on mission today, maybe you need to stripe down the layers of cover and gird yourself with a towel and walk around with a basin of water and wash some ones feet. Not probably the most socially acceptable picture, but still I didn't say your layers of clothes that is just what you thought, your cover could be your attitude toward others, your cover could be just about any barrier we put between ourselves and others. Knock it down strip it off and let Him work thru you to be the example of Christ in your day.

People don't mind it when you do charitable things for them, philanthropy is not a bad thing but if your only reason for being charitable is to make yourself feel like you have done your bit then you are smoking something to strong. When you walk out the door today how are you going to be an example of Christ, the Christ who washed the feet of those who served Him, the Christ who healed the leapers and only one came back to thank Him, the Christ who sacrificed Himself on a cross for your and my sins.

Resolve

Romans 14:13 -Therefore let us not judge one another anymore, but rather resolve this, not to put a stumbling block or a cause to fall in our brother's way.

"First do no harm," not a part of the Hippocratic Oath and I am just not sure where it comes from but it is a good rule to go by huh docs? That the actions that we do first bring no harm, that the cure is not worse then the illness. After all you wouldn't amputate an arm for an ingrown fingernail? No of course not, I know Ron and Patrick you are saying well if it is infected and gang-green or whatever. Some times we shoot from the hip thou and figure we know what is going on and take action to cut it off, when maybe all we need to do is increase antibiotics er something. Guess you can tell it's a good thing they don't let me do surgery huh. Hey Bob don't be afraid I am not going up to the OR.

Is this our approach to discipleship? First do no harm, or are we teaching church instead of teaching Gospel? I love it when some one tells me it's a sin to do something and when you ask them to show you in God's word they say well in the church constitution its wrong? Tell me if you don't follow your church constitution is it a sin or a pho-pa (no I don't know how to spell it). Now I have committed many a pho-pa but none of them were sins. I never did it with malice in my heart or to get even or any of that, its just well I wasn't disciple in the tactfulness of church cliques. We are quick at times to call something wrong that is not wrong, in so doing we judge and place stumbling blocks in the path of a brother or a sister.

Some one once told me that the best answers come from God so rely on what God tells you. Is this what we do, or do we rely on what "they" say? Who ever they are, I have yet to figure that one out. They must be people who came before, some sortta committee or board that decided what was and is acceptable and what was and is a pho-pa but they called it a sin. When was it that we started relying on a constitution or by-laws to teach, to discipleship to conduct services rather then relying on God's own word?

What stumbling blocks do we put in some ones path, hmm could it be when we don't challenge what they say and don't look it up so we teach the they said instead of the He said. I am sure there are other stumbling blocks, some conscious and sub-consciously put in a path. That is why we must resolve, we must put an extraordinary effort to make sure we don't teach a cure harsher then the disease.

I wonder what Christ would teach today if He were here today? Oh He would teach the same thing that is in red letters in your bible. How well we know those words is reflected in our attitudes, in our discipleship of others and in our relationship. Christ didn't bring harm to anyone, even the money-changers after all He could have made them a pillar of salt instead of just driving them out, a dead man can not repent.

When you look at your day what will you resolve to do, what will you teach, how will your words that you pass on edify the body? First do no harm and don't judge others but look at what you place in their path. Hmm Love them first, let some one know how dear to you they are. Love will conquer all, Christ's love covered all God's love sent Christ.

Want

Psalm 23:1 The LORD is my shepherd; I shall not want.

I was fishing down at the river yesterday, after all the rain in the
morning it turned out to be a fairly nice day. All the streams were
up and flowing fast, they were brown with mud and there is no way
any fish could see a bait/lure thru all of that muck. As I came down a
hill I noticed that where the creek flowed into the river it was muddy
but about half way over it was nice green water (it never looks blue).
So I figured that I would get to my spot and I would be able to cast
over the muck and catch something in the green still water. Wouldn't
you know by the time I got to my spot there was a guy there already
fishing, man that stunk, so I had to go down a little further and that
is where the water was rushing not flowing mind you but rushing by,
aint no way I would catch a fish there. I just wanted to fish where the
water was clear and still that is all I wanted to do and that guy if he
would leave I could fish in my spot after all, the audacity of the guy
didn't he know it was my spot he was in. Yet they guy was fishing
to eat and I was fishing to catch and release. So who was God taking
care of their wants?

There isn't a one of you who has a want that God hasn't met or
taken care of. There are some things that you would like to have
maybe but all of you have a coat to wear, clean water to drink and if
your pantries are empty it is because you haven't gone to the store
lately. Maybe we should think of our real needs instead of our luxury

needs? I don't know but some trips that I have been on where we think we are meeting a need we see that the people are happy and joyful not because of what they have but because of "Whom" they know and of their families. I would venture a guess to say if your or I lived in a home that the walls were built out of pallet slats with a rug or blanket draped over we wouldn't be so happy would we.

Tell me is your want really your need? Is what you desire necessary to your happiness? IS the LORD your want? I know when we go to the mall or fishing store outlet that we walk in going I'll take this or I'll take that, maybe we say that would be nice to have or that bass boat with the glitter and the biggest outboard that will get us across the lake at mach 3 is something that we want. But in your heart those are not wants they are desires.

What is it that you really want, check your heart, is it happiness for your family is it assurance for yourself, tell me please what is it that your heart truly wants. To know the Father better, to know Him more what is it that you really want, scrape off the fluff and stuff and ask your self what is it that you really want. It is no mistake that this is the first part to Psalm 23, which goes on to talk about where He leads you and where He helps you thru and what He has prepared for you. You see if you can't listen to Him your river will always rush by so you will be thirsty, you will have fear in the shadow of the valley of death because you don't have assurance and your table will be un-set.

You see you can have the biggest and best of everything but if you have not met God your needs will leave you empty and lost. Look at your wants are they what you need. Tell me do you need God today, is He your want first.

Today

Psalm 95:7 -For He is our God, And we are the people of His pasture, And the sheep of His hand. Today, if you will hear His voice:

Are you a sheep that is hard of hearing?
It is funny when you're a kid and listening to music on your headphones you would crank the music up and then your folks would say "turn it down or you'll hurt your ears." How many of you have said that to your own kids now? My daughter got a mp3 player from Santa and she listens to it almost all of the time and I heard my wife tell her "turn it down or you will hurt your ears." It just strikes me as funny when we find ourselves repeating what our parents said to us when we turned the music up and hurt our ears. Yes, we have had to say it more than once, she seems to forget and goes back and turns it back up the next time she listens to it. What is the acceptable volume of music in our lives, do we need to scale back the volume so we can hear Him as we should?

Have you ever noticed animals out in a field? They got no worries because yes their animals they don't know what lies ahead. Sheep just wander around eating here and there, chewing the grass down and setting down when they want. Sheep in a pasture don't have to worry about punching the clock or satisfying the boss or making budget or turning a profit or meeting regulations or what the spouse needs or how the kids are doing once weaned or car payments or house payments or whatever they just gotta be sheep. When you drive by and blow your horn to see if it will get them to stampede or at least turn (yeah like I am the only one who has done that) around but they just do there thing not worried about the noise.

I wonder if each of us went thru the day turning down the stuff in our ears so we can hear God as we should and acted like the sheep of His field of his pasture of His Creation how much more we would be able to experience. You see just because our lives are full of activity doesn't mean that our lives are full. If your day planner is full of where ya gotta be and whatcha gotta do are you really living a life that is full? I wonder, maybe not – maybe you have filled your life with the rushing water and not being led to the still water. Go ahead and look at what it is you gotta do today, what is important to do? Have you talked with God yet today, have you listened for His response, no rather did you really take the time to hear His voice or did your morning routine dictate how much time you would give Him to respond to ya.

Christ never hurried to get anywhere did He? I mean I didn't find anywhere where it said "and Jesus rushed off to get to Capernaum" or where He taped His sundial watch getting His apostles attention because it was time to go get in the boat to cross so He could show them how to walk on water. I know that is kind of silly but still Christ knew that God had a plan, how do you suppose Christ knew, well Jesus spoke with His Father and He listened to Him.

Today if you will hear His voice will you recognize it? Is the volume turned up too much in your life? Then turn it down or you will hurt your ears and harden your heart.

Walk

Psalm 23:4 -Yea, though I walk through the valley of the shadow of death, I will fear no evil; For You are with me; Your rod and Your staff, they comfort me.

Matthew 28:20 -teaching them to observe all things that I have commanded you; and lo, I am with you always, even to the end of the age." Amen.

Walk without fear, but walk in the hope and love and mercy of the LORD your God.

Have you thought that how you walk today people will be learning from you, that if you walk with fear of the world people will learn from that? Walk boldly knowing that this is but for a time, that there is a gate at the end that is narrow for you to walk thru.

Look, I just can't tell you how important it is for us to walk the way we are supposed to walk, each taking our own steps along the narrow path. It is just as important though for each of us to help each other especially when we stumble to get back up and to be restored. That we shouldn't fear the valley that is dark and but that we should keep in mind that His rod and His staff protect us because He is with us even to the end of the day.

Some of you are hurting, some of you are wonder what to do, some of you just want to get something that will help you thru the day and some of you are wonder what in the world I am talking about. That's cool; Obie is probably getting a chuckle out of this so far because I may be rambling a bit more than usual. But what I want to remind you of is that you are not alone, that God is here with you, yes right there with you and He will not abandon you or leave you to your own devises. That if maybe you don't feel Him maybe you should lean closer in.

Faith must be an important part of your life, not just saying I have faith but living with the knowledge of faith in your life. Does that make any sense to you? Let me give you an example then, if you have no faith what do you expect will happen when you open the door, just taking things as they come or do you have faith that God has a plan and that His plan involves you. It does you know, Allison and Rod do you know that God knows how many hairs you have on your head, Doug and David do you know that God was with you in your mourning and just wants you to lean toward Him and not away from Him.

We could go on couldn't we, after all we each at times wonder why or where God is in our lives, why He would let this or that happen to us. Doesn't He know us, why then why? Then tell me where you are leaning, toward Him or away from Him. Your witness is pivotal when you consider that others are watching how you get thru times of trial and struggle. You and I may struggle and stumble, we may skin the stew out of our knees, reach out to the staff and hand that will pull you up.

God has placed each of you in a mission field; this field may be the person next to you at the office. This person sees how you get thru trials; you are there for a reason.

Shine

Numbers 6:25 -The LORD make His face shine upon you,
And be gracious to you;

How has the LORD blessed you, even if you are looking at your cup as half full it is still not empty? There are so many ways that God looks after us each and everyday that we say it is to hard to count, but then why are we so disappointed when God answers one of our prayers NO. Could it be that we are still children, still sheep in His pasture, that sometimes we only notice the rain when we lift our head up from the green grass?

When ever I think of this verse I think of a big spotlight being shone (is that right shone) down upon you and following you thru out the day. When I was in high school I was in the play Arsenic and Ole' Lace, yes I was the psycho path Jonathan Brewster, anyway I hated the spotlight on me, shining in my eyes drawing attention to myself. Not that I don't mind being the center of attention, James just said I have a big personality, anyway again. It's just that the light let everyone see that my face was smaller than my nose, look ya'll that is one of the reason I wear glasses to hide a beak. ANYWAY! Man get over it, we all have flaws that we don't want anyone to see, not all of them physical huh.

Now with the LORD'S face directed toward you, at first that can sound intimidating or even a bit nervous which is good. Maybe you need to deal with what is making you nervous first, probably that sin that got exposed when the light shined on it. In God's light there is no shadow, no place for sin to hide. Kind a like that deer in the headlights look, you know the look that says Holy Cow don't run me down!! Look if it is exposed then you can deal with it, and hey come to think of it God is right there so it is not like you gotta wait to deal with it. Confess the sin and turn from it and turn your face to God to meet His gaze at you.

It may sound a bit blustery or whatever, but I like to look back at God when I feel His eyes on me, I kind a smile back cause you know what He likes a good laugh. No, I can't prove that biblically but since He is the King of Glory it can't make me feel anything but joy and that makes me happy. Doesn't it make you happy knowing that the God who created it all, who made the sun to rise and set, the God who breathed life into you, the God who has given us so very much is looking at you, even now. That is the ultimate warm fuzzy if you ask me.

Tell me does His grace abound in your life, or have you even thought about His grace lately? Now that's a bit scary, not thinking about His grace I mean. Tell me what do you think about His grace, is it something that makes your heart skip a beat? To think that God whom you serve David and Doug and Walter and Hugh and Tim and Jan and Jo Ann and Billy and Doris and Yvonne is this day looking at you and being gracious to you? Wow, man for Pete's sake that is awesome aint it. We don't deserve His grace, not done a dog gone thing to earn it and yet because we have called upon His Son's name, turned from a life of sin and stepped into His light we have been given grace, mercy, love, joy, and on and on and on. WHOOPIE, PRAISE GOD (I know whoopee is not a churchy word but hey deal with it)

Body Odor

******Warning: The following writing is rated
Pew-Wee********************

There is nothing as sour as the stank of body odor, that noxious aroma of un-washed filth and sweat. When some one comes up to you in a crowd and then the odor hits your nose and if it is a nice humid day in Clay County Alabama it is all you can do not to be repulsed by it and want to walk away, because it is not just smelly it is stanky. You think, how can some one live like that, how can anyone walk around with yellow stained shirt from their own sweat, don't they notice that they stink. I know Debra and Dorothy why are we talking about body odor, couldn't we be talking about something like lilacs or honey suckle they smell good. Well ya'll sin is like that pungent stench of body odor, but unless you turn from sin and wash in the blood of the Lamb then that is what you fill the nostrils of God with, your nasty stanky sweaty odor of sin.

Ephesians 5:2 -And walk in love, as Christ also has loved us and given Himself for us, an offering and a sacrifice to God for a sweet-smelling aroma.

So today are you going to walk in love, as Christ? It is your choice you know, no one is going to make you sin. No if ands or buts about it today you will make a choice either to walk in a fragrant aroma or to walk with yellow rings. When you think about it really there just is no one to blame for our faults but ourselves, yes even when others put stones in your path you have the choice to keep your eyes open lift your foot over the stone and go about the way of Christ.

You see today with the choices you make will reflect your relationship with Christ. Right, isn't that right? Or do you step outside of your relationship with Christ when dealing with others or when dealing with certain situations? Hmm, think about that a second and I know you gotta be a certain level of "politically correct," but can you really step in and out of your relationship with Christ just because some one may be offended. Don't let their odor get on you. I know it's not easy, God never said it would be, Christ said that people would hate you because of Him.

We are to walk in the love of Christ and reflect that love that we cherish so very much. I guess that is one thing that we all could probably do a better job at, you know walking like Christ in love. Sometimes we want to get out of the way of those who haven't washed instead of going to dinner with them; we would rather keep the leapers outside in a cave rather then invite them in. And for Pete's sake we aint gonna give them the choicest place at the table but keep them out the back door in the alley. I wonder where you and I would be had we not been invited to the table, where would we be if we never came to Christ, would we still not recognize our own body odor.

You see no matter how many new clothes you may get or how hard you scrub with soap or what perfume or cologne you put on you may still have a pungent aroma of sin wafting about you. Man will recognize you new clothes and you just got outta the shower smell but God will notice your sin. Who is your example of walking in love Christ or Man?

Glorify

John 21:19 -This He spoke, signifying by what death he would glorify God. And when He had spoken this, He said to him, "Follow Me."

I wonder what we will do today that will glorify God? There are times when I really don't feel like I could ever be good enough to bring glory to the Father, that the things I have done in the past are just a big black splotch. Do you think that is where forgiveness comes in, that God doesn't use white-out but erases it completely and then re-writes on the sheet of paper forgiven? Hmm I wonder if we wrote in pencil on a piece of paper the sins we had done then erase them and then knock the eraser dust off the page and make sure that there is nothing left then write forgiven on the page. That is what we are when we come to Christ admitting we are sinners not varying degrees of sinners but that we have sinned against God, that we accept the gift of the cross and believe that God raised Christ on the third day. We are forgiven, forgiven restored to the fold of God and today because of forgiveness we have the opportunity to GLORIFY GOD!!

These words that Christ spoke to Peter are words for us today. Now for those of you who are thinking that I am saying some one will gird you and take you where you don't wish to go the answer is yes. Maybe not off to death, but maybe some one will drag you thru the mud because you choose to stand up for Christ. That instead of taking the "PC" way out of the predicament you find yourself in that you stand up and GLORIFY GOD. We don't really want to suffer for Christ thou do we, we like the security of the walls of our church buildings, (I have to say buildings or double D will email me back saying we ((people)) are the church)). We are like Peter out on the boat fishing, just knowing that we should be doing but lacking the conviction to do what Christ and God have called us to do.

I would love to challenge you and the church you attend to look at the ministry of the church but that really isn't it. Where is your, that is you sitting there reading this, where is your ministry, is it still in the boat, was it that one big event at Thanksgiving, is your ministry going or staying, how today are you glorifying the Father. Look now all you Baptist don't have a hissy, but ministry is not about numbers it is about a number and the number is One. We get pre-occupied with numbers and forget it aint about us in the first place, rather it is about the One who forgave you, the One who has forgiven me. That when we serve Him with our heart and soul first, that He knows that we are not perfect is a given and still He wants you outta the boat seeking Him.

When was the last time you "Followed Me," can you recall the time where God said go here. I know we will go when we get good and equipped waiting till the funds get in and the training is accomplished. So our answer to "Follow Me" is okay but wait a sec would ya God. How will you bring Glory to the Father today, simply by Following Him? In an earlier sequence in this section Christ asked Peter if he loved Him. Three times as a matter of fact Christ asked this question, "Do you love Me?" it wasn't until the third time that Peter got it. How many times will Christ have to ask you if you love Him before you get it, enough to follow where ever He leads?

Choke

Matthew 13:22 -Now he who received seed among the thorns is he who hears the word, and the cares of this world and the deceitfulness of riches choke the word, and he becomes unfruitful.

When I was a kid, we had this garden that we had to get all of the weeds out of. What a pain in the, well you know. Starting in the front and working thru it to the back of the garden where the pumpkins were. Now I am not talking about your average garden which you would call a plot but this thing was 90 x 50 yards or so it seemed. If you didn't get the weeds out then two things would happen, the yield would be less and it would be even harder to harvest the crop, sure I didn't much care if the potato crop choked off and died but the tomatoes man oh man I wanted a high yield and those babies. When you got older, things during the summer seemed to get busy so you didn't have the time to get the weeds out, you had to go work at a farm, baseball and mowing lawns occupied your time. So the tomatoes would get overgrown and you had to work even harder to get the weeds out. Do you know anyone who needs to get the weeds out of their life before they are choked off?

There was that time that you were excited about your life with Christ, well after you accepted Christ that is. Everything was new; you had that hunger for reading God's word and the zeal for worshipping in your Father's house and going to church to meet with all your brothers and sisters in Christ. Life was good there at first wasn't it, after all what did you know but the LOVE of GOD the joy of walking with Christ and the thrill of being led by the Holy Spirit. Do ya remember that time when you knew that Christ was there for you, to sit back and just feel His presence and to be able just to be still in that moment and breathe?

So what is different now? Are you spending so much time planning what mission trip you want to do instead of listening to God, are you investing time in a committee about what to do with the old chairs that aren't being used instead of asking God how He can use you to fill those chairs, are you wondering how you can get on the deaconate instead of waiting on some tables? Did you think it was just the things outside the church walls that are choking off your relationship with God, sure I could have talked about work and recreation and those are fine sure, we may be investing a bunch of time to those things? But what about the time that we spend at church, have we let the hustle and bustle of the world seep into the church?

There are some really busy people out there but their fruit has been choked off by well their busyness. What fruit do you really bare, is it fruit of the Spirit or fruit of your labor. What's the difference you ask, well when it is fruit of your labor it is look what I have done and when it is the fruit of the spirit it is WOW look what God used me for. If you find that what you are doing is keeping you away from God and more involved in doing stuff no matter what it is then you are too busy. Maybe it is time to get the hoe out and whack some of the weeds out so you can really grow and produce fruit worthy to be picked off of the vine.

Challenge Yourself

Exodus 20:[14] "You shall not commit adultery

Ya know what we hear the Ten Commandments but do we live by them, do you apply them in your life, and every aspect of your life or just on a Sunday morning? I gotta tell ya to look around then and see if you are participating in breaking the Ten Commandments, if you break one then you break them all. Even if you don't consider yourself and adulterer or a thief or a blasphemer or a hypocrite, we say "but I never," really you never?

Tell me something are your Sunday's as busy as your Monday's have you forgotten to keep the Lord's Day HOLY and separate a time to rest? We are not very good at resting are we? Sure we have all those funky gadgets that we play with, we are people of leisure but still we don't know squat about resting. Sunday is just a day off for many people, it has become a day to go out to eat and then split up and go about your own hobbies, and some of you work hard doing your hobbies. We don't like to rest we gotta be doing something. God created all things is six days and He rested on the Sabbath and made it Holy for us.

I picked this commandment to get your attention, because I know people hear the word adultery and their ears prick up a little more. Why is that, are we interested in the gossip or are we concerned that our nation is becoming an adulterous generation. We have not taken the commandments as commandments but as suggestions with no thought to the thought that there is a penalty for breaking these commandments.

Can I ask you something, it's just between you and I. Have you polluted your mind by the things that you watch or the things that you read or the things that you have let come into your life. May I be frank with you, is it just playful banter or is it in God's eyes sexual harassment? It is just funny how we think that human resource managers came up with the term, they may have coined the phrase but God gave us the commandment. Ya won't have to worry about getting sued you will have to answer to God. He is your judge not a guy or gal in a robe.

How are you doing with the commandments? Do you take the Lord's name in vain; do you have any other gods before Him? I don't mean to come off as a downer today but ya know what we need to take the commandments serous and I fear we don't. Isn't it sad that we get all vexed because some one can't display the commandments but yet we don't know where in the bible they are and we know them only vaguely?

Look I am not saying I am any better, far from it; I also need to work at holding these commandments close. Hey Ya'll we are in this together aren't we, right, then start holding each other accountable, don't come down on each other as a hammer because there may be a plank in your eye, but hold each other and me accountable in love.

Rust and Moth

Matthew 6: 19-21 Do not store up for yourselves treasures on earth, where moth and rust destroy, and where thieves break in and steal. [20]But store up for yourselves treasures in heaven, where moth and rust do not destroy, and where thieves do not break in and steal. [21]For where your treasure is, there your heart will be also.

At the house I grew up at there was in the back corner a place we called the grove. It had like six trees in a 15 x 15 foot space, not very large but hey it seemed large back then. We would dig in that place planting all sorts of treasure in holes. The grove was a special place cause it had one stump in the very back corner that you could crawl behind and just be alone. I learned to treasure those moments more than I treasured the stuff in the holes.

Bank accounts, check books, money pouches and stuff are what a lot of people treasure, unfortunately even some within the church. The outlook is that these things are theirs and yours if you belong to the right group or go through the right channels. How do you, how can we let people know that we aught not worry about the stuff the junk in our lives. We should however concern our selves with the treasure of Christ.

More and more as the days go by I can see where God has not only blessed me but where He has over-flowingly (not a normal word I know that) blessed you and I. Call me radical but you see Christ is the true treasure not your check book or bank statement. We have concerned ourselves with the rust and the moth instead of salvation and evangelism. Yes Tim there will always be opportunities to witness to tell folks about Christ, we need not apologies for it or think we are being confrontational. We are just sharing the wealth.

Just as at night you lock your door to your home or when you go to the mall you lock your car so to have we locked our hearts, sealed them up. Unfortunately though since we haven't used our hearts daily there has been some rust collecting. Well knock it off, unlock your heart and share the love you have inside you with the world. You want to save up for retirement cool that is fine but let me say retirement will only last till your dead then it comes to eternity which one will last longer?

What is it that you really treasure? Where is your heart at today? Express the joy, share the love give honor and all ALLLLLLL PRAISES TO HIM.

Peace

John 14:27 Peace I leave with you; my peace I give you. I do not give to you as the world gives. Do not let your hearts be troubled and do not be afraid.

Have you ever just felt so relaxed and clean that you felt spotless? Have you ever felt so good that no matter what the day will bring that you know that God will bring you through it? Have you just felt at peace with God and yourself?

No pain, no hurt just peace.

As I read and learn God's words and feel the gentleness of His spirit it is this peace that I seek. I often wonder if other Christians feel the same sense of peace in His word. This joy from hearing God speaks through His book. It is to me still just a new sensation a new and wonderful thing just to be in awe of God who surrounds us. I would suggest that you tap into it but I am sure that you do don'tcha?

You see I know that the world will fling its junk today. I know that there will be folks who don't know Christ as their Lord and Savior who are as lost as the night is dark. That is how they will act and I should expect that. As the armor comes on it isn't a physical suit of mail and metal but rather it is the spirit of peace and that is God.

Christ will not leave you, He is there with you now do not be afraid, have the peace that surpasses all understanding the peace that comes from Christ.

Old Problem

Hebrews 10:25 Let us not give up meeting together, as some are in the habit of doing, but let us encourage one another-- and all the more as you see the Day approaching.

S ome one once told be to make something a habit you have to do it seven times without missing a day. Now I am really not sure of that philosophy how ever it does seem biblical because it has seven in it. Okay Adam maybe not biblical but it is odd that some people think doing something seven times in a row will make it a habit. In the same sense no matter if you have been doing something 21 times in a row or for years that it just takes one excuse for people to stop doing something.

Why is it that some people don't go to or seek fellowship with other Christian? They would be quick to point out that they are believers though if asked. So how is it that they have abandoned the fellowship or that they flop around saying they are looking for a church. It is humorous to me that we find people saying they can do it by themselves, that they know enough and read enough to get by without having to go to "church."

You see it isn't the building we go to though is it? I mean Russell are you planning on going to church Sunday so you can sit in your assigned seat to make sure it is there? Tim are you planning on going to church cause that is your job? Kevin is church the only place that you sing at or folks will let you sign at? Of course not, you go to be encouraged and to encourage. Hopefully we do both on Sunday, maybe we should be doing that today after all the church really is the body of Christ and maybe you know of a Christian who is hurting.

Encouragement is a funny thing just at there is two sides to every story so to is it with encouragement. Have you ever saw someone sitting in the back row daring you to welcome them, doing what you can to welcome them and then finding out that what you did wasn't good enough cause some one else didn't encourage them. It is an excuse that is used, but when you boil it down it is after all just an excuse.

Sure we need to encourage those to come, to take a part, to get "plugged in." It is also their responsibility to get in the habit of coming in and getting hungry for it. So hungry that if they miss a Sunday they would feel as if they missed it they would starve. When you do get down to it the it really isn't a program, service, music, pew, or what not rather the it is always a He. Do you really need encouragement to see and hear Him?

Family

Matthew 1:1A record of the genealogy of Jesus Christ the son of David, the son of Abraham:

My family tree is real long and has a bunch of branches; the Irmiter name is not in danger of dying out anytime in the near future or next couple hundred years. In having a large family tree as it where you know who your brothers and sisters are and where they came from and what the do and did cause you grew up with them. It is those in the tree that started the branching out that we don't know much about cause the records from here to Germany (in my case) have been muddled with time. I know the Irmiter's came from Germany and that they were in Chicago and then one moved to Iowa but hey who were these guys and why did they do it? I have not a clue other than to get away or to get land or to prosper where they could.

Look here, Jesus Christ is your brother, He is God's only Son. Adopted or what it makes no never mind to God you are His children. We say we are brothers and sisters in Christ but then really do we act like it? Sure we fight and squabble and fuss at each other just like real brothers and sisters, right?

Do you know where the family of God came from? Do you know your ancestors and what they did and what they overcame? Doink, open the bible and find out then. Is there any better tool at your disposal to find out about the family of GOD? No, I don't think so.

Everything is laid out for you in black and white, in some cases big brother's words are in red to stand out more. Through it all are our Fathers words. These are not stories or fairy tales but rather these words are His for you to read and to hear from Him.

Your genealogy does it have Christ in it? Have you come into the body of Christ or do you prefer to be a distant cousin who knows who Christ is but doesn't have that family relationship. "Lord, this is Doug my Brother, this is Walter your adopted son, and" Christ will say "They came to you thru me." "Welcome home, enter and be well," God will say

I Don't Know

Luke 2:15 When the angels had left them and gone into heaven, the shepherds said to one another, "Let's go to Bethlehem and see this thing that has happened, which the Lord has told us about."

Last night I went to the Jolly Senior's Christmas party and it was quite nice. Food, fellowship and good song made for an interesting evening. Adam belted out Holy Night, which has recently like in the past couple of years become one of my favorite songs no matter the time of year. No matter if it is July or December truly a night where Jesus comes into a heart or into a village it is a Holy Night.

So I thought of those shepherds again out in the pasture tending to their flocks. Looking after sheep by looking out for predators whether they were two legged or four legged. When an angel appeared to them and scared the "dickens," out of them. THE DICKENS get it. (Sorry) Anyway, they heard from the angel then the host choir group got jiggy with it then they were left alone.

The shepherds didn't say, "Let's go check this out that the angels were talking about." Rather they said what "the Lord has told us about." You see on this night the angels sang and rejoiced the shepherds heard and obeyed for they did go see what it was about. What they saw energized them to go and spread the word.

Now I don't know about you but isn't that what fellowship is all about. Going to see Christ getting energized then going out and spreading what it was all about. Thinking about how those guys made their walk into Bethlehem, were they thinking well if we're gone who is going to watch the sheep, should I send a message to the wife so she doesn't worry if I am late getting home, man I would rather be golfing or fishing, it can wait really the angels didn't say I had to go this very moment. Not at all they were simply obedient to what the Lord had instructed them to do and didn't let distractions from stopping them.

This Holy Night where the stars are shining brightly. Where your soul feels His worth fall to your knees and hear the angels still singing. Because through it all Christ has come.

So when you go see God on Sunday or Saturday sees God let His love shine from your heart be open to His words and His touch. Then go spread the word.

Serve or Served

Matthew 6:24 "No one can serve two masters. Either he will hate the one and love the other, or he will be devoted to the one and despise the other. You cannot serve both God and Money.

Okay for starters this isn't about money; you could in fact put a lot of things in the place of money for instance church things like programs, furniture, seats, people, and pastor and on. A couple of people have been talking about being saved and having that relationship with God thru Christ His son. I mean these guys and ladies have great faith and love for the Lord and truly I look up to them. Through all of the debate I can only say this; if you see whom it is a person serves then you see what a person serves.

We look at each other and say wow that person really gets it, that guy really knows what's going on but then when they stumble and fall we question how could that happen to them. Doink they are human we will stumble and fall. I know in my great wisdom and maturity that I will make mistakes and that you may say well how could that have happened to him. Doink once again we are human.

That is where God steps in and helps, this is also where you can tell by the fruit that we bear if a person gets it or not. You see if you understand that we are all sinners and that no sin is any worse or at a different level then any other sin then you will also realize that God can and will forgive you of that sin. He will also restore you, sure you must back away from the functions in the church that you are doing not because you lost respect but rather because the most important thing is the relationship between you and God that you must work on solely.

Would you rather serve or be served, it may sound simple or strange but it is really what cuts to the core of your heart. I feel that if a person would rather serve others, then they get it. Serve does not mean sitting in a chair and dictating to people what to do but serving means cleaning up after something, opening a door, helping, lending a hand. I ask you to look at what you are doing in the body of Christ is it for your name or His, are ya just trying to stay busy with activities or are you trying to build up the body for His Glory.

Kind

Proverbs 12:25 An anxious heart weighs a man down, but a kind word cheers him up.

Have you shared a kind word with anyone today? It is never really that early to share a kind word with someone is it and in the same respect it is never to late either. As long as we have breath in our bodies we can always share a kind word.

In the past year I have tried to do just that for all of you. Some times the words have been better then others, some have been written well while others have been written without punctuation. It is however a kind word that comes through which is my hope. I just want you to know that you are not in this alone.

When you look around you have seen friends, relatives and maybe even yourself have been in need of an encouraging word. Even I have needed these devotional times to help me work things out. In comments that you have sent I have also been encouraged and I thank you for that.

A kind word is not mushy or touchy feely thing that once you pass it on then it is gone. Rather it is something that not only stays with the one who is encouraged by it but in a way it also encourages the one who said it. If through sharing a kind word it brings a smile to their face and a smile to yours then isn't it worth it. What better of an encouragement would it also be if you shared Christ with someone and they not only listened but also acted upon it?

It is in fact today that you might need a little boost in your walk. There is nothing more encouraging then the words of God. I guess you can find encouragement in them because they are true and trustworthy. God has never ever let you down He has always stood by your side. What is encouraging for you today, what will lift your spirit?

God will.

Boldness

Acts 4:29 Now, Lord, consider their threats and enable your servants to speak your word with great boldness.

When I was in the 7th grade I wasn't very tall okay I was short real short. I remember playing basketball one year, no this is not why I don't like basketball, anyway, it was a Saturday morning and it was an away game and we were smoking the other team so even I got in. I was playing guard and got the ball and had a clear path to the hoop. Man I should have gone it would have been an easy two or at least a foul but I didn't I froze cause there were some big guys down there by the hoop, when your 4'8" everyone is a big guy. I didn't take it to the hoop. I passed off hoping the other guy would make the shot so I would at least get an assist. What I got was a coach who pulled me and told me to sit down.

That is what we do, we pass off cause we think some one else could do a better job or they are better equipped or what not. For crying out loud give me the proverbial break. We spend too much time worrying about the threats. The threats both imagined and real we contemplate ourselves right out of the game. What it is though is someone's eternal resting place. Of where they will really spend eternity and I am not talking about a wooden or metal box. I am talking about Heaven or Hell.

What really are people threatening you with when you share God's word with them; mostly around where you live it is simply rejection. I am not talking physical or hazardous but rather just verbal. We are put off with hearing "No," really is that why you have stopped being bold cause some one told you NO. Wow how sad.

In this prayer it is being asked that the Lord consider the threats. What is a threat just words, you can't threaten me physically cause if you touch me then that is an assault. So it was asked to consider the threat, and that's what God does He considers them and then says hmm that's something I can help with so you don't worry I'll take care of ya. More than that really cause then He enables you the servant to speak with boldness, oops so sorry let me look at that OH with GREAT boldness. I gotcha so that is what we are going to do today huh is speak with great boldness? Let God consider the threat when you are in Mexico, Lanett, Tuscaloosa, Omaha, Spencer, or elsewhere He can deal with the threat and He will enable you to share His message to whom ever you meet.

Simple

Psalm 116:[6] The LORD protects the simple-hearted; when I was in great need, he saved me.

Selah

Open your heart today and let the Lord fill you. Close your eyes and open your ears and listen with your heart. Turn off tune out all of the distractions in your life and just be.

Selah

Rejoice in this moment with God as He comes to you in His fullness in the quietness. Listen to the words that He brings to you. Let His love consume you.

We often make things seem more difficult then they need to be or really are. I have seen churches put emphasis on money, programs and stuff rather then on the one whom provides the money who supply's the stuff and whom the programs are really supposed to be about. When all God really wants is a relationship with you.

It is funny but I have heard twice from two different people that we have to keep the main thing the main thing. The main thing is not the biggest and the best, the main thing is not who has the most folks in their pews, or largest check book or most CDs. The main thing is a relationship with God thru Jesus Christ.

God will always take care of you, He knows your voice, and He knows your needs and your wants. Most importantly however is that He is the one who saves you. Through no work of my hand can I save another or even myself. Through no word that I can type or say can I ensure some one's salvation. Simply through Jesus Christ I can come to have a relationship with God.

It is okay to be simple hearted to have one goal you don't have to be an overachiever you just have to know the one who wants to achieve much through you. Let me just ask you one question today. Br. H, Br. R, Doug, Walter, Shelly, Deanna, Rachel, Dr. Wynn, Randy, Kiley, Allen, Jack, Linda, Mrs. Fincher, and all of you is your heart on the main thing today is your heart on God is your message whether you present it from the pulpit or to an orphan child on a street is it on the main thing is it really?

Perspective

2 Corinthians 5:7 We live by faith, not by sight.

Have you tasted an apple lately? I mean we all have our favorite apples don't we some like red delicious while others like granny smith it takes all kinds. You have your expectation of what it will taste like when you bite into it. It will be sweet or sour, it will crunch and juice will run down the corners of your mouth and you will bit through a worm. Eegads not the worm, that wasn't a part of what your expectations were. Really you took great care to pick out the best apple you could find looking for bruises and tale-tale signs of infestations your faith was placed in what you saw and touched.

Is that how we go through the day only placing faith in what we see, what we can place our hands on. I know I have talked about this before but as with so many things I think it is a good idea to constantly challenge ourselves on. We live by faith that the next moment will be better then the next that today as we come together that there will be a tomorrow.

We can look at how bad we are feeling today and say well this bites and it rips but what has that gained you. Really are you any better of cause your crying in your soda/beer? Probably not, you are probably worse off now because you have to sit back and get over being depressed before you can deal with the problem, good job!

What better way to deal with something then to let God deal with it and have faith that He will take care of it? You are not omi anything He is, you are not that great of an organizer He is, you lack some leadership skills but He does not. Here is the hardest thing for me, by placing my faith in Him I have to take my hands off of it and sit back and watch. Ask Tam she will tell ya that I have to things just so when I am doing them.

We live by faith is not a once and awhile thing is it an everyday every moment every second thing. You don't just have faith in a idea or a plan or scheme but in the God, the one and only LORD. How can you and I possibly tweak God's plan, smack ya up along side of the head cause you and I can't. We can just be a part of it.

If today you are placing your faith in your skills and your talent then I tell you that your faith is missed placed. Live by faith act like that apple is from God and that is all that matters.

Tired

Isaiah 40:30 Even youths grow tired and weary, and young men stumble and fall;

We at times get tired not from just the 15hour days of work and church but of the constantly being on the go. Work starts at six am after work you take a break then onto church then visitation then grocery shopping. Looking at what to do where to go and what to buy for parties at Christmas time. Hours on the road to here and there, I guess the gas companies love that. There is even a countdown in shopping days till Christmas. AHHHHHHHHHHHHHHH HHHHHHHHHHHHHHHHHHHHHHHHHHHHHHHHHHHHHH

I am just flat tired.

Isaiah 40: 31 but those who hope in the LORD will renew their strength. They will soar on wings like eagles; they will run and not grow weary, they will walk and not be faint.

It isn't the bows or the eggnog it isn't the lights or the trees it is solely a time where we can and should reflect more on Christ. We get tired we get frustrated we get bored and all of these things can be rectified with Christ. You see if you are tired sleep, get some rest, if you are wore out take a nap, if you are frustrated then simplify your life by focusing on Christ if you are bored well then do the same.

What I mean is do you know the why of what you are doing, are you doing it for you, do you really think you got to do it all? Well of course you are tired and frustrated cause guess what you are not perfect you will ware yourself out. It is only in the daily renewing of our strength that we can make it. If you are physically tired rest, if you spiritually wore out seek the strength that comes from God, in other words get alone with God.

I don't think I can recall anywhere in the bible that God told us to do everything by ourselves. As a matter of fact we soar better when we soar as a flock; we can fly higher when the strength of the body climbs into the air as one. It is not your strength but the power of the Father. He is the wind beneath our wings.

That Many

Luke 1:14 He will be a joy and delight to you, and **many** will rejoice because of his birth,

Have you thought about who "they," are? Who is the them in the they that are doing all of that talking and planning and so on. Who are they and why don't they mind their own business. Okay now that I have that out of the way, you are one of the **many** that this verse was talking about.

The list of names of people that rejoice at the birth of Christ has been long and distinguished. Presidents, Kings and Farmers, (okay Doug and Fishermen) have come and lifted their voices in honor and worship and praise to the Son who was born in a manger in Bethlehem. It is funny when your in a crowd that all the voices merge into one an undistinguishable voice. Unfortunately that only happens at football games or baseball games and not at church. But look here it can happen we can come together and rejoice in the Lord, we can lift our hands along with our hearts and praise God for nothing more than because He is God and if He hasn't blessed us then being God would be worthy enough to be praised.

Matter of fact we don't have to wait till Sunday do we Russell, I mean hey can't we praise and rejoice where we are? Look can't we praise God at work can't we rejoice today because of His Birth? YES YES YES. We don't have to wait we can right now rejoice. You this day can be one of the many who rejoice because of the birth of the Christ.

He came under the radar of Herod and the world didn't take much notice only a few came to see this child in the manger. Last night I went to a Christmas party and while Adam was reading about Christ who was born Crystal's baby started to coo and cry a little. I don't know but it reminded me that this is how Christ came into the world. He was born and was a baby and did the baby things. When the Shepherds came around was Jesus asleep in the hay or was He hungry.

You are one of the many, aren't you? I wonder if Mary and Joseph really had any idea how many would rejoice at the Birth of Christ. Are you going to rejoice, how about today?

Possible

Matthew 19:26 Jesus looked at them and said, "With man this is impossible, but with God all things are possible."

Why did Christ come, seems a little hard for a Monday morning huh well it is really simple, to make the impossible possible.

Life is not the ant and the rubber tree plant, sorry it is a nice story but alas it is just a story that some use to motivate folks to not give up. That's cool and all but why not get motivated by God's word this morning. You can see something and say well I can't do that and that is as far as you will ever go. Sometimes we stop at the foot of the mountain because you don't think you can climb that high and for the most part you are right. Then again if the rope is weaved together with God's own hands and He is your climbing partner can you think of any better place to be?

We as Christians should stop thinking in terms of black and white what is solely before us, things that we can judge and plan but rather we should see what God has in store for us. There is no better way to get through today then if you release it into God's hands. It doesn't matter a great deal to me if you are a cook or accountant, nurse or cardio – tech if what you do today you seek the impossible with God you will find it possible.

You and I come up short we just do there is nothing really too wrong with that unless we use our lack of skill or knowledge as a crutch that is wrong. It means that we lack faith that God will provide for us what we need, and that is just wrong. Dare the impossible in God's sight He will make it possible. Dream the dream live in the possible, live in the light that brings life see it clearly don't let doubt or self dependence get in your way rely on the Father who loves you and He will be there as your climbing partner as you scale the mountain.

Meaning

John 6:47 I tell you the truth, he who believes has everlasting life.

I was listening to Chicago 17 and *You're the Inspiration* the other day well actually it is playing now. When this first came out I was just out of high school and to most folks it has some sort of sentimental attachments but then as I listened to it the words took on a different thought. I know it is not a Christian song in any stretch of the imagination up till now but who better to get inspiration from then God huh can you answer me that.

What do you get inspiration from, a song, a story, a devotional, a picture or just what? Sure maybe all of these things but really there is more than that isn't there, sure there is and He is called God, He is the Great I Am and He is the inspiration. We can look all around and see what it is that He has given us and done for us and how He leads us on. When you stop and look at a sunset or sunrise you see God's hand.

You see this everlasting life is something that is just as real as God, just as real as the sunrise. Christ is so much more than a picture of a babe in a manger but He ascended in the end to sit at His, our Father's right hand. Who is it then that you believe in that now He sits upon His throne. God.

Everlasting life begins or began today or when you first believed in Christ, but let me ask you something. Do you live a life that shows you believe that you have eternal life or are you just so focused on the what if and the whys of life. Eternal life is just that it is everlasting and with God it will be so much more then anything ever you have experienced while your two feet have been on this earth.

IF God is your inspiration then you will not only want to live but you will also want a life that is lived for Him.

Remember

Psalm 3:3 But you are a shield around me, O LORD; you bestow glory on me and lift up my head. [4] To the LORD I cry aloud, and he answers me from his holy hill.

Selah

It seems to me that today would be a good day to look at our lives and acknowledge what a wonderful God we serve. It also accurse to me that we are in no less of a battle this day and age as David was in his time and just as it was true for David so to is it going to be for us. GOD will be and GOD will answer our cry.

David was attacked physically with sword and spear, he was chased out of town and hid in a cave. The weapons have changed but the desired outcome is still the same. If your going to stand up for God then you will be attacked, if you are not under attack then are you really standing up for Him at all.

The world has weapons of words, court orders, ignorance and hate and we protect ourselves by retreating in the cave but we don't call it a cave we call it a building. When was the last time you really stepped out for Christ?

Do we put on our armor daily and if so do we then go into the fray, do we have faith that truly God will be our shield around us? It's okay if we admit it because once you see the problem then you can solve it or maybe we can CRY OUT IN A LOUD VOICE to the

LORD who will hear and will answer from His Holy Hill. Our God THE only God is not impotent or weak nor are His servants.

Your shield is the shield of the Most High; your armor has been forged through time and with loving hands with great care. When you are in need He is there to lift up your head when you may feel you don't have the strength to go on. To you I say not only stand the gap but also put on His shield, there is nothing that we can do by ourselves but with God all will be glorified.

Blessing

Luke 24:51 While he was blessing them, he left them and was taken up into heaven.

How blessed are you no really have you ever thought about those words before you said them? I don't mean this flippantly or anything like that but really how blessed are you? God's blessing are a continual thing just as when Christ was ascending to heaven to take His rightful place He was still blessing those around Him, just as it is today for the blessings have not stopped.

You have a wife or husband who loves you even though we don't show it all the time they way they would want us to we know that they still love us. You have children who have been a blessing to you, sure they have made you angry and sad still how much more joy have they brought you. You don't have a house but rather if you are like I am it is a home, Thanks Tam. You have friends like I do that would be all of you and some really close friends whom if you are like me if they wanted to attack hell with a bucket of water you would go with them. You have cars and trucks, clothes and suits, food and water all that you will ever need and more. Do you still not see God pouring out His Blessings still?

Okay that is cool so look deeper. If you have acknowledged Christ as Lord and Savior of your life and that you are a sinner who was saved by the shedding of His blood for you then on the third day He was raised from the dead by His Father, our Father. Still not convinced you are blessed well then I am sorry because you will not understand it. Up until you acknowledged Christ you were just a spoiled brat with your hand out, after you acknowledged Christ you became a new creation, yes you did cause now you understand that it wasn't stuff but blessings that you had received.

Christ even now is sitting with DAD and asking Him to continually pour out His blessings upon us. In the quietness of the morning when my mind is in idle I ponder the blessings of family and friends and who each one of you are and I know that you to me are a blessing from God Himself.

Tam, Amanda, Daniel, Doug, Julie, Walter, Russell, Kevin, Will, Jan, David G, David J, Steven, Tim, Hugh, Jo Anne, Deanna, Rachael, Helen, Kathleen, Danita and all of you.

What are we seeking?

Matthew 7:7 "Ask and it will be given to you; seek and you will find; knock and the door will be opened to you.

As you look around and go through your day what is it that you're after, what is it you seek and where is it that you have looked? Poser, no I don't think so but I hope the answer is clear.

Do we ask? Do we seek? I have nothing but questions this day. Are you seeking what God has in store for you have you asked Him what it is all about? Have you looked for the answer or ran away from it, do you dare knock on the door? Are you waiting till Sunday for the pastor to fill you in on what God has for you?

All I can say is don't be afraid, don't worry and be encouraged cause God Loves you and that is why when you ask you receive and when you seek you will find and when you knock the door will be opened for you. It is with your heart that you do all of these things not solely with words or actions but with a true heart of love.

I cannot explain it but to compare it to God or me. You see when some one asks me something I can't always provide, when they seek something from me it wears me out, and yes some times when some one knocks at my door and I know who it is and what it is they want I may not open the door. Where as God can give you what you ask, can provide for what you seek and will open the door for you if only you knock. God is not just a figment of ones imagination but rather

He IS. Who else can do the things He does, who else provide the things He does?

It is what you are seeking and why you seek it that matters, are you seeking happiness then where are you looking, have you really asked in faith, have you opened up God's word to find the answers, are you knocking half heartedly or with the expectation of the door being answered?

Seek God first, ask God First, Knock on His Door and He will let you in. If on this day you feel just a little run down then have you been looking for happiness in the wrong place? What are you going to do to change that?

7 a.m.

Ecclesiastes 3:[4] a time to weep and a time to laugh, a time to mourn and a time to dance,

What time do you have, you got time to laugh do you got time to dance do you have the time to weep? Why not, if you don't have time to live then what is it you are doing? I am sorry but I don't get it, if you can't express joy and celebration and even getting tear up about stuff then what are you doing just going through the motions. If I may how is that working for you, feel like you have missed out on some stuff.

There is always a time to laugh, I have seen some of the most gut busting side splitting laughter at a visitation/wake when people remember what they did. I am sure mine will be a quiet event where people can only stand around and say how solemn I was and how quiet. Forget it people remember the most awkward moments in their life and that makes us bust a gut.

A time to dance could this be when your first child was born or when you got married or when some once accepts Christ or when some one is baptized or when some one goes out on mission. When do you dance, I guess this is kind of like saying make a joyful noise well it doesn't say dance well like a ballerina or what ever it just says there is a time to dance. But alas we only dance to the tune we want to hear and ridicule or ignore the tune others dance to.

Weeping is the one that I most often have problems expressing. You see I had just never been a weepy sort, pout yes weep no. I find of late though that tears well up when I hear of folks that don't have family around during the holidays or kids without parents or a mom or dad at any time. What do you weep for, if you think you weep for yourself then look at it again is it weeping or pouting?

I guess all in all when you think about how it is that God has changed you and how He continues to mature you in faith and in love then do you hold it in or do you express it. You see if you hold it in then you will be filled and it will stop and grow stagnate there will be no more room in your heart but for yourself. If you however let it out and share the joy, the pain, the happiness with others then it will always stay fresh and vibrant.

Live the life that God wants to share with you.

What is in a Blessing

Numbers 6:22The LORD said to Moses, [23] "Tell Aaron and his sons, 'This is how you are to bless the Israelites. Say to them:

> [24] " ' "The LORD bless you
> and keep you;
> [25] the LORD make his face shine upon you
> and be gracious to you;
> [26] the LORD turn his face toward you
> and give you peace." '

[27] "So they will put my name on the Israelites, and I will bless them."

May the LORD *barak* you and shamar you, may the Lord shine His paniym upon you.

Barak – baw-rak is bless, there are about 20 + things that go into the definition of this way to bless, from encouragement to kneeling to a thank you. Which in and of itself is what a blessing is, it is something more than we can touch and taste it is what has been given to us. It is the breath that you take it is the sky you view it is the kind words that are shared between friends it is the honor of giving of time. You can not think of just one way that you have been blessed you have been barak(ed) in so many ways but let me ask you have you been a barak to someone today.

Shamar – shaw-mar is to hedge about; to guard. This is not you who guards yourself is it but it is God who guards you, this hedge that has been placed around you has been placed there by God. We don't often think that of God's protection on a day to day basis but it is. To many times we only think of His protection after we have gotten into trouble or the arrows have already flown. We step out of His protection because why, we think we can do it ourselves. Stand in the hedge that God has placed around you. Can't see it well look at your family, look at your friends I can't tell you how many times Walter has helped to remind me of God's protection and in this way God has strengthened the hedge even more.

Paniym – Paw-neem is countenance, and what is His countenance but His presence. If God used words to create the earth and stars and well how about everything then what do you think His countenance can do? We all know people who when they enter a room those already in the room take notice is this not the same thing with God. If He is with you do others take notice, sure they do. It is not really all that much of an imagination stretches as a matter of fact why you think you can meet someone who is a Christian and within moments you have a kinship, doink it is God's paniym.

Lights On

John 1 [4]In him was life, and that life was the light of men. [5]The light shines in the darkness, but the darkness has not understood it.

W ho drives with their lights on all of the time, night or day? Why?

1. *What are the safety advantages of DRLs? Daytime running lights are a low-cost method to reduce crashes. They are especially effective in preventing daytime head-on and front-corner collisions by increasing vehicle conspicuity and making it easier to detect approaching vehicles from farther away. Insurance Institute for Highway Safety*

Even in the day the world is in darkness what is darkness in this sense? Sin, evil, what?

We are supposed to be the DRLs and Christ is the light that shines from them. People are supposed to be able to recognize the light in us that shines forth from us. Are we finding that we have tried to drive with the lights off cause it makes us less conspicuous? Sure we figure we can flip on those lights if we sense danger or when the sun goes down. We can have the bumper sticker on and the license plate frame that reads God is MY Pilot but what shines is the most important thing.

Do you understand the light? I mean hey do you get what the light is about, do you stand in the light, and are you a light reflector? In many ways I once fought the light, its not that I didn't know Christ but still I fought against what the light revealed in my life. We have so many petty things that the light reveals each day to us yes we got some major things also. You see this light is not there in a blaring sort of way making you blind but rather it is there to help you see.

This light is not of man but of God as a matter of fact it is GOD. See God is not out to get you to belittle you or put you down but with His light you can see. Because of Christ the whole word could see both Jew and Gentile all now have the opportunity to walk in the light. Sin doesn't understand the light the only thing sin knows is that it is revealed by the light.

Are you walking in the light or do you have one foot in darkness? Why?

Have you decreased?

John 3:30 He must become greater; I must become less.

John 4:34 My food," said Jesus, "is to do the will of him who sent me and to finish his work.

Have you found that you have been on the decrease here of late, not talking about a diet or getting demoted or anything like that? Is it your will that you are after or some one else's? As a matter of fact what is this whole *will* thing anyway?

Tseba (tseb-aw) wishes, please.

Isn't it about time that we stopped with the fluff and stuff and really just got down to basics? No I am not talking music or traditional or contemporary or blended or what not simply this, who's will are you trying to go by? John came before Christ and knew that when Christ came and started His ministry that he would diminish in prominence. Even Christ knew that He was not there to do what He wanted to do but rather He was there to do the will the tseba the wishes of the Father.

Should we think of ourselves more better (yes I know) than Christ? You see do you really think that Christ wanted to come as a babe, to go around preaching and teaching and being constantly harassed with question and comments from those who should have known better, do you think Christ really wanted to die on the cross. Are any of you or am I running to put ourselves in such a predicament, nope I don't think so. Christ did all of these things for us because this is what His Father wished or willed Him to do and Christ was obedient to His Fathers will or wishes.

If it were all about you it would be okay but it is not, what right we have to tell God No. I understand that we do tell Him no a lot more often then we tell Him Yes. No Father I just don't feel like reading your word, No God I don't think I can make it to Sunday School, Nope I aint gonna sing that song God just cause I don't like it and No God I just told it like it is and if their feelings got hurt well then so be it. Is it ever God's will or wishes to be away from you by His choice, is it His will or wishes that you only worship Him on your grounds, really is it His wishes or will that we should assault one another with harsh words. IS your faith about doing what you wish?

If it is still about you then you have not stepped to the side and grown less and you have not allowed Him to increase in your life. Simply this, the choice is yours are you going to do His will or your will?

How

Romans 12:21 Do not be overcome by evil, but overcome evil with good.

It is just a word and it is so basic that it is missed, overcome. You cannot overcome evil by yourself you need to overcome evil with good and God is Good. Really does it seem overwhelming that you should overcome evil only with God? Think about it, rather think about what it is that has been trying to overcome you is it evil or just evil in disguise?

Our thoughts and actions what we do and how we act reflect what it is that we are overcome with right? How we live our lives is much more than just what others see. Now I don't want you to get this wrong but so much of the stuff in our lives may not be evil in and of itself however if the stuff in our lives keeps us from a one on one relationship with God then what have we become overcome with.

Sometimes I wonder if we put as much effort into a growing maturing relationship with God as we do into slinging stepping worrying prideful things of my way or your way or traditional ways or modern ways then how much better off we would be. You see I know that is something that is totally individual only you can answer that, only you can see what it is that you have let overcome your life.

I do however remember and think of what it is that I once thought would make me happy. The stuff the things the dollars just about everything but God, never really thought about how God can overcome the sorrow the hurt. He does though you know; He can overcome everything as a matter of FACT His Son Jesus overcame the grave.

Overcoming adversity doesn't matter as much as how you overcome adversity does it.

This next year what is it really no scratch that not next year but how about today what is it that has gotten in the way? Travel, work, cars, boats, golf, games, or just plain stuff what ever it is that is what you need to look at.

Today and Tomorrow

John 4:24 God is spirit, and his worshipers must worship in spirit and in truth."

The lady at the well ya know she was not sick, or crippled or about to be stoned she did not go to the well because Jesus was there she went cause she had to get water for cooking or cleaning. What does that have to do with worshiping, I don't know but maybe it was the everyday routine of what she was doing. Look is it so hard to see yourself going through your day doing what you normally do and running smack dab into Christ. Maybe now just maybe though we should be the ones looking for the opportunity to witness to someone at the well.

Is church about worshiping is spirit and in truth or is it about doing things an established way a set guideline to meet your maker. The routine of life is a traitorous thing because it is almost the biggest distraction that we have because we have seen it all before.

Worship is not about anything more then God and expressing your love solely for HIM. Take a breath, inhale the goodness and the sweetness that is the LORD, and take it in. The simple breath that you take, the air that fills your lungs, the oxygen that is absorbed into your bloodstream that is pumped throughout your body that permeates every fiber of your being. Ex-hale as streams of airflows out of your lungs past your vocal cords and out of your mouth, this air still contains live saving oxygen.

So to it should be with your worship as you breathe in the spirit and it fills your every fiber of your being an indwelling of love that supplies everything, it is not just absorbed into your blood stream but also into your heart, your soul your thoughts and your actions. As you ex-hale you have the opportunity to share the truth with some one else today, that very moment there is enough breath to share the love of Christ with some one.

In your routine of work or play, in your daily grind of doing the normal things the normal way understand that He is with you, in your breath in the truth that you speak and share. Worshiping is not about filling a pew or being Baptist, Catholic, Lutheran, Methodist, or Presbyterian but rather it is if you have the spirit of truth in you and that you worship in spirit and truth.

God is the breath of life, not just life here but life with Him for eternity

Fish where the fish are

Matthew 4:19 "**Come**, follow me," Jesus said, "and I will make you fishers of men."

I went out deer hunting this past New Year and I know your first thought is the deer have nothing to worry about. True enough the deer had nothing to worry about and according to the guy I went hunting with it was a combination of the things that I did wrong, one not the most stealthy of people, two I wore leather shoes and apparently they smell human, three we went out at the wrong time of day. I happen to still think if was the neon sign that I carried with me that said hunter here with a neon finger pointing at me.

It occurred to me that we are a lot like the hunters as Christians we act like we got to be wearing this that or the other thing. That we have to go through this program then this discipleship class then this step then look at this target group or that section or this list and on and on and on. When really all we have to do is COME.

You see we can talk a good game about how we are going to reach people for Christ, okay I mean me. That if we/I do this then I'll be ready but what happens then is there is still an excuse that comes up to keep you from coming. It is true when it is said that this world is dying and waiting to hear the good news, what they are waiting on is you and I to get equipped how much longer are they going to have to wait?

Look let me make this plain for you, that sister of yours who thinks that Jesus was just a good philosopher like Mohammad or Buddha when are you going to stand up and say look sis I love you but you are just wrong. How about that brother who is drunk at family reunions when are you going to tell him about being drunk with the Holy Spirit. You see if you don't step up to the plate then who will, are you waiting for missionaries to come to your house so they can tell them. If we keep waiting guess what will happen our friends and families will spend eternity in hell.

You just come and follow, that's it just come can you do that? Sure it aint hard to open a door and follow Christ. Let Him make you the fisherman let Him make you the fishers of men. It isn't your tools but His; it is not your education or skill but His.

Get up Go out and Follow

What's Next

Psalm 150

[1] Praise the LORD . [1]

Praise God in his sanctuary; praise him in his mighty heavens.

[2] Praise him for his acts of power; praise him for his surpassing greatness.

[3] Praise him with the sounding of the trumpet, praise him with the harp and lyre,

[4] praise him with tambourine and dancing, praise him with the strings and flute,

[5] praise him with the clash of cymbals, praise him with resounding cymbals.

[6] Let everything that has breath praise the LORD .

Praise the LORD .
You ever just need a boost, I mean an extra kick in the pants? That is what I need today just a little smack, don't even think about it Kevin. After Christmas, after the New Year's, after hearing about the mission trip to Mexico, after Thanksgiving really after being on top of the mountain and seeing wondrous things that God has done. It is almost as if my body wants to go back down to get some rest. Or is it just me?

Then I think about what comes next, today and tomorrow come next and why should I not seek after God today. Maybe you don't think this is the right verse to talk about seeking after God well have you ever thought that praising God is all about being in His presence. I mean that look at verse one, Praise the LORD, Praise the Great I AM, Praise Yahweh, Praise the personal GOD who lives. Where is He at but in His Sanctuary in His mighty Heavens?

Why do we praise Him but because we have seen His acts of power we have felt His Surpassing Greatness. Your body maybe tired may need just to get some rest after running all over Alabama, Mississippi, Tennessee, Minnesota, Iowa, Nebraska or Timbuktu but in your heart your soul leaps for joy and resounds with praise for the God you have seen.

How on this day are you going to praise GOD, with harp, lyre, tambourine, dance, strings, flute, clash of cymbals, no no with resounding cymbals really it doesn't matter what you use as long as you PRAISE THE LORD. How about this thou that since you have breath that is since you have wind, since you have a soul why not praise God with your voice, your soul your heart! Let your heart be filled with joy for the Lord sits on His throne in His greatness and He thinks about you and looks after you even now, just as He will tomorrow and the day after and the day after.

The Vigil Is On

Luke 12:40 You also must be ready, because the Son of Man will come at an hour when you do not expect him."

What is it that you are keeping your eye out for? Have you ever had a spotter who would sound the alarm if your parents were coming, now not that I was ever a bad kid, right Rachel and Deana (nudge-nudge)? Anyway we would have some one keeping an eye out so we could get things straightened out as quickly as possible, like a minute or two was enough time to get things cleaned up after some of the messes we created. Inevitably we always got caught. Then when we got older we would send our younger brothers out and see if they would get caught and by some strange reason we still got in trouble. Go figure?

Are you ready for Christ to come back? No really are you ready for the sky to split and for the heavens to open up and for Christ to come and claim His church. Really then what is it that you are doing right now that makes you think you are ready. Relying on what you did in the past just aint going to be getting it. We are supposed to keep vigil until He comes back or He calls us home take you pick but either way it isn't up to you or I.

We have had our day, now it is time for the younger folks to do it, I am tired, I am retired. But I don't know how, I haven't ever done that before, look the older folks have done it let them continue to do it. Isn't that where we have gotten to, haven't we stopped looking at Christ and started looking at what we are doing? Have we been doing the things we do just so's we can say we did them or are we doing them because the Master told us to and we don't want to be found slothful when He comes back.

Hasn't this been a large part of why Satan has been laughing cause when we sit down and focus on ourselves we don't see that another day has passed and another person has not been witnessed to or told about Christ? When we only see ourselves then we have taken ourselves out of God's plan, for His plan is not just about the one but also about the many.

In time we grow still, in time we grow complacent, in time we grow comfortable and comfort is nice. Look it isn't our physical comfort we should be about though; rather it should be the one who provides the comfort. We should be on vigil in anticipation of Christ's return, in your life you may be just the beginning or you could be in the early morning hours but whatever the time what ever the condition you must be keeping watch for His return.

Said

Matthew 3:17 And a voice from heaven said, "This is my Son, whom I love; with him I am well pleased."

How many of us have stories to tell about what Christ has done for us in our lives?

It is not difficult to think of is it, those things that you consider blessings or how He helped you get through school when you were away from family, or how He brought you to Valley Alabama, or just about any number of things that He has done for you. Isn't it easy to think of the things in your life that God has done for you Mark? Look Christ hadn't even done really anything spectacular that is documented yet when God spoke these words, really the only thing that Christ had done so far was to be born and to be obedient, way before the feeding of the 5000 or the healing of the blind, leapers, cripples, sick and possessed. Even before changing water into wine.

This is my Savior who died for me and rose again, this is my teacher who taught me to love you before myself, this is my God who was there in the beginning and spoke the world into existence this is truly the GREAT I AM. If telling anyone about your love of Christ makes you a holly roller then by all means roll on, if letting people know that you seek to please your Father in heaven first and it makes them uncomfortable then go ahead and make them squirm. I am sorry but we are really supposed to please the Father.

In this next year what will you say in words about God, how will your actions bring a smile to God's face? Is it that you said that you are going to read the bible thru and thru or how about you are going to read the bible thru and thru to learn and grow and apply what it ALL says? What about you are going to turn over a new leaf when in fact the other side of a leave is virtually the same as the other why not burn the leaf instead?

What will be said of you this next year is not as important as what you will say? Will you Kevin talk about Christ more, not just in song but one on one with words, Russell will you be so centered on Christ that even on the golf course folks will see that you are a Pastor, Doug will you be bold for Christ will you seek His face every day, Rodney will you give your life to Him and rely on God? What joy Paula it will give God when we place all of our faith in Him, that our bodies may be tired but our souls will be joyful?

When will we hear God say to us, these are my sons and daughters in them I am well pleased?

What is it?

Matthew 21:14 The blind and the lame came to him at the temple, and he healed them.

What is it that I am missing, what is it that I don't see am I blind am I unable to see what it is that makes me lame?
What is it that you are looking for?
I think of times in my life where I have just sat in church and closed my eyes and thought of You Jesus and what You have done for me. Not just the cross or the tomb or the manger but today sitting there thinking of You and just seeing with my heart the love you have. I think sometimes it is a good thing to close my eyes and not be distracted by the physical perception of people. I guess that is kind of why I like doing heart checks not for others but for myself.

You see we have all come to the temple blind and lame at one point or other in our lives in one fashion or the other. Look we didn't see with our hearts we didn't look with love we only saw what we saw and perceived what the input of that data was. This is where our infirmity lays this is where we are lame by our own heart closed up and sealed.

Blind and lame = attitude and action

What happens when God opens your eyes, you no longer bump into the wall or door. What happens why you are healed when you have been made to see and your lame(ness) has bee dealt with? Open your eyes and see what it is, open your eyes and see who He is.

How much more rejoicing there would be if we let God do church and heal our sight and cure our lameness. Why are you going to church on Sunday, what is it you hope to see, do you need to get healed?

Recognized

John 21:4 Early in the morning, Jesus stood on the shore, but the disciples did not realize that it was Jesus.

I am the worst at remembering names, faces maybe I can do okay on but names nope. Even the first time I met Tam the next time I saw her I couldn't remember her name. I remember there were a few of us sitting at some tables outside of the NCO club and I was waiting for some one to call her by name. Well here were a few guys who had walked with Christ for three or so years and didn't realize it was Christ on the shore.

It was not until the nets had been re-cast on the other side of the boat and the catch had been hauled in partially that the disciple whom Jesus loved realized it was Jesus who told them where to fish. Only after something happened did they realize that it was Christ, then instead of dropping everything one got dressed and then thy towed the fish in and then they counted the fish and checked the nets. Sure you could make a case that Peter may have when up to Christ and gave Him a hug then helped the others.

Here is my question, how do you recognize Christ?

If that seems difficult to answer then how can those whom we are supposed to witness to how can they recognize Christ in you?

Since we are supposed to be Christ-like, striving to be like Christ should our actions and words be what Jesus would do and not just wearing a bracelet that has WWJD on it. The world is looking for God sometimes they only find a god in stuff and smoke. We should be recognized as Christians not by the size of a building or the bank accounts or glitz and glamour but rather by how are hearts are focused on love and serving and teaching and building up of the person and encouraging and striving to be a light in the world. After all we are just a tool to be used by God we are just the flashlight case to God's light that shines forth.

Do people recognize Christ in you?

Sense

Matthew 9:29 Then he touched their eyes and said, "According to your faith will it be done to you";

How in tune are your senses, do you need Christ to touch your ears, eyes, nose, mouth or heart?

Whether it is hunting, fishing or playing golf it is amazing to me how much your senses have to be dialed in. When fishing you feel the bite of a fish which is 10 to 15 yards away, but just sense that it is a fish rather then dragging the line over a rock, you wait for the bang–bang-bang so you can cross its eyes as you set the hook. When hunting you wait looking and listening for the turkey or deer, sitting still ears and eyes scanning your surroundings but not wanting to move too much because the prey is also looking and listening. In golf when you draw the club head back and when it has reached its peak you accelerate it forward to strike the ball and sensing how it hits the club face you can tell if you shank it or slice it or just hit is straight and long (my favorite).

What senses will you use today, probably all of them do ya think? Okay maybe physically that will work but what about according to your faith, which senses are you going to use today? Yes by your faith are you going to see, by your faith are you going to listen, by your faith will you smell and taste with your heart will you sense the things that are going on around you.

Their eyes were blind but their faith was not, they were healed weren't they, just as your sight was given to you when you accepted Christ as Lord and Savior. Your eyes were open you ears open your sense of smell and taste not for flavor or sent where broadened. There was a change in you; after all it was your heart that changed.

When you see with your heart your senses pick up the different things. It is not a time for us to be self-absorbed by what we only can see, or touch, or taste, or smell or hear. Rather it is at time to be led by our hearts, your heart is filled with the Holy Spirit it will expand your senses.

Let me ask you something, do you know someone who is hurting, do you know someone who needs to hear the good news, do you sense the Savior close at hand? If you can't then maybe you do need Christ to heal your heart, or eyes or ears or touch so you can feel again so you can see and hear again so you can experience life more abundantly so you can have the joy of using all of your senses to worship GOD.

Intentional

John 13:38 Then Jesus answered, "Will you really lay down your life for me? I tell you the truth, before the rooster crows, you will disown me three times!

As I sit here this morning or dwelt upon last night, what are no rather what are my reasons for being a Christian and how is my Christianity intentional. It seems to be that one thing keeps coming up for me lately is Peter and his ups and downs. Let me ask you a question well how about this why don't you look at the question that Jesus asked Peter but in turn really asks all of us. "Will you really lay down your life for me?" Have we disowned Christ three times before the rooster crowed?

Have you and I really laid down our life for Christ, have we gotten rid of the stuff that hinders us from really serving Christ fully? At times that is a resounding yes but unfortunately that is usually just on Sunday at church when it should be a Monday at work. How do you make your Christianity intentional but unless you grow in Christ and do what He says through the Holy Spirit and not do stuff just for the sake of doing.

Now I am not talking about getting rid of golf or fishing or needle point if that is what floats your boat but rather the stuff that you and I do that gets in the way of witnessing for Christ. We talk about following through on stuff but so seldom do, we say well that would be a good idea but I got to get this done first. It seems we are still worried about people standing around a fire warming themselves wondering if they will point their finger at us and call us Christian's.

Well we are and we are supposed to be different we are supposed to be Holy, we are supposed to be making a difference we are supposed to be bringing the light into the world, we are we are we are but we don't. If we only bring the light with us when we come to church how bright is that light going to appear when it is surrounded by light itself? It won't stand out it just won't.

Really will you lay down your life, your comfort, your pride, your weakness, your sin for Christ really will you do that? Not sometime in the future but today try now. My reasons for being a Christian is solely cause someone knocked on the door and I invited Him in and now I choose to live for Him. Daily seeking daily being intentional about how we can support and encourage and grow His Kingdom, Thy Will be Done Oh LORD.

Sin

Luke 5:8 When Simon Peter saw this, he fell at Jesus' knees and said, "Go away from me, Lord; I am a sinful man!"

Why does God want to use us when we are weak and sinful? Now I know that each of you are far better than I, knowing that I am just weak and have to be constantly watching out for where to avoid sin then blinking and finding myself in sin. It isn't the sin that God uses but the sinner, it isn't the sin that Christ came to make clean but rather it is to wash the sinner clean of their sin. Nothing gets out the stain of sin like the blood of Christ.

Peter knew what he had done in his life, he knew the things that were sinful and probably kept on doing them up until this point. Having done them and knowing that they were wrong and then having Christ in your boat or house or heart and being convicted of those sins fell Peter to his knees. Peter knew who he was, Peter was a fisherman who lived on the wild side, maybe spent to much time living in sin then even learning to fish but that is a different story.

Why Peter, why Fran, why Doug, why Hugh, why Tim why RV well why not, who better to work through? What better place to start, after all if it was just up to man then it wouldn't matter but since it is up to God why not use folks who people will see and say not that must be God cause that aint the Fran or Doug or Hugh or Tim or RV that I know.

Christ didn't let Peter off of the hook, (fish joke) but rather He reeled him in (another fish joke) and caught him and taught Him the released him back into the lake (third times a charm fish joke). Do you really think Christ is going to let you off of the hook if you whine your way out of stuff? No Christ sorry I just aint good enough, doink HE KNOWS THAT! You see HE IS GOOD ENOUGH to use you, through you.

I am not nowhere near good enough to think God could ever use this Iowa country, one of 17, worked on a farm, de-tasseled corn, walked/ran on the wild side boy but you know what He don't let me off of the hook either.

Let me just ask you one thing more. If you are away from Christ for even one minute do you feel the separation or are you just waiting for Sunday to get a fresh touch from Him?

Shallow or Substance

Hebrews 11: 1 Now faith is the assurance of things hoped for, the conviction of things not seen.

There is an old adage in golf, drive for show and putt for doe. You can drive it 300 yards and get it on the green in two but if it takes you 4 putts to put it in then that is still a double bogey so what good has that done ya, putting is where the score is. How is your faith is it out there going three hundred yards then when it gets down to having to really use your faith then that is where it takes you a while to get it.

You see we struggle at times with a lot of junk, with things that we can no more control then the sun coming up this morning. So to is the marching on of life and death it will happen and there is nothing we can do about it. That being said what is it then that you and I have faith in, where we will be after we pass away from this life and meet our Maker. Can I just get personnel with you after all it is just you and I here.

Open up your eyes and meet your MAKER today. Faith, assurance, hope, conviction none of which you can see and touch. It is what is just as much as it is what it will be tomorrow. Moses didn't live a life that didn't have hardships, Sarah didn't live a life that was full of her children, the both lived by the faith that they had in God that God would be true to His word. They were obedient and yes they were disobedient at times but the one thing they didn't do was quit.

Have we quit, has our faith been shallow, have we said God this world is to far gone for even you to make a difference. Faith with Substance is not a faith that withers but a faith that continues to grow a Faith that sees that instead of a world far to gone but a world that is ready for God. If God moves today will you join Him, if God starts revival with the members of His Body latch on and get their feet with Him, is the body ready are you ready.

Our churches should not be the pretty oh and ah three hundred yard drive put the consistent stroke of a putt that sends the ball to its home.

RE-vive- all

Psalm 80:18 Then we will not turn away from you; revive us, and we will call on your name.

Have you ever left a banana sit out until it is brown and yellow till it looks like it is only fit to trash and then wondered who it was to take that banana and put it in bread and make banana bread. The banana found new life as a different item. Okay I know it is scary some of the things that I think of.

Really you and I are the bananas sorry if you don't find that appealing. We are though we have been bruised with the sin in our lives until we accepted Christ's forgiveness we were sitting on a shelf and getting ready for the trash heap. Even now that we have Christ's forgiveness we still find ourselves having at times turned away from Christ, we find excuses that we are not good enough or its to hard or this that or the other thing and yes Dr. Wynn I know how you feel about excuses.

How about today, how about today we do not turn away from Him, how about we ask Him to fill us and revive us and then after we have been revived we call upon His name. He wants to revive us ALL. Revival is to have everyone be revived but it has to start with Him and your relationship with Him.

The Dump

John 15:1 "I am the true vine, and my Father is the gardener. [2]He cuts off every branch in me that bears no fruit, while every branch that does bear fruit he prunes [1] so that it will be even more fruitful.

I was cleaning out the garage a couple of weeks ago and it is funny how much "stuff" we have acquired. Sure it was after Christmas so we had the boxes and paper from that, then there were items that didn't sell at the garage sale, then there were things that I had no idea where they came from. As a side note, no Tupperware was damaged during the cleaning of the garage; all of it was treated humanely. All of these things ended up at the dump for what use were they if they just sat around and collected dust?

Have you gone to the dump with things in your life? Why not are you still holding onto stuff thinking that one day you will use it? Well if you are holding on to the stuff then what are you using to hold on to God with?

Christ the vine, God the gardener, you a branch and what you do the fruit. If you are connected to the vine are you bearing the fruit that you should be or is there even room on your branch for fruit, if your branch so full of leaves that the sprout of fruit can't make it through. Well what do you think happens to a branch that doesn't bear fruit, it gets cut off.

As a Christian we need to be pruned once and a while, maybe day to day so that there is room for the fruit so that we can be even more fruitful. To many times we like the junk oops sorry stuff nope one more time the leaves, we hid behind them and cling to them but what each leaf is simply is an excuse we use not to bear fruit. Then when we do give just a little of our time with a half hearted effort then the fruit really isn't even worth the effort it is as if it has rotted before it could be picked.

If you and I don't care about what kind of fruit we bear then why should God? He does though; He does care what kind of fruit you bear and that is why the pruning shears are in His hands and sometimes pruning hurts.

When was the last time you the branch used the vine to talk to the gardener? When is the last time you went to the garden house seeking the Father? I would like to say something catchy and funny here but it escapes me so the only thing is just this. The gardener loves ya, and is waiting and pruning and nourishing you, He is waiting for the fruit but waiting is not forever we must bear fruit.

Road

Matthew 7:14 But small is the gate and narrow the road that leads to life, and only a few find it.

When I was a kid and would travel the back roads in Iowa some of those dirt roads grew kind a narrow and you would keep an eye out for dust clouds so you could slow up and get on the other side of the road instead of driving down the middle. It would not be a good thing to come up on a tractor but since it was flat enough you could see for miles ahead of you and avoid the hazards, most of the time.

The gate is small and the road is narrow but there is still a gate and still a road. What would it be like if there were no gate and no road? Thru Christ there is both but only a few have chosen this road. We don't have to look out for dust clouds heading our way because we should all be heading the same direction.

This road is not strung with obstacles or pitfalls but rather it is smooth and easy to walk. I think the problems come when instead of walking down the center of the road we walk down the side maybe just to see where it is everyone else is at or maybe we try to keep one foot on the road and one foot in the ditch. That is where the pitfalls and obstacles are right along the road in the ditch.

Have you ever thought that when you are walking that there is a point in your gate that one foot is down and the other is lifted? I know it seems strange to think about it but it is true, unless you drag your feet Kevin I know. Should we as Christians be dragging our feet anyway? When I think of people dragging their feet I think that maybe they really don't want to get where they are going.

When we stumble it isn't because of the road but it is where we placed our feet.

I don't think of this road as just a simple cow or goat trail but as a one-lane road winding through forests and hills. There is room for many more on the road the gate may be narrow but it will not close until the last of those who have traveled the narrow road pass through it. If we cling together on this road and encourage others to stay on this road then that is only just part of what we are to do. You see not only do we stumble and fall off of this road but so do the people on the wide road; they wonder off and notice this narrow road. They find that they can not get on it unless you share the message of salvation with them and then Jesus will bring them on the road and we are to take them in and help them to get their bearings or their feet.

What are your feet stepping in, are we dragging our feet, are we taking new Christians on the road and building them up are we encouraging others on the road? It is funny about those Iowa roads that even if they are narrow and dusty that they still lead home.

Way

John 14:6 Jesus answered, "I am the way and the truth and the life. No one comes to the Father except through me.

I can't think of many more controversial lines then this one can you? The world will say you are intolerant and unforgiving if you profess that there is only one way to heaven.

SO BE IT

I say this to you all, so be it, we are not unforgiving nor are we intolerant we just know the truth. We do not have to shy from it or change from it. No it is not about softening the message because it is not our message to soften but His and if He wanted it another way then He can we must follow His lead.

You see there is nothing hard about it; there are not 7 steps to heaven or this level of heaven or working your way up or going around the side. Maybe its just me and my tactless ness oops I meant my tactfulness but the only way is straight through Christ. Not as in a military obstacle but as a choice to let Him take you there because He knows the way and is willing and able to take you there to His Father's place.

I can almost picture Jesus standing there hands outstretched and open telling the disciples this in a smooth soft tone, none confrontational, not arrogant or with pride but with total desire that they understand that there is only one way and this way is open to all. Look I don't know about you but it fills me with great joy knowing that I have already accepted this way.

Look I don't want to come off as lofty or anything but do you have joy about choosing Christ, are there regrets of things that you had to leave behind? Then did you really choose at all or have you only just realized that Christ is the way, the only way. SO we will live our lives the way we want to and then when we are ready then and only then will we truly accept Christ as Lord and Savior.

It is not hard so don't make it seem that way, it is not difficult so don't live your life as woe is me. People will choose Christ when they see that Christ is making a difference in a Christian. If all we can do is fuss and fume then where is this joy of knowing that you are going to be with the Father one-day cause you choose Christ.

One Heart

One heart pumping blood to the whole body, through each vein and artery right on down to the capillaries to nourish each cell otherwise the body dies. Circulation is important isn't it, I know this guy who when it gets cold out his hands turn almost ghostly white because his circulation slows down and he has to warm up his hands so the blood flows down to his finger tips.

Casting Crowns has this song out "*If we are the body,*" in the song it ask why aren't these hands or legs or words doing what they are supposed to be doing. It is a good song and good to think about. I had a guy once tell me that he liked the Hymns because he could sit back and think about the words that are being sung.

Why is the body not doing what it was intended to do could it be as simple as there is a circulation problem? Maybe we are not beating with one heart maybe we are just acting like a body and not really being a body?

Matthew 22:37 Jesus replied: "'Love the Lord your God with all your heart and with all your soul and with all your mind."

When you and I love the Lord, rather when you and I LOVE THE LORD with all of our hearts it circulates to our entire soul and permeate our minds then our actions will be out of Love. We need to get this right; we need to stop thinking that church is about us and get back to thinking that we are church for God. There is nothing more or less than when we come to His house with the heart of worship and then, note the then; after we leave that we continue to be the body.

It is not just a Sunday morning or evening services that we work on our circulation but rather it is Monday afternoon waiting in line at Wal-Mart and you see some one struggling with their kids or at work on Thursday morning when people are just waiting for the weekend or when you hear of some one who's husband left them or someone who has just had a rough day where is the church where is the body at this time.

When in Matthew Christ was talking about the heart, soul and mind you will notice that He said *ALL* not most of or part of but all. We sometime don't do that do we sometimes we only come together part way or on our own terms well is that living a surrendered life, probably not huh? You see if we don't let God have the All that Christ was talking about then that means that there is a circulation problem, the heart isn't getting the blood to all of the members of the body.

Will you look at your circulation this morning, will you see if you love the Lord your God with all your heart with all your soul and with your entire mind? Will you see if there is blockage, will you see if maybe you need a pipe cleaner to open up the flow of blood?

Fight or Flight

John 10:12 -The hired hand is not the shepherd who owns the sheep. So when he sees the wolf coming, he abandons the sheep and runs away. Then the wolf attacks the flock and scatters it. [13]The man runs away because he is a hired hand and cares nothing for the sheep.

One of the key phrases that has been going around or maybe it's just me, could be you know how I can be, and is to *"take ownership."* Referring to what ever it is that you are doing to treat it as yours, that you are in control and that it rests with you. If it makes it or if it fails rests entirely on you. Sure you can call someone for assistance but they probably won't care as much as you do, they are just advisors or hired hands and their heart isn't in it.

Where do you see yourself in this verse? What does it mean to you? I know I express my self on a variety of views and will on this one also but understand that I do know that you may see something else in it. All I can do is share with you my heart about this and really if that helps ya that is cool but it also helps me.

So let me ask you are you the hired hand, or the sheep, or the wolf which one? Yes I didn't say Shepherd in this one cause hey that is Christ and no one else. Are you the hired hand who is there to look after the sheep maybe the shepherd is away looking for the one who wandered away and left you to look after the flock, is your heart in it. Now most of the pastors that I have met I would tell you yes their heart was and is in it. They try to lead the flock and tend to their needs and keep them together. Are you the sheep a member of the flock who try to stay together because there is strength in numbers and you feel good just standing there and just go about your business, just being a part of the flock is satisfying. Are you the wolf? Let me see a show of hands of those who thought they were the wolves, didn't think so.

Lets look at what a wolf does though, it picks the stray off, it doesn't go after the ram or the hired hand but that one who is wandering on the skirts of the flock. It attacks the vulnerability of the flock, because now maybe just maybe the sheep have strayed away looking for sweet grass instead of just being a part of the flock. WHAM the sheep is dead. A victim of not recalling what the shepherd said and did when He left the flock with the hired hand, after all whom do you think it was who called the hired hand in?

Hired hands what can we do to not flee from the wolf? Look the shepherd knows what's going on do you think He has abandoned you when stuff hits when the wolf strikes? Nope He hasn't He that being Christ is still with you He has given you a policy and procedure manual called the Bible for you. You are just to use this word, His word to keep the flock together and if the sheep are really His they will recognize His word and not flee from it when the wolf approaches.

Who's listening?

Psalm 5:3 In the morning, O LORD, you hear my voice; in the morning I lay my requests before you and wait in expectation.

Have you ever called some company and using their 1-800-656-help line and you are greeted with a "you have reached the widget manufactures of America, please listen to the following options," For English press one For Spanish press 2. Press one go ahead, would you like customer service press one, for sales press 2, for accounts payable press 3, to speak to an operator press 0, go ahead press 0, for an operator in English press one, for an operator in Spanish press 2 for all other languages press oh I don't know 3. No wonder by the time you reach an actual persons desk they are either out or not even there so go ahead and just leave a message.

Well guess who is listening to your prayers, that's right Hugh you get a star, O LORD's listening He hears your voice. There is no first dial the prayer line and then depending upon what your request is hit the appropriate button and leave a message. We don't have to go through the run around to get to God He is always listening; as a matter of fact He is always present. One thing, does God know your voice rather does He recognize it?

Yes I know God knows all things and yes that He knows who you are even to the extents of He knew you before you were in the womb and He knows how many hairs are on your head. What I am asking I guess is God expecting to hear from you or do you just drop a line every now and then?

What is it like to talk to God; Our Father who is in heaven, hallowed is His name. Do you remember when the you were so excited to tell your parents of wife something that you could barely contain your glee and how they were excited with you, or when things weren't going so well and you went to them for encouragement cause you know that they will put there arms around you and let you know you are loved. Well do you wait in expectation of God answering your prayer this morning or are we just going through the motions. Are we just figuratively laying down the request before Him or are we actually saying, God I can't do this I don't know how, Lord I am tired of trying to do it myself I need help, GOD Abba Father thank you for being here for me and with me thank you for the day that you have made.

Expectation of seeing God today do you have it, do you expect God to answer your prayers, open your eyes open your heart, open your ears and look.

Live

John 14:18 I will not leave you as orphans; I will come to you. 19Before long, the world will not see me anymore, but you will see me. Because I live, you also will live. 20On that day you will realize that I am in my Father, and you are in me, and I am in you.

A re you alive, sure you got the blood pumping and a brain cell are firing but is your soul alive?

It is a sunrise that makes me think of what the world sees, it is the birds that swoop down and scoop a fish from the river that makes me wonder if the world only sees the beauty of the even and not the love of the creator. We are not alone; we have not been kicked to the curb and abandoned. All we have to do is call out to our Father and He will come.

I recall what the world sees, I remember standing in the Taunus Mountains in Germany looking across a valley and seeing the stream running and being so quiet that I could hear it. I remember feeling the warms of the sun and the coolness of the breeze. You see I remember these things and knowing now that I still missed a lot.

I recall standing next to a lake with a fly rod in my hands and setting the fly on the water near some cover and a fish breaking the surface and swallowing the fly, I remember setting the hook and brining the fish in. I recall the mist on the lake as the sun broke I remember looking across the lake with the fish in my hand and the still beauty of the moment and the light reflected and dance on the waves and I recalled that I am not alone and that my God made this moment for me to remind me of His greatness and His love.

You see we forget that He lives and we are to live, we are not to close off ourselves to everyone outside of the church but if the lost are to see Him they must see Him in us. We should not be just talking about a pretty picture but also about the one who created the picture. Our Father, my Father your Father He lives so live for Him.

Today, now, this moment

John 3:16"For God so loved the world that he gave his one and only Son, that whoever believes in him shall not perish but have eternal life. [17]For God did not send his Son into the world to condemn the world, but to save the world through him.

What is it that you take away from an awesome Sunday, is it the words of the pastor or the words of the speaker or the emotional high of a song? What is it that we need today, now this moment? Could it be that this sums up Gods love for us that He sent His only Son into to world that all who believe in Him should not perish but will have eternal life that He didn't send Him to condemn the world but that through Him the world could be saved?

Right now this moment is not just a tick of a clock it is part of your eternity with Him it is right now today this moment. You can either live like you know it or live like it doesn't matter. We can have faith in God's words for they are true each and every time they are spoken or each and every time that they are read. What are we afraid of, being different standing out in a crowd, so what you're supposed to.

The flame that burns can be a roaring fire or it can be a smoldering ember, but before it can be a flame or fire or even before it became an ember first it had to be a spark. That friction when you strike a match, before the stick ignites and is placed on the fuel is when the fire began. We can kindle each others flames we can grow in to a raging fire fueled by the Holy Spirit over taking the world not a fire that destroys but a fire that brings Christ into the lives that we are in touch with.

Who will you tell today, now this very moment about Christ? You see that person that you don't get along with that person whom you can't stand to be around cause they just drive you nuts, well maybe Christ died for them also. Look we won't get anywhere all of our words will be just fodder for the fire that stays in place unless we put motion to our words until we go each day from our homes on mission for Christ to spread the good news.

Are you ready for God to open a door and give you the opportunity to share His Love with someone? Hope so; strap it on big daddy because they are coming your way.

Siyach – Meditation

Psalm 104:34 May my meditation be pleasing to him, as I rejoice in the LORD.

Has there ever been anything that leaves you speechless, something that has so captivated your heart and vision that you struggle to find the words for? The birth of your children comes to mind, when you first hold them in your arms, when you experience first hand creation. As I read through this chapter I could only think of God and how He felt when the first flower bloomed when the first breeze blew when the sun first shown. You see He was at work and through the energy of His labor things were made (maaseh).

The flower, the sun, blossoms, pleasing, meditation and creation, have you ever noticed the similarities between a sunflower and you? No I am not talking about the petals or the seeds or the vines or the roots or the stalk but rather its nature. You see a sunflower will always face the sun; the blossom will always rotate with the sun throughout the day. Just as you and I look upon the Son each day so do we keep our eyes upon Him?

May our prayers and thoughts be pleasing to Him, as we rejoice in the Lord but more than that though. How pleasing are our contemplations, our utterances, our communication, our talk basically how pleasing is our prayer to Him? Sometimes I just shoot through a prayer without much thought or meditation about it, I don't take the time to be still and form my thoughts I just blurt the words out without much in the way or worrying about "Thy Will be done," just more or less bang, bang, bang over and out amen.

Let me ask you something when was the last time you told God thank you specifically for something that He created for you? Not Thank God for the birds (turkey) the fish (bass) or the fairway (golf) but really thank you for the work of His hands. Thank You Abba Father for the turkey that you created for the bird that both is wonderful to look at and brings nourishment Lord both for my soul and for my body only a Great God could create a bird pleasing in all ways.

God wants you to passionately serve and worship Him, I am only saying is the way that you worship or serve or communicate or meditate pleasing? If you don't think it is then what are you going to do to change it?

Give it up.

Psalm 51: The sacrifices of God are a broken spirit; a broken and contrite heart,

O God, you will not despise.

Striking how David's words rings true even still to this day, then again the truth is a funny thing. You see the truth has always been true and always will be true there is no deviation or tweaking that needs to be done to the truth. I was reading Exodus and listening to how the Israelites came and gave freewill offerings not out of a sense of well if we gotta but out of a sense of we wanta. For some reason the word freewill interposed itself on thinking about some of the conversations I have has here of late with a couple of you.

You see there has been some discussion of why don't some people seem to get it? They attend sporadically at best when they do come it is with a sour face, they only want to see things their way, and what could we do to reach them. I don't know, I have no idea what I can do to reach the lost attending church. Then again is that really the answer or just an excuse, what an excuse Dr. Wynn, yes-yes I know. It is easy to say I don't know it is harder to come up with an answer. After all what do we do but just sit back and talk about it and really how much do we pray about it and ask God for direction.

Can I ask you something, duh, but has God ever turned you away when you have come before Him with a broken and contrite heart? Has He ever left you alone when you have come to Him with a broken spirit? Not the God I know has ever left anyone when they are truly seeking Him. Could the reason why people don't get it is that they don't have a broken spirit or contrite heart? Is the reason why we get befuddled and confused and narrow vision because we are to busy looking to see if they get it that we don't see that we don't have a broken spirit also when we have let God down and sinned. I know it is easier to look away from the mirror then it is to look at it.

I just happen to think that we should be not just saying we are sorry because it is easy but rather that we aught ta be sorry for what we have done or didn't do. Our own sin should make us humble and contrite it should break our heart that we have sinned against God. It should not be well God this is Fran guess what whoops messed up again sorry bout that, hey tell ya what I'll do better next time...................

First you got to look how your sincerity is then you gotta look again, don't look away and don't turn away. Face it we could all probably do with a little brokenness about failing Christ.

Ephesians 2:4But because of his great love for us, God, who is rich in mercy, [5]made us alive with Christ even when we were dead in transgressions--it is by grace you have been saved.

Abide

1 John 2:28 And now, little children, abide in Him, that when He appears, we may have confidence and not be ashamed before Him at His coming.

1: to wait for: **AWAIT**
2 a: to endure without yielding: **WITHSTAND b**: to bear patiently: **TOLERATE** <cannot *abide* such bigots>
3: to accept without objection <will *abide* your decision>
intransitive senses
1: to remain stable or fixed in a state
2: to continue in a place

If Christ was to come back at 9:00 today what would He find ya doing?

Can you have joy abiding in Him, yes I think so nah scratch that I know so. Ya'll ya know what, God doesn't expect you to be walking around with your hands clasped in front of you with that somber sour face on. As if the least thing would bring shame upon God. Please give me a break. He does however expect us to keep His commands doesn't He? I know some of you will be diligently reading His word when He comes back and others of you will be out on a foreign mission field but for me I will probably be cracking on some one. Yep Jesse and Rod when Christ comes back will we be prepared and will we be in a situation that will cause Him to shake His head in disgust or in humor?

As we endeavor to make it thru today I hope that we are not just looking at surviving, at time that is all I can do also, but that we endeavor to abide in His words and in His actions. Wouldn't it be a cool thing Russell that before we laid our head down on the pillow tonight that we could look back on the day and say "I walked the path," and no I am not talking ancient Indian game path. That we looked back on the day and said today I abided in Christ and thank you Lord for giving me the strength to do so.

It isn't easy is it Nancy to abide in Christ with every action and every thought of each and everyday, to think to hard on it would cause you to get a head ache. Yet this is what we are to do. We can not do it alone, but then you are not alone are you, after all God did send the Holy Spirit to help you and well didn't He also give you those people you call friends. Sometimes we don't abide in Christ because we aren't really listening to Him, following the Holy Spirit and avoiding those who call us to be accountable.

Endure without yielding, without yielding to the temptations of this world and keeping you focus on that narrow gate. Will you yield today to the temptations of this world, what will cause you to slip? Never ever forget something ya'll when we slip we can get back up, what if Christ came back after you slipped and you were I the middle of a repentant confession and instead of feeling the forgiveness sweep over you, you actually hear His voice say "you are forgiven, arise and abide with me for ever."

Let not the wind knock you down, keep your feet planted firmly on the Rock.

9 781597 819916